SQUEEZE THE SPONGE

A No-Yawn Guide to College Writing

RHODA JANZEN

FLIP FLIP
LEARNING

Squeeze the Sponge:
A No-Yawn Guide to College Writing

uses Rhoda Janzen's powerful, hilarious, and emotionally generous voice as an award-winning professor and best-selling author to offer undergraduate students an inspirational writing guide.

The interactive version of *Squeeze the Sponge* includes the following features:

▷ Collaborative discussion activities in real time;
▷ Auto-graded quizzes at the end of each chapter with a timer feature and built-in cheating prevention measures;
▷ Annually updated links to relevant online sources;
▷ Detailed instructor PowerPoint presentations for each chapter;
▷ Simple and intuitive instructor assessment tools;
▷ Easily accessible from any browser and compatible with all major devices, including desktop computers, laptops, tablets, and smartphones.

Interactive
ISBN: 978-0-9910375-9-9

Print/Digital Bundle
ISBN: 978-0-9910375-6-8

Flip Learning is a small and innovative publisher of page-turning textbooks authored by renowned scholars who are also recipients of distinguished awards for undergraduate teaching.

WHAT INSTRUCTORS ARE SAYING ABOUT *SQUEEZE THE SPONGE...*

"This is a genuinely unique and wonderful text. It combines the intensely readable personal touch of the how-to writing handbook with the no-nonsense nuts-and-bolts of the freshman composition textbook. I enjoyed reading it and suspect most students will as well, and was struck throughout by the author's powerful, consistently engaging voice: This is a composition textbook that is actually fun to read!"

– **Ira Allen**, Assistant Professor of Rhetoric, Writing, and Digital Media Studies, Northern Arizona University

"This text displays a remarkable voice and degree of engagement with the reader, built both from understandable anecdotes and the author's own experiences. Its tone is decidedly non-textbook and this is to its great credit as a potential stand-out among prospective teachers of writing."

– **David Grant**, Associate Professor of English, University of Northern Iowa

"The author makes herself known to the students. She has a strong voice and personality, writing from a first-person P.O.V. rather than relying on a deceptive third-person impersonal 'authority' that distances readers. Best of all, the author works by building on what she knows students are already able to do."

– **Elizabeth Lowry**, Lecturer in Rhetoric and Composition, Arizona State University

Published by Flip Learning

Copyright © 2018 by Rhoda Janzen

FlipLearning.com

Second Flip Learning bundle edition 2018

ISBN-10 0-9910375-5-3
ISBN-13 978-0-9910375-5-1

Original cover artwork by Drew Spielvogel

For information about special discounts for bulk purchases,
please contact Flip Learning Sales at sales@fliplearning.com.

Printed in the United States of America

3 5 7 9 10 8 6 4 2

ACKNOWLEDGMENTS

I wish to thank my former teachers and program directors for having introduced me to a rich variety of games and activities that made learning more fun. I've been using some of those games, or adapted versions thereof, in my own classrooms for thirty years. Mentors at the University of Florida, The Los Angeles Institute of Reading Development, and the University of California Los Angeles modeled wonderfully creative pedagogy that has shaped and enriched my own. To these institutions and professors I will always be grateful. May the baton pass to the next generation of future teachers!

ALSO BY RHODA JANZEN

Mennonite in a Little Black Dress

Babel's Stair

Mennonite Meets Mr. Right

RHODA JANZEN is the author of the #1 *New York Times* bestselling memoir *Mennonite in a Little Black Dress* and a recent finalist for the Thurber Prize for American Humor. A poet and American literature scholar, Janzen holds a PhD from the University of California, Los Angeles, where she was awarded the University of California Poet Laureate in 1994 and 1997. She is currently Associate Professor of English at Hope College in Holland, Michigan, where she teaches literature and writing. Janzen has received UCLA's Luckman Award for Distinguished Teaching and a National Pew Charitable Trust Award for Innovation in Teaching.

CONTENTS

1 Matcha and Meatball

1.1 Use What You Have Been Given

Y'all know the Mennonites, right? Like the Amish, except with slightly different theology and better pie? For Mennonite reasons beyond my control, I found my freshman year in college a tad overwhelming. I was the gal with the rape whistle in my purse, and maybe a cold meatball in a baggie, nervously aware that I did not know anything about anything, unless you count meatballs.

Rumors flew thick and fast about an especially intimidating professor. He read the dictionary for pleasure! He competed in Ironman Triathlons! He had built a laser in his backyard! All we knew for sure was that he rolled into every session just as the second hand swept the twelve, an entrance so terrifyingly prompt that we suspected him of hiding nearby

Matcha: beverage of the enlightened

with a stopwatch. Here was the signature rumpled cashmere jacket, the hip owlish glasses, the cross-body manbag that dared someone, anyone, to ask about the difference between nihilism and existentialism. He'd swirl his mug of matcha, steamwise, as if to demonstrate its fine bouquet.

I think we can all agree that a hot caffeinated beverage improves every seminar experience. But this professor went out of his way to present himself as a *connoisseur* of matcha. He spoke in lordly tones about the many imported varieties. Something in his manner suggested that we who drank lesser beverages were culturally blighted. Naturally I sat in the back, thumbing through my mental Rolodex. Matcha, matcha? What *was* it, and why had I never heard of it?

Yes, he matcha-shamed us, this fellow. But more importantly, he set up a scary paradigm that still seems unhelpful to me. With every lecture, every comment, every quiz, this professor reinforced a learning environment that positioned the students as *not having.* We students lacked knowledge, we lacked skills, we lacked cultural sophistication. We lacked what we needed to succeed in college, and the only way to get it was to

A) admit there was a problem, as at Alcoholics Anonymous,

and

B) make a desperate grab for what he could give us.

Did we admit our ignorance? Sure. When you're in a position of powerlessness, the two most obvious strategies are admission and denial, after all.

Well, soon enough my world righted itself. The matcha in the mug was a tempest in a teacup, as Cicero would have said. But this was years before I read Cicero. Nothing outrageous happened. I figured out the difference between nihilism and existentialism, right on schedule. And in subsequent decades I thought of that professor only when matcha came up in conversation—which is to say, not very often. Nothing like a couple of decades to adjust your vision.

I bring up my freshman year in college for one reason only. I want to make it clear that in this textbook I am purposefully rejecting what I call the Matcha Approach. And so, freshman students reading this book, you're not missing anything. You don't need to grab for what anybody has. My counsel to you is simple and straightforward: just use what you have been given.

Yes, I am arguing that you already have everything you need in order to succeed in the field of college writing. You got into college, didn't you? How about you relax and trust the system? The reason you were admitted into college is that you *deserve* to be admitted. You didn't fake anybody out. You didn't bamboozle a soul. As a freshman I was worried that I had somehow managed to hoodwink the admissions office into thinking me smarter, more capable, than I really was. Guess what, though? The people in the admissions office who studied your transcripts and read your application essay and discussed your entrance exams actually do know what they're doing. They recognize potential when they see it. And this means you already have everything you need. You are well equipped.

In fact, you *already* know how to write, reason, and argue your case. You *already* know how to compare stuff to other stuff. On Facebook and in email, you have already established that you can sound like you, and not somebody else. You students reading this right now already know how to communicate information on paper in such a way that the reader can catch your drift. And you already have years of practice at adjusting your writing according to expectation and audience. I therefore want to suggest that we all give ourselves a pat on the back. Let's sit down and enjoy a Red Velvet cupcake as a tribute to the excellence we have already achieved! Allow me to point out that you'll be in a better mood if you look at what you have, as opposed to what you don't have. You can learn in fear, or you can learn in confidence. Take your pick.

What are the qualities that you need that you already happen to have? Common sense, creativity, and logic. Style, personality, opinions. Literacy, awareness, the courtesy to ask what others think. The ability to recognize excellence when you see it. Cupcakes, meatballs—in short, whatever's hidden in your bag. You need what you've got, and you've got what you need. What I'm saying is, you are in a position, right now, today, to become an even better writer than you already are.

I'm not pretending that the academic bar hasn't just been raised. It has. Few will disagree that university-level writing applies a more rigorous standard of excellence than that which may have earned you an A in high school. Yet it may be freeing for you to know that you don't have to be a brainiac, or an English major, or a dork to bump your writing up to the next level. No matter who you are, no matter what intrigues or bores you, your high school education has prepared you to nail down some useful strategies that will propel you to success.

The plan is to show you how to improve what you have. At my end, I promise to talk in a normal voice, not in a professorish tone that makes you want to skip to the end of the chapter to see if there's a helpful summary. Although I am right on schedule for middle age with bifocals and a couple of rooster potholders, I remember my own college years perfectly well. Personally, I would have appreciated a textbook written by someone who wasn't trying to be high-falutin' all the time.

Fortunately there's no rule that insists we all have to prepare for academic assignments by reading academic-sounding textbooks. Me, I don't care whether you drink matcha or rooibos or water from the hose. My idea is to talk about college-level writing expectations plainly and to give you some practical tips that will truly advance you. Speaking as one who learned to write well in college, and then made plenty of money from my writing later, I'm not interested in covering every little thing that can be said about college writing, or covering every permutation of every possible writing assignment. To me it seems more practical to lay out a starter kit that will be useful for most *assignments*. My idea is to spotlight a few skills that you can adapt as needed to a variety of college writing tasks. I aim to demonstrate that the skills are the same, whether you are writing about an essay, an article, a poem, a movie, a lab report, whatever.

I want to use what I've been given, too. And what I've been given is a unique perspective: the chance to live and work and publish in two worlds. Please know that even though this is a nontraditional textbook, I do cherish the global scholarly community with its rich exchange of ideas, its research protocols, its savvy epistemologies. Yet I have also grown to love the world I inhabited on book tours: the book groups, the public libraries, the radio listeners with their frank questions. These folks were reading books only for insight or pleasure, not as part of a professional conversation. From them I learned as much as from my own college students.

In the academy we have wonderful, insightful scholars whose work has changed the way composition classes are taught. Rhetoric-composition scholars have been game-changers in so many ways: their work in genre studies, their analysis of how texts function socially, their studies in literacy technologies and pedagogic theories, and on and on. But my own background is different. Therefore my textbook may be a bit unusual—not because I disrespect the textbooks that have already been written but because my own experience has given me a different sort of book to write.

I don't want to talk *at* you. I want to talk *to* you. I promise not to make small things seem more important than they are. Conversely, if something is likely to tank your grade, I will say so. And I swear right up front that I will not include any gimmicky exercises that make you roll your eyes, such as writing a letter to Death. We've all had enough dear-death experiences.

See that tiny cloud on the horizon? It's the dust of Matcha Man galloping away. It is my hope that the material you read here will make you feel better, not worse. I deeply believe that we should enjoy our studies, not merely endure them. May these pages trigger a chain reaction of ideas rather than a contagion of yawns! And as you begin your studies, may your confidence grow and your best writing begin.

2 Considering How You Will Be Graded

2.1 Being Graded on What You Write

Have you noticed that most textbooks are silent on the subject of grades, as if to pretend that you would joyfully practice academic skills for the sheer pleasure of the experience? The grades that you get color the way you feel about your writing. Correct me if I'm wrong, but contemporary textbooks seem to have overlooked that fact. My niece Joon used to clap her hands over her ears and shout "Lalalalala!" when she didn't want to hear something. While I am personally sympathetic to all forms of denial—been there!—I do wish textbook authors would just admit that the writing experience changes pretty radically when you are being *graded* on what you write. Some folks do write for pleasure, and I'm one of them. My tribe is a global community of list-makers and journal-keepers, scribblers and bloggers. If somebody dies, we volunteer to write the epitaph. If nobody dies, we send out a breezy newsletter.

When you are of the same tribe, terrific. When you're not, terrific. You can experience grade anxiety either way, and it's not doing anybody any favors to ignore the reality of the assessment process.

Over the years I have heard students vent about negative experiences with this or that prof's grading. I've heard students complain about this or that course grade. Though I do my best to sidestep gripefests, I still catch the occasional downdraft. And I'd like to suggest that this downdraft presents a view of writing classes that will not help you advance in college. It's a view like buckshot to the behind: ouch, painful position ahead. Sometimes students speak as if their grade in a writing class is an utter crapshoot. Essay assignments can produce a vague quease because you are at the mercy of seemingly erratic, unpredictable writing instructors. Perhaps the instructor uses the Staircase Method! (Heard this one? Instructor chucks the lot of papers from the top of the stairwell and assigns grades according to where the essays land: top step, A; middle step, C; bottom step, D.)

I would like to assure you that your instructors are not random, careless people. They are dedicated professionals, committed to your learning. In fact, college instructors care so much about your learning that they have been willing to devote an unusually long time to their professional preparation. Other careers with comparable training periods pay more. Your instructors have chosen this field because they think your learning is important.

I cheerfully allow that academia makes it a point to honor diverse pedagogies. But this view that the student is somehow at the mercy of the quixotic writing instructor is, and I say this respectfully, wackadoodle. It is cuh-razy to hand your power away. Don't turn yourself into a victim! Ascribing all that power to your instructor undermines your *own* agency, as if you have no say in the development of your own skill set. You do. No matter what the situation is with your instructor's bee and/or bonnet, you have control over your own writing. I urge you to take it.

Like you, professors are trapped in a system of evaluation. If you are attending a college that uses letter grades as its primary form of assessment, please know that the grading scale ain't arbitrary. Profs may not like it. You may not like it. Grade inflation notwithstanding, the letter grades are supposed to be standardized nationwide, though of course they might inch higher or lower depending on the conferring institution. After a lifetime of receiving the same five letter grades in school, sometimes we lose sight of the underlying message. Here is a handy translation.

A: "In a perfect world, I would read this essay proudly to the guy at my neighbor's pontoon party."

B: "This essay is like a pair of useful black pants."

C: "Having read this essay, I am in the mood for a tuna sandwich."

D: "Oh dear, this student must have had a late night."

E: "As middle fingers go, this one offers an unambiguous declaration of other priorities."

Notice that when a writing assignment earns an average or a

below-average grade, your instructors are not assuming that you cannot write better. We are assuming that for whatever reason, *you have chosen not to*. This assumption should cheer you up. Most instructors at the college level honestly figure that you can indeed write well, should you choose to prioritize good writing as an academic goal.

I am one of many professors who aren't crazy about having to give out grades. In the collective faculty fantasy, which is the only time academics all agree, students bring a picnic lunch and flock around us to learn for the sake of learning. But we are not Socrates. You are not Xenophon. It doesn't work like that. In real life professors assign grades because to do so is part of our job.

I take my hat off to instructors who try to shimmy around conventional letter grades by inviting students to assign their own grades, or who offer assignments with lots of wiggle room for nontraditional assessment. Some instructors say, Certainly you may substitute an interpretive dance for a term paper! By all means, you may submit a poignant black-and-white photograph instead of an essay! Go ahead and title it "Hang in There," especially if it features a duckling snuggled against a squirrel nutkin, in an adorable teensy hammock! While I am sympathetic to these alternative expressions of creativity, I don't think they'll help you much in the professional world after college. You know what will? Learning how to write better.

Some instructors shrug at grade anxiety and say, "Just don't take the grade personally." That's disingenuous, because a grade *is* personal. It's personal in the sense that a person is trying very hard to write better, so as to become a more well-rounded, more employable person. Grades matter. And when you get a grade you aren't expecting, it *is* tempting to shift the focus onto the instructor.

Tempting, but not profitable. In fact, harmful. My suggestion to you, the student, would be to focus on the improvement rather than the grade. You may have graduated from high school only months prior, but this isn't high school. You don't have to be intimidated by your instructors. We will not treat you like kids. We will treat you like the adults you are. So many college students don't figure this out until their junior or senior years: you can march straight to your professor's office hours and boldly go get the help you have already paid for. Instead of talking about the grade you got, ask for some specific strategies to *get the grade you want.*

3 Considering Your Audience

3.1 Introductory Activities

Shapes

Instructors should prepare a plain envelope for every partner pair the day before this activity is conducted in class, and then fill those envelopes with the same set of six abstract shapes, cut out of plain white paper.

In class, invite pairs of students to ditch their desks and sit back to back on the floor, legs akimbo. One person should give directions while the other takes directions. From the moment the activity begins, the direction-taker must be utterly silent, not a peep. The silent partner sits with six shapes at the ready, waiting benignly to follow instructions from the talker. Because the silent partner is facing in the opposite direction, he or she cannot see what the direction-giver is doing: arranging the six shapes into a pattern between outstretched legs in such a way that each shape is touching at least one other shape.

Pairs are not competing with each other, or the clock. The object of this exercise is to get the silent partner to recreate the pattern exactly as the direction-giver has arranged it on the floor. The talking partner gives directions over the shoulder, step by step, until the whole pattern has been explained. At no time can the talker see what the partner is doing, which means that the direction-giver needs to speak in a loud, clear, slow voice. The partner, being silent, has no way of demanding a repeat or a clarification.

When you finish the activity, turn around and inspect your patterns, noting what did and did not work. Then put your heads together as a class, and answer the following questions:

▷   What was the hardest thing about replicating the pattern?

▷   What was the most helpful thing the direction-giver did?

▷   How is the role of the direction-giver like being a writer?

▷   How is the role of the silent partner like being a reader?

▷   Make an educated guess based on your own communication patterns. For you personally, what will be challenging about considering your audience when you write for college assignments?

Cold Shoulder

Find somebody in the class with whom you haven't yet partnered. If possible, arrange your chairs closely facing each other. (If the seats are fixed, you might want to try this on the floor, sitting directly opposite each other.) Now, before you begin, think of a childhood story that illustrates the cosmic silliness of Murphy's Law—that is, if something can go wrong, it will. Don't pick a traumatic, life-changing narrative. Pick an aw-shucks, eye-rolling narrative. A birthday party imploded, a ball game tanked, a long-awaited treat fizzled.

Face your partner with blank face and cold shoulders. Stiffen up in your chair, feet on the floor, arms locked. Being careful to sound as bland as possible, take turns narrating your childhood incidents. Do not gesture. Do not let your voice assume nuance, inflection, or personality. Channel your Inner Robot. Your partner will sit there and let you talk, but because she has a glazed eye and a torso cut in stone, she may remind you of the Great Pyramid of Giza. Like our friend Cheops in the necropolis, she will have nothing to say. She will make eye contact, but trying to connect with your partner will be like staring at the Sphinx.

▷ Which was harder, talking like a robot or listening like a blank wall?

▷ Did you spot any evidence to suggest that your partner heard and understood what you were saying?

▷ Did you communicate your story accurately? Pick a word to describe how you felt while you were sharing your story.

> ▷ What about this exercise resembles the relationship between writer and reader? What's different?

3.2 Effectively Communicating Across the Gap

When we speak language with our mouths or sign it with our hands, the words and signs can be delivered even if we stiffen up and even if the listener does not encourage us with yummy noises and body language that cue social interest. Think about all the things that we usually rely on: the torso that angles subtly toward the speaker, the faint nod, the warm eye contact. Together these things combine to say, "Keep talking, I'm listening!"

In person-to-person speech it is easy to see, however, that the *effectiveness* of the communication isn't just about the words or signs that comprise human speech. The effectiveness of our speech is enhanced by things other than words: inflection, tone, gesture, expression, occasion, context, and reception, to name a few. Check out Amber Galloway Gallego[1], who earned a master's degree in ASL (American Sign Language/English). She really puts her interpretation skills to creative use. Described by *Vibe* as "the most recognizable sign language interpreter in [the United States]," Gallego has made

---

1   Visit link: https://goo.gl/4yh5ty

a name for herself signing for rappers and hip-hop artists such as Snoop Dogg, Kendrick Lamar, Eminem, Iggy Azalea, Wiz Khalifa, and Nicki Minaj.

What Gallego has demonstrated is that effective communication is a property of context and audience. However, there's a pretty profound gap between communicating with an audience who is present and a reader who is absent. In that gap we note both physical distance and time. Writing is almost always done in private. If it's shared with an audience—that is, a reader—it will be shared with somebody who isn't sitting right there in the room with the writer. The writer typically retreats to a private spot to get the job done. The scholar Walter J. Ong, thinking about the ways in which the transition from orality to literacy changed human culture, once pointed out that writing involves a fundamental irony: in order to connect, we have to withdraw.[2]

So that means the gap contains even more than physical distance and time. It contains conjecture, imagination, and speculation, because how do we even know who our audience is? If a writer is expecting a certain kind of reader, there's a lot of slippage there for him to be wrong. What if the actual reader turns out to be different from the one he has imagined?

How writers handle that gray area, the gap between who they guess their audience is and who their audience actually turns out to be, is a matter of constant, in-the-moment decision making. Sometimes we make these decisions consciously, sometimes unconsciously. Sometimes we even make them on

---

2   Walter J. Ong, *Orality and Literacy: The Technologizing of the Word* (London: Methuen, 1982).

autopilot, as when we suddenly find ourselves pulling into the driveway but can't remember the commute. That happens. But usually it is helpful to be aware of the gray area that stretches between writer and reader like no-man's-land.

A composition class not only wants you to be aware of that zone; it wants to put you in that zone on purpose. By giving you the opportunity to get feedback from peer readers and by giving you the chance to revise your writing with feedback from those same peers and from your instructor, the composition class invites you to practice thinking about your audience in ways that will strengthen your writing. Thinking about your audience can save you from making gaffes and goofs. Without the feedback loop, for example, you might make unhelpful assumptions about who your audience is. You might underexplain, or overstate, or tiptoe around an issue that begs to be acknowledged.

Let's frame this in explicitly positive terms. Thinking about audience doesn't just prevent you from messing up. It actually *helps* you achieve a proactive goal foundational to all academic writing: the ability to write generously and respectfully about positions that oppose your own. If you don't sit down and actively train yourself to think about your readers' beliefs, values, and arguments, you might end up not even *caring* about perspectives that challenge your own, let alone writing about them with accuracy and respect.

3.3 To Think or Not to Think about Audience

Peter Elbow, a scholar who specializes in the teaching of composition, reminds us that some writers choose not to think about audience on purpose. Typically they make that call when they're in the first-draft stage, writing like a banshee to generate material on the page. Do you know any artists who believe that invoking *any* idea of audience, whether informed or misinformed, interferes with the very act of creation? I do. These writers would say that their first responsibility is to the *idea* they're writing about, not the reader. Plus, notes Elbow, speculating about what your reader thinks or doesn't think can totally freeze you up. It can mess with your voice and stiffen up your writing. It can result in a fake-sounding self-consciousness, as when contestants in a beauty pageant parrot a glib answer they think everybody wants to hear: "My platform is after-school literacy programs for at-risk youth, and world peace!"

Here's a question for you. Would you write what you write anyway, even if there were no one around to read it? I did that once—twice, if you count a childhood in which I churned out endless pages in green crayon, parked on the Tinker Toy drum in my brothers' closet. The more recent experience seems more otherworldly, though. A couple of years ago I accidentally wrote a whole book in thirty-four days, hiding out in my parents' gazebo. It was a sweltering summer in California's Central Valley, the heat far too extreme to be sitting outside all day. Nonetheless I sat still as a papery moth hour after hour, day after day, in triple-digit temperatures. Why I did that I cannot say. My dad says that occasionally he'd bring me a handful of cherries from the tree in the backyard or an iced tea. I didn't even notice. I ate the cherries and drank the tea, but I was utterly gone.

During that time I certainly was not thinking of an audience for my writing. And if I had been, I would have guessed that my audience would have consisted of a wee handful of scholars like me, folks who published "serious" writing in journals that only a few like-minded writers enjoy. Here's the kicker. If I had known in advance that the book I was writing would become a best seller, I would have been way too intimidated to write it. My comfort zone was writing for other writers. Turns out that the book I was writing was not for other writers at all. It ended up being for people who had messed up their lives and who had run home desperate for love and pity. In short, it was for a far, far larger audience than I would have ever guessed. That alone would have stopped me cold in my tracks. If I had thought about book tours and radio shows and international translations, I would have run screaming for the hills.

But the story doesn't end with my naive failure to anticipate audience needs, desires, and concerns. Eventually I *did* think about audience. I had to. My editor wisely twisted my arm. Before that book went to print, I was pushed to enter the gray zone, the weird space between what a writer assumes about a reader and who that reader actually turns out to be. And of course I eventually saw that it goes both ways.

At my editor's urging, I eventually began to make (tenuous, imperfect) assumptions about what my readers needed to hear from me. I was writing about a community of origin that not many people knew much about, so I needed to provide way more information than I had up until that point. This process turned on what I was guessing about my readers. And my guesses weren't even well-informed, since at that time I hadn't even read much in the genre of books that my readers typically purchased (memoir). My expectations of who my readers would be were shaped almost exclusively by my work as a professor. Yet when the book came out, I swiftly saw that the *readers'* experiences and expectations shaped their vision of who *I* was as a writer, too. Every week I got hundreds of letters about my upbeat book that had affirmed the importance of family and community. Then in the same week I'd get hundreds more that applauded my courage in calling out an oppressive, conservative community. These readers all read the same book. Yet their own attitudes and experiences caused them to come to very different conclusions about who I was.

Which is all to say, a composition class isn't just about what and how you write. It's about for *whom* you write, the actual readers external to your text, in this case your peers and your instructor. A composition class is about examining your own attitudes, reactions, and expectations that may or may not be a match for your actual audience. And it's about all the things you can intentionally do to close the gap between the unexamined image in your head and the intentional writing you do on the page.

4

Firming the Frame

4.1 Topic vs. Core Argument

Most people have their own version of the perfect date. When I was seventeen, my idea of romance turned on the dreaminess of ballroom dancing, plus everything it evoked in my imagination. For me ballroom dancing evoked crimson lipstick, a libation involving Pernod, and a man who could raise one eyebrow. However, nice Mennonite girls did not dance salsa, sip cocktails, or wear lipstick. Sadly, if Mennonite guys were raising one eyebrow, I didn't know about it.

On my Perfect Date a witty, sophisticated man would whisk me off to Santorini. There we would mambo in the moonlight, he in gray flannel, I in a frock of iridescent malines. I would travel with a round hat box and my date would tip the porter, because this fantasy always commenced in the

Gare de Lyon. *Au revoir, mes amis*! Jean-Claud and I are off for a madcap weekend in Greece!

In real life my boyfriend went by T-Bone, not Jean-Claud. He worked in the mailroom and played in an alternative band called Dorian Gray. He didn't have a Santorini budget. If he had extra money, he spent it on striped pants. Also it was 1983, not 1933. Hard to mambo to Kajagoogoo's "Too Shy."

I could already couples-dance, sort of, if you counted what you do at prom. Not that Mennonites were allowed to go to prom. Mennonites had a *banquet*, boo. Ours was titled "The Time of Your Life," with big fake clocks positioned strategically here and there, as if to remind teens that unless they did something about it, the apex of glamour would crest at a seated banquet in Fresno, with the smell of chicken cutlets and hairspray. Never the rebel I wanted to be, I obediently waited until I was out on my own to sign up for ballroom lessons.

I was ready! I had the shoes, the puffy dress, the accurate facts from many helpful library romances! These strongly suggested that the woman's job was to cling to the man like a sparkly limpet while he danced her round and wondered aloud if she had been skiing with mutual chums since the trip to Biarritz last December.

Turns out that the dance frame between the guy and the girl was the exact opposite of pliant. Both space and posture were firmly fixed. It required constant awareness to maintain the tautness of the frame. "IMAGINE A GIANT BEACH BALL ON YOUR CHEST," urged my instructor, a loud talker with one gray tooth. The dancers who had appeared to be gliding effortlessly were not effortless at all. And it wasn't that they seemed effortless in *spite* of the taut frame. No, they seemed effortless *because* of it. Sheesh. Of course I saw that in order to learn ballroom, I would have to let go of my old ideas. In fact I could not dance a single step until I was ready to correct my misconception and firm up the dance frame.

Let go of some stuff, learn some stuff. This is what you have to do when you start writing for college assignments. Like someone who already knows how to dance, sort of, you already have a general idea how to write. You've turned in plenty of high school essays. Presumably they all had an introduction, a body, and a conclusion. Paragraphs, check; thesis, check; quotations, check. But get ready. Having written some essays in high school doesn't necessarily mean you have been practicing the conventions of academic writing that you will need at the university level. In college the lights aren't comfortably dimmed, for starters. The lights are blazing and your instructors are studying your every move to see if you know how to hold a frame. And that's a good thing, if what you want is to be a confident writer.

And so, friend, I have an imaginary beach ball for you to tuck under your chin. I am the guy with one gray tooth, and I have some useful information to shout in your personal space, if you'll receive it.

Let's begin this section with a distinction that will help you set up a firm frame for any academic essay. This distinction between topic and idea may look small, but I'm telling you as a professor with thirty-five years of college classroom experience: nope, not small. Large. Huge, in fact. Without this distinction you'll find yourself with that frustrated feeling you get when you can't figure out what your instructors *want*, for heaven's sake.

I will tell you what they want. They want you to be able to trust your ability to set up an argument. If you don't know the difference between a topic and the idea behind it, you'll find yourself too tense to trust your own ability to set the thing up. A topic is the subject matter. A topic is what something is *about*. In a picture it's the visual focus. In a literary or cinematic text it's the plot. In an essay it's the subject that the author is writing about. Consider this bad vacation photo taken by yours truly. The items in the picture below belonged to some folks who were tenting close by.

"Hey, whaddya say we bring our personal fireplace implements from home along on our trip to the Keweenaw Peninsula!"

A photograph is just like an article, an essay, or a story in that it is always about something. The topic, or subject matter, is whatever you can see in the picture. In this photo the topic is some random stuff somebody brought along camping.

I was, like, "Honey, sneak over there and take a close-up of those fireplace implements!" My husband said he didn't want to violate their personal space. Also he wants to go on record as saying that bringing personal fireplace implements from home may actually *enhance* the camping experience. Let us hope so.

The core argument of the photo, or what used to be called *theme*, is not the same thing as the topic. If the topic is "personal fireplace implements at a campsite" the core argument is "some people choose to pack weird and random items when camping." The topic is the thing floating in front of your eye. By contrast, the core argument is the thing that expresses a whole idea. Unlike the topic, the core argument usually points to a larger meaning, an *interpretation* of what the text is about.

It doesn't matter what kind of text we're talking about here. It can be a photo, an ad, a poem, an essay you read for a college class. It can be a blog, a speech, a report, a comic book. A novel, an old episode of *Orange Is the New Black*, somebody's dissertation on stratigraphy, the evening news, whatever. The texts may differ, but the task is the same. Your job is to find the central idea.

Think of the topic as the main thing you see on the page/ screen/surface and the core argument as the main message you are left with when you're ready to walk away. For example, when you're in the audience at a play, you see what's happening onstage: the props, the characters, the lighting, and so on. That's topic. When my husband and I went to see a high school production of the Charles Dickens classic *A Tale of Two Cities*, we were amazed that any high school drama teacher would have the brass to take on a play about the French Revolution. I mean, all that blood and gore, not to mention the tall powdered wigs! You'll be happy to know that the director creatively improvised La Guillotine. Time and again, we heard an audio loop of a tremendous offstage blade dropping with a whack and then a thunder of heads rolling down a distant ramp. Walt Disney it was not. At intermission, the lobby was abuzz with parents, all of whom had plenty to say about the emphatic and perpetual thud of the guillotine, the heads rolling, the shouting of a bloodthirsty crowd. Some parents were appalled at the soundtrack. Others loved it. Whether they loved it or hated it, they were all talking about the director's production choices. That's topic.

The performance got a standing O. Four hundred proud moms and dads leaped to their feet in frenzied applause. My husband and I did not personally know anybody in the cast, so we exited the theater chasing stray thoughts about the tall powdered wigs (me) and the mechanics of the oblique guillotine blade (Mitch). For a while Mitch let me free-associate vis-à-vis the tall powdered wig of yesteryear.

You do you, Marie.

Portrait of Marie Antoinette ca. 1775

"You could keep a sandwich inside one those things!"

He finally interrupted. "Lookin' like ol' boy didn't realize that the new regime would be just as bad as the one it was replacing."

That's argument.

Notice that you can talk about the argument only on the other side of the performance. You land on an idea that you can't get to without having watched the whole show. A core argument is always a *complete idea*. It will always be a bona fide sentence, too—the real deal, not just a chicken nugget. The core argument that it makes may not be an in-your-face, I'm-right-you're-wrong sort of argument, but it does assert a position. It offers a takeaway. What is the text trying to get us to think, do, or believe? When my husband suggested that Dickens, the author of *A Tale of Two Cities*, hadn't quite thought through the revolution he appeared to support, Mitch was no longer talking about what was happening on that theater stage. He was talking about core argument. And the Dickens theater production that we saw that night did seem to suggest that the end can both justify and transform the means, a position that my husband clearly doesn't share.

You cannot articulate a core argument in just a word or phrase. For instance you can't say that the message of this play was "the moral problem of political revolution." When you do that, you're reducing argument to topic. You're not stating a whole idea. All you're doing is stating that a moral problem exists. But you aren't stating what that moral problem *is*.

On the other hand, you can articulate a topic in just a word or a phrase. A topic doesn't even need to be a complete sentence. Here are a couple of examples of topics, drawn from a variety of cultural texts:

▷ Fun in a blended family
 (*The Brady Bunch*, Sherwood Schwartz)

▷ Ah, an open can of whupass!
 (*Mixed Martial Arts Showdown*, World Series of

Fighting)

▷ Love, sweet and unsinkable!
(*Titanic*, James Cameron)

▷ America haunted by the ghost of slavery
(*Beloved*, Toni Morrison)

▷ Lip gloss as totem of popularity
("Lip Gloss," Lil Mama)

▷ Surviving a Nazi concentration camp
(*Man's Search for Meaning*, Viktor Frankl)

▷ Transgender empowerment
(*I Am Cait*, Caitlyn Jenner)

Topic Swap

In small groups, list the topics of any ten well-known texts that seem to comment on the culture that has produced them. Pull from any genre—music, film, art, television, literature, online gaming. Then on a separate piece of paper jot down just the topics, minus the texts. Swap with another group.

▷ How easy was it to identify the texts of another group?

▷ Did your group come up with any wrong answers that were interestingly right?

4.2 Discerning Topic from Argument in *Cinderella*

2015 film adaptation of *Cinderella*

Many freshmen arrive in college having accidentally kerfuffled topic and argument. They treat them as if they're interchangeable, and, yikes, they aren't. If this is something you need to *un*learn, now's the time.

Let's use a text we all know to practice distinguishing topic from argument. My topic for *Cinderella*, for example, would be

▷   Upward class mobility

If you've ever read *Cinderella*, or seen one of the many movie versions, you will probably nod at the topic I picked. Most readers agree: righto, *Cinderella* describes a woman's movement from poverty to wealth. At the beginning Cinderella is lonely, unhappy, and poor. At the end she's married, happy, and rich. Events that take her from a position of marginalized lack to affluent centrality literally do occur in the story. There's a scale. Up she goes. Upscale. If you were so inclined, you could make a little list to document her rise. A fairy godmother, an opulent ball, a weird but sexy shoe, a makeover. If you were reading a print version of this story, you could turn to various pages to document these things.

In approximately fifth grade, you learned how to tell the difference between the main stuff (Cinderella goes to the ball) and the minor stuff (Cinderella cleans the fireplace). By high school you learned to recognize the four or five major events that drive the plot, the things without which the other things could not happen. Now that you are in college, you are expected to distinguish event from idea, detail from what that detail suggests. What I'm saying is, you cannot be an effective writer *in any field* unless you get the difference between topic and argument. Whether you're trying to write a good essay or a good lab report, you need to signal from the outset that you have given some thought to what the text/experiment *means*. It is not enough to document what *occurs*.

Notice that when you hear people arguing over what a text is "about," the discussion almost always turns on what that text *means* (argument), not on what happens (topic).

That's because the topic is usually not up for interpretation.[1] Nobody's arguing about the plot of *Cinderella*. All readers of the American version agree: yup, a gal experiences unhappy servanthood. By story's end, she's better-off, so yay. Furthermore, most readers agree on many other aspects of the topic. We agree even on minor points such as the littleness of the foot, the slipper made of glass, the meanness of the stepsisters. Your topic is your topic. It's clear because it's supposed to be clear.

The argument, though, might be less so. That's because the main message is always an abstract idea rather than a concrete object. Because it is an abstract idea, it may not be stated explicitly in the text. If you spot a concrete object that seems to be generating a pattern of significance, chances are you have a symbol, not a core argument. Even if glass slippers suddenly go viral and everybody runs out to Neiman Marcus to buy some, the glass slipper all by itself cannot be a core argument.

Glass slipper as symbol

But a glass slipper can be a symbol. A **symbol** is a thing that literally occurs in a text, something you can see, hear, smell,

---

1   With a few famous exceptions, that is. One really renowned example of a story with an ambiguous topic is Henry James's 1898 novella *The Turn of the Screw*. Even though everyone reads the same story, they can't agree about what is actually going on in the plot. Is it a story about a couple of creeper kids possessed by the ghosts of dead people? Or is it about a governess's descent into madness? Head-scratcher.

or touch. Then, in addition to having a literal role in the text, it drags in a larger meaning, like a kite with a tail. Symbols occur in all kinds of writing, not just in literature. They even occur in life, so don't make the mistake of dismissing them as the special purview of poems and stories. A symbol is almost always interesting because it offers a double whammy of significance. One, it plays a structural role. Two, it plays a semantic role. It is always its own concrete self, but at the same time it signifies some larger meaning. Let's take the real-life example of a wedding ring. Everyone agrees that a wedding ring is a symbol. On the literal level it is an actual piece of jewelry, a fairly expensive ring right there on the left hand. If you're happily partnered, the literal value of the ring, although costly, is actually worth less than the value of the meaning it represents—constancy, true love, public declaration of commitment, sorry folks! this one's taken, all that.

If you can show what larger meaning Cinderella's literal shoe represents, then a glass slipper can be a symbol as well as a shoe. But in college you can't just assert that something symbolizes something else. You actually have to demonstrate a logical connection between a literal thing in a text and the larger thing it is supposed to represent. One of the most unusual, memorable things about Cinderella's shoe is that it's made of glass. You could say that because glass breaks easily, the slipper calls our attention to the fragility of Cinderella's social and economic position. Cinderella is in a really strange, liminal position, at once the daughter of class privilege (rich house, dead dad) and servitude (hard labor, poor conditions). Trying to negotiate two identities—well, that's fragile. On a whim the mean stepmom could throw Cinderella out on her butt, and then the daughter of class privilege would instantly become a penniless, homeless orphan. No job security: that's fragile. And here's another fragile thing. Cinderella keeps getting mixed messages from her stepsisters, who tell her yesyesyes, you can go to the ball, but also nonono, not until you've finished this impossible task. You could say that Cinderella is, like her own foot, encased in fierce unrelenting fragility.

Glass slipper as motif

Sometimes a text repeats something over and over in different ways, shoes here, slippers there, feetfeetfeet. If so, what you have is a **motif**. A motif is not the same thing as an argument, either. This is because an argument must be a complete idea, not a concrete object you can see, touch, smell, or taste. A slipper *is* a concrete object that no one wants to taste, except maybe a fetishist. If I had a glass slipper, I could clean it with Windex. I could give it to our Prince, who, if he turns out to be a fetishist, might slobber on it a little. But I could not say that the glass slipper is an argument.

Imagine polling five people, none of them a fetishist. You ask them just one question: "Hey, what happens in the classic fairy tale *Cinderella*?" Chances are your five respondents will all offer pretty much the same response. *Girl marries up*, they'll say. But if you were to ask the same five respondents a slightly different question, the responses would no doubt change. Now you're asking *this* question: "What does *Cinderella*, the classic fairy tale, *mean*?"

You are under no obligation to badger your family and friends with this question because I have already done it for you! I asked five people: two professor friends, an unknown guy sitting on an Adirondack chair at my neighbor's pontoon party, my brother-in-law, and my ninety-one-year-old aunt. Also, my nineteen-year-old niece tardily threw in her two cents for free. Here's what I got:

▷ **English Professor #1:** Cinderella is saying that women must be physically beautiful in order to succeed. They must comply with their culture's prescribed gender roles, especially regarding their symbolic smallness, their obedience to authority, and their willingness to listen to their biological clock.

▷ **English Professor #2:** *Cinderella* is about how we know what we know, with the glass slipper representing epistemology. The presence of epiphany is defined by its abrupt, almost magical appearance, as when the Fairy Godmother waves a wand and the shoe suddenly appears on Cinderella's foot. And the absence of epiphany is defined by the trope of the quest, as when the Prince conducts a kingdom-wide search for the foot that fits the shoe. [Dang, right? But to be fair, this professor was enjoying her second G&T.]

▷ **Random Guy at Pontoon Party:** *Cinderella* is a warning against sibling rivalry. Support your family, or you'll become bitter and ugly like the stepsisters.

▷ **Brother-in-law:** If you have a good attitude, good things will come your way.

▷ **Niece:** Rich or poor, everyone deserves love.

▷ **Aunt:** You should wear comfortable shoes.

Obviously there's no one right answer. But it seems to me that some of the answers could be better supported than others. What do you think? A central argument, which is often implied rather than stated, is hospitable to interpretation. I didn't stop to ask my five respondents to support their interpretations with evidence from the fairy tale itself. That's what I would have done had I been their teacher in a classroom.

College writing assignments ask you to prioritize ideas over topics. Good college writing doesn't focus on topic. It always goes straight for the idea that the topic implies. It might *refer* to topic, but only as a way to talk about argument. The plan later will be to use the text to support your interpretation of the main message, which is why a clear articulation of the core argument is the single most important thing you can do to set up your writing for a college assignment. So let's talk about these core arguments. First we'll tackle the necessary task of how to know what your own argument is. Then, because most college essays ask you to write in response to something you've read, we'll move on to discussing some good strategies to figure out the main message of the texts you write about.

5 How to Know What You Are Arguing

5.1 Thesis Statements: Four Categories to Remember

No matter what your assignment is, all thesis statements can be scooted into one of four helpful categories. If you understand the four categories, then you automatically understand the strategy you need in order to deliver a paper that supports its thesis. These four categories, called *claims*, represent four different approaches to structure. Once you recognize what kind of claim you are making, you know what kind of argument to set up. Thus your job is more than just writing a decent thesis statement. You actually need to think about what kind of strategy your particular thesis statement invites.

5.2 Value

Of the four kinds of claims, the claim of value is the only one I cannot recommend for writing that you have to turn in for a grade. Perhaps you might like to reserve this sort of claim for social events involving, but not limited to, tweeting, ranting, going home for Thanksgiving, and political discussions involving awkward silences and alcohol. Am I being mean? No! That is, sort of! In fact, the claim of value may be just the ticket in your personal writing, for instance on Facebook and in texts to your friends. Claims of value can be funny, memorably dramatic, and richly expressive. But if you produce academic writing that bases a whole argument on a claim of value, professorial eyebrows will be raised. Tutors will be assigned. Average grades will be given.

Here's why. A claim of value is a statement of opinion loaded with emotionally charged language or subjective words or phrases that mean wildly different things to different people. Value claims often use hyperbolic superlatives such as *best*, *worst*, *least*, and so on. Although often irresistible, a claim of value initiates an argument you just can't win.

Please join me in imagining that you were part of the loyal underground fan base for the 90s rapper Vanilla Ice long before he signed up to appear on *Dancing with the Stars*. You know Vanilla Ice's real name, you follow him on Twitter, you think he looks much better now that he is the age of your dad. Perhaps you have recently seen him—Vanilla Ice, not your dad—playing Tuscaloosa with Salt-N-Pepa and Coolio, on the rousing "I ♥ the 90s" tour. Also, at parties you sometimes rap the lyrics to "Ice, Ice Baby," maybe even doing the signature move with your foot.

Here comes an attractive acquaintance at such a party.

You: Know what? Vanilla Ice is the best entertainer of all time!

Attractive acquaintance: Vanilla who?

You [*doing the thing with your foot*]:

"Rock a mic like a vandal!
Light up a stage and
wax a chump like a candle!"

Attractive acquaintance: Nice talking to you, bye!

At this point you have probably intuited that you will never be able to convince this attractive acquaintance of the many rich contributions of Vanilla Ice, aka Robert Van Winkle. Why? The attractive acquaintance has a very different idea of what constitutes good entertainment. You can talk about the retro originality of Vanilla Ice's lyrics all the livelong day, but the attractive acquaintance

Vanilla Ice performing with MC Hammer in 2009

plainly doesn't admire retro originality.

You can't win a value argument because a claim of value isn't arguable. The central claim may indeed deliver your position in clear language [*Vanilla Ice is the best entertainer of all time!*]. Yet the claim itself contains a loaded, highly subjective term [*best*]. Doing that retro move with your foot, there at the party, you begged a much larger question, namely: What constitutes good entertainment in the first place? Vanilla Ice can be either champion or chump, depending on your perspective. Vanilla Ice, and I mean this respectfully, is the Rorschach inkblot of 90s entertainers.

Does this mean you can't write about Vanilla Ice in a college paper? Not at all. In the twenty-first century you can pretty much write about anything at the university level, provided you say something smart about it and link it to a larger cultural discussion with intriguing implications. When you signed up to go to college, you agreed to find out what other people think. You agreed to research their data, expose yourself to their professional opinions, and join a conversation that involves listening, quoting, responding, and writing. One of the cool things about our exponentially increasing databank of shared cultural knowledge is that there are experts in any field you can name. This gives you huge freedom in choosing subjects that interest you personally. One time one of my students wrote a great paper about people who think they see Jesus in yams, or tree bark, or rust stains on the underpass. You'd think that the topic would be a stretch, right? Not so. That student located plenty of lively cultural discussion vis-à-vis Jesus yams, and plenty of theologians and cultural anthropologists whose work applied to them. At issue here is the *language* you use, not the topic you choose. You can write about anything that interests you, divine yam portents and/ or Vanilla Ice.

The problem with value language is that it is both slippery and extreme. Whenever I see it in a student essay, I think of those yellow caution signs that declare a recently mopped floor, a wee man flailing backward: *Cuidado!* Danger! Value language doesn't necessarily mean you can't craft an effective argument, but it comes with a high risk of destabilizing that argument.

Look for words or phrases that have a built-in emotional trigger all by themselves, even when you lift them out of their context. Some words by definition are intended to yank a negative emotional response out of you. They don't even need to appear in sentences with other words, other thoughts. Think about loaded terms such as

> *dreadful, appalling, harmful, immature, bad, worse, worst, disgusting, ugly, nasty, skanktastic.*

For sure you want to avoid writing a thesis with slippery terms like these, or even their more academic-sounding cousins,

> *deleterious, provincial, fundamentalist, reprehensible, jejune, chicanerous.*

And please note that not all slippery language is negative. Some terms are sneakily employed to pull a *positive* emotional response from you. That's just as bad. Like their negative counterparts, positive value words can whip up an emotional tizzy even as stand-alone terms:

> *happy, beautiful, noble, great, better, best, delightful, cozy, amazing, fabulous.*

Here's a typical value-claim thesis that might sneak into academic writing:

> Ed Ruscha's paintings provide a brilliant illustration of the unusual media, surreal images, and arresting dissonance of the midcentury American pop-art movement.

You can prove that Ruscha's unusual media, surreal images, and dissonance exemplify the pop-art movement, but you cannot prove that they are brilliant. And anyway, the object of your essay is not to demonstrate how brilliant Ruscha is compared to other visual artists, whose work you won't even be addressing. Your object is to demonstrate the ways in which *Ruscha's* work reflects pop art. That you can do. But when you use slippery subjective terms like *brilliant*, you are setting out to argue something else.

Ed Ruscha's *The Old Tech-Chem Building* and *Blue Collar Tech-Chem* paintings

So, to wrap up, you might want to consider using one of the other three types of claims when setting up your thesis.

5.3 Fact

A claim of fact tacitly promises that the author will provide evidence that demonstrates the validity of its claim. What I'm about to say may seem strange, but stay with me. Structurally speaking, a claim of fact doesn't have to be *true* to be classed as a claim of fact. A claim of fact can assert anything at all, likely or preposterous, nutty or insightful, true or false. This is because right now we're not looking at the content of the claim but rather what kind of claim it is.

A claim of fact is merely a neutral-sounding sentence that presents as a demonstrable statement. "Hey," it seems to imply, "check it out, I can deliver some evidence. So keep reading." For example, a bystander asserts, "The officer shot an unarmed suspect." That's a claim of fact whether the suspect was armed or not. The statement functions as a claim of fact in what may later become a contested argument. Can the speaker prove that the suspect was not armed? Maybe she *was* armed. Maybe the weapon will show up later when police release the video. Maybe she *wasn't* armed, in which case the officer's choice to shoot may jump-start a national conversation about police bias. Even though only one of these two statements can be true, they are both claims of fact:

| The officer shot an unarmed suspect.

| The officer shot an armed suspect.

With either claim the reader is likely to keep right on reading. Both statements promise not just further discussion but actual evidence. Any alert reader would sit down to the table with a polite request for more. "Please pass the proof!"

A claim of fact, whatever the content, will work just fine in your academic writing as long as you are prepared to offer evidence that your claim is so. We make claims of fact all the time, sometimes without using careful or appropriate academic language.

> Neanderthals freely ate one another.

> The ancient Egyptians sometimes mummified small crocodiles.

> Rasputin influenced Empress Alexandra Fyodorovna.

The only time claims of fact aren't suitable for a thesis is when they're super easy to prove. You could document them in one or two sentences, which would be great if you were writing the teeny house of college essays. But most college writing assignments call for more than a paragraph. A typical college writing assignment is 3–5 pages because your instructors want to give you a chance to *develop* your thesis, not just document it. So if you want to build your essay around a claim of fact, try for a thesis that invites elaboration or discussion.

> **Nossir:** Neanderthals freely ate one another.
> **Better:** Neanderthals were apex predators.
>   (You can locate cannibalism as one of many forms

A lifelike model of *Homo neanderthalensis* at London's Natural History Museum

of cultural predation.)

Nossir: The ancient Egyptians sometimes mummified small crocodiles.

Better: Animal mummies help us understand ancient Egyptian religious practices.

(You can discuss the slender crocodile mummy as an animal sacrifice, a beloved pet with iconic religious significance, or a tasty snack to be enjoyed en route to the afterlife.)

Nossir: Rasputin influenced Empress Alexandra Fyodorovna.

Better: Rasputin's reputation was so damaged in the press that his actual influence on Empress Alexandra Fyodorovna is difficult to trace.

(You can discuss the smear campaign orchestrated

by Rasputin's enemies as part of the political unrest preceding the Russian Revolution.)

In sum, claims of fact are doable. Make sure that your main claim allows you to ground the statement in a larger context and to raise issues that matter.

5.4 Cause and Effect

Cause and effect is where academic writing starts to heat up. If you want to set yourself up to win, shoot for a thesis that promises to prove that A causes B. You don't have to use a claim of cause and effect in order to craft an excellent thesis, but this kind of claim is pretty easy to work, even for writers who are just beginning to learn the conventions of academic writing. Ask yourself what the main event of the essay will be, the most important action. If this piece of writing were a three-ring circus, what would be happening in the big ring in the middle? Once you've decided on the main event, ask yourself, "What causes the main outcome? What force or social condition is responsible for this outcome?"

Notice that you personally are not answering the cause-and-effect question. This is the place to analyze what the *author* is saying. Here's what cause and effect looks like in action, in a paragraph about a short story written by the American author Toni Cade Bambara.

Toni Cade Bambara's "The Lesson" suggests that poverty perpetuates ignorance. Conversely, in Bambara's urban world, it is only education that results in the self-awareness necessary for change. When the college graduate Ms. Moore takes a group of rowdy children to F.A.O. Schwarz for an object lesson in class privilege, the children begin to understand the implications of their economic marginalization. Up until the moment when Ms. Moore takes the school children to the expensive toy store, the narrator's behavior has been disrespectful, violent, and bullying. After the lesson, however, Sylvia understands the difference between what is probable (more poverty) and what is possible (success). Sylvia's realization changes the reader's interpretation even as it changes the course of her life. Thus Bambara's lesson is not that we are sometimes complicit in our own marginalization. The lesson is that our future doesn't have to look like our past.

See the A that causes the B? Education brings insight, which in turn invites change. You can frame a cause-and-effect argument lots of ways, but these are some of the tried-and-true equations with which writers argue that A produces an effect on B.

▷   this abstract idea manifests in that concrete action
▷   this movement engenders that legislation
▷   this decision affected that outcome
▷   this media message foments that reality
▷   this factor contributed to that result
▷   this call invites that response
▷   this action comes with that consequence

Human beings define themselves by logic. That's why the cause-and-effect thesis is so easy to set up. We think like that *anyway*, even when we're not writing a paper. Think back to some of the scary stuff our ancestors did, such as child sacrifice. We know now that our ancestors had that logic all catty-wampus. The rain comes and crops grow whether we harm or cherish our children. But even the *illogical* cause-and-effect arguments must have been pretty persuasive, right? Whole cultures got on board.

False cause

Some composition textbooks itemize the fallacies that can screw up your writing. I personally enjoy reading about those fallacies, but, then, I am also the kind of person who savors long-winded, heavily footnoted inquiries into the religious practices of pre-Columbian peoples. Since this is supposed to be a textbook about good writing and not bad logic, I will choose just one fallacy to warn you about. I pick the granddaddy of fallacies, a real doozy. It's the one that messes up your sense of cause and effect. This fallacy is called False Cause. If you're looking to irritate your friends, you may also feel free to use the Latin label: *Post hoc, ergo propter hoc.* (After this, therefore, on account of this.)

A claim qualifies for False Cause when there's just not enough evidence to conclude that A causes B. Perhaps you already have enough evidence to show that A is happening. You can also demonstrate that B is happening. But there's not enough hard evidence to show a *causal* relationship between the two. When I show you how this fallacy works, below, you will probably recognize it as the troubling kernel of all essential stereotypes—meaning those stereotypes that assume people act a certain way because of an essential condition into which they are born, such as race, gender, or sexual orientation.

Accidentally making a False Cause claim doesn't mean you're intellectually limited. It just means that you're human. We all sometimes come to False Cause conclusions not because we're mean, or bigoted, or narrow-minded but because we're hardwired to learn from our past experiences.

Inductive logic

Letting your own experiences shape what you believe turns on a certain way of thinking called **inductive logic**. We are all inductive thinkers. And inductive logic is curiously susceptible to False Cause thinking. I want to make it very clear that I am not trashing inductive logic. We need it, and inductive logic is in itself a good thing. But there's a certain sort of risk that attaches to it.

Check out the difference between these two types of logic, both of which help us maximize our intellectual and psychosocial potential: inductive and deductive. They both involve ratiocinative movement, but they are streams flowing in opposite directions.

▷ **Inductive logic** moves from the **particular to the general**.

▷ **Deductive logic** moves from the **general to the particular**.

Imagine you are five years old, standing on a stool to help your daddy make pancakes. Daddy gives you a ladleful of batter to pour into the pan. But you overreach and accidentally burn your little hand. Tears, kisses! Faster than a burn can heal, an idea is rising like a phoenix from the ashes of this poignant childhood experience. This idea is helping shape your understanding of kitchen protocol. In other words, you have already begun a slow-mo realization about life and pancakes. You have already taken advantage of a particular, specific incident to move toward a general conclusion. And it is inductive thinking that has presented you with your tentative cause-and-effect conclusion. If you touch that burner, guess what? You get burned. A causes B.

Your memory may flicker over the pancake incident the next time you are standing at the stove. Now, at age seven, you are big enough to sidestep the stool. You are making your dad's girlfriend an omelet. When you reach over the hot skillet to pour in the beaten eggs, do you pull your hand back in time to avoid the burn? Yes, you do! Here's a second specific incident that has reinforced the truth of your earlier conclusion.

Now we skip ahead many years to college, when, after an evening out, you and some friends have the serious munchies. Somebody suggests grilled cheese, topped, perhaps, with left-over General Tso's Chicken. (It all sounds good to you right now.) So you get busy. Burner on, check. Bread with cheese, check. The mysterious General Tso, whoever he was, would be pleased and astonished by this delicious innovation!

Do you burn your hand on the burner? No way, not even in this kooky late-night mood. Why? Because by now you have cooked often enough to have come to a firm inductive conclusion. Namely, if you touch that burner, you'll get burned.

Is your conclusion valid?

Um. This brings us to the San Andreas in California. The state of induction has a fault line in what is otherwise very useful logic. That burner will burn you, sure enough—as long as the burner is *on*. But what if it's off? A cool burner offers no threat to any hand, though if you want to go stand there with your hand spread out on it, okay!

The problem with inductive logic is that we may be tempted to come to a premature conclusion with the persuasive, but limited, evidence of personal experience. Now you can see why this baby is so dangerous. If five out of five blondes are bad drivers, when are you safe to conclude that blondes are generally bad drivers? If you know of three different religious families who are stockpiling canned goods for the Apocalypse there in their underground bunker, when are you safe to conclude that all religious folks are nutters?

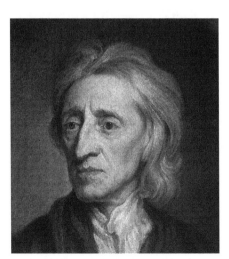

Portrait of John Locke ca. 1697

We would be dummies if we failed to learn the lessons that personal observation has to teach. In fact personal observation is one of the main ways human beings gather knowledge. Back in the day, the seventeenth-century Enlightenment thinker John Locke pointed out that we all amass knowledge through the experiences of our five senses. Locke's ideas about how we know what we know helped us develop a modern understanding of the sentient self, meaning a self defined by a continuity of consciousness. Our level of consciousness is continually morphing based on incoming data, which means that consciousness is not a goal we achieve but a process we live.

Moreover, the conclusions we make using inductive logic play a *constructive* role in the identities we develop. Imagine if, in the pancake scenario, you made an early decision to resist your natural impulse toward inductive logic. "By jingo, I will give this hot burner a fair chance! I refuse to jump to conclusions about the likelihood of its ever hurting me again!" Such a response would be unwise. To think inductively is as unavoidable as it is practical. We would expose ourselves to a world of hurt if we stubbornly refused to learn from experience—either from our own or from the experiences of those we trust. Consider how learning from our collective experience is the inductive rationale for studying the human record. The idea isn't to learn history. The idea is to learn *from* history.

So here we are at a conundrum. Inductive logic is necessary for our growth and survival. Yet it is also at the heart of all stereotypes involving essentialist conditions of birth, gender, race, and so on. How do we know when inductive logic is good and when it's bad? Do a quick scan of your mental files for the stereotypes that have been saved to the hard drive of your mind. Perhaps some of these include stereotypes about groups other than the one you identify with. The stereotypes are mostly negative, right? Isn't it curious how stereotypes are rarely positive, causing us to *admire* the group in question? That should be our first clue that something is amiss.

The problem with stereotypes isn't that they over-rely on inductive logic. The problem is that they never acknowledge the obvious limitations of this way of thinking. The next time you are listening to a talk show or the next time you are reading an op-ed piece, see if you can detect an example of stereotyping. (It's often easier to spot when we don't personally know the speaker.) If you do manage to identify a moment that turns on accidental stereotyping, chances are you will have also found a nice clear case of False Cause.

It's worthwhile, too, to mention the opposite of accidental stereotyping. Is there such a thing as *intentional* stereotyping? Sure. There's the kind we see in old-school texts such as the 1962 classic film *To Kill a Mockingbird*, where intentional stereotyping fuels a lynch mob. In that movie the folks perpetrating race stereotypes totally know they're doing it, and they're only too eager to act on those stereotypes. Although civil rights and better education have improved some of our social conditions, stereotyping on purpose still plays a huge role in American culture. Today we might see intentional stereotyping in ways that purport to be less violent. Sometimes it's called *marketing*, sometimes *stand-up*. Think, for example, about what our comedians are trying to achieve. They're trying to get us to laugh ruefully at ourselves. In educated circles today stereotyping may seem as problematic when people don't *know* they are stereotyping as when they do. Some even find it less offensive, maybe even downright funny, when the stereotyping is intentional. One thing is sure, though. While False Cause essentialist thinking may have a role in shaping American everything from ads to improv, it has no place in academic writing.

Deductive logic

The opposite of inductive logic, **deduction,** can also go askew. This is the sort of thinking that moves from general to specific, as in the scenario below. I'll begin by making a general claim, using language that suggests a principle or a general law of cause and effect.

> If you eat 26 family-size bags of Cheetos in one sitting, you'll get sick.

True, right? No problem with the logic? A causes B. Now let us move on to the next claim in the logical progression. This next one is already less general, moving toward the specific:

> I have just eaten 26 family-size bags of Cheetos.

If the logic of the initial premise is sound, then there can be only one possible conclusion, yes?

> Therefore, I will soon get sick.

It's good logic, if bizarre nutrition. But imagine what would happen if we set it up this way instead:

> If you eat 26 family-size bags of Cheetos in one sitting, you'll get sick.

| I am sick right now.

| Therefore, I have just eaten 26 family-size bags of Cheetos.

Why is the logic suddenly wonky? Because the speaker may have gotten sick from a non-Cheeto cause. Who knows, maybe this speaker doesn't do Cheetos on principle. Maybe he has overindulged in Ding-Dongs or Pop-Tarts. Maybe he has an ongoing flirtation with the Keebler Elves. Or maybe he's sick because he recently donated a kidney. Or maybe he suffers from motion sickness, there in the backseat of a NYC cab. We can all agree: many are the non-Cheeto vomitous interludes.

Thus deductive thinking can also go astray. I'm sure it comes as no surprise to you that every human activity has the potential for screw-up. And yes, the particular flaws that inhere in induction and deduction recur with alarming frequency in our cultural conversations. That said, the cause-and-effect thesis is still one of the easiest to set up and carry out in academic writing. People with college educations—professors, bosses, employees—are in the business of making persuasive cause-and-effect arguments, whether they're theorizing what killed the dinosaurs or researching how to improve their bottom line. Because this kind of claim will be equally useful while you are a student and in your professional life thereafter, I strongly recommend that you go out of your way to practice setting up cause-and-effect paradigms.

5.5 Solution and Policy

Civil War reenactment at Kennekuk County Park near Danville, Illinois

The fourth kind of claim is especially appealing to activists, pragmatists, dissidents, believers, and Civil War buffs who enjoy complicated period reenactments of the Battle of Shiloh.

One humid July morning my brothers reluctantly mustered for pop-up camper duty. None of us wanted to sweat it out in an odorous camper with mildewed flaps. We wanted to be at home in California, swimming in our friends' pools. However, whether we liked it or not, our parents rounded us up once a year for an embarrassing cross-country car trip. On the way we were required to play learning games such as "Name the State Capital on the Tin Garbage Can Mom Brought Along Because It Featured a Map of the United States." Our vacation destination was always educational, perhaps an underground cavern with stalactites. All six of us squeezed into a wheezy VW van with curtains. Please know that in 1970 air-conditioning had certainly been invented. We just didn't have it. Girls cooked and did the dishes, boys farted and caught toads. Everybody wore matching homemade shorts.

Don't think I am making this up. I can photodocument.

So it was on this sultry July afternoon that we piled out at a remote woodsy campground in Tennessee. Like previous campgrounds, this one offered stinging black flies, a snake or two, and an outhouse with spiders. Yet this particular facility stood head and shoulders above the rest. It one-upped the competition with a patch of olallieberries, fuzzed with prickers. My mother handed me and my sister two Styrofoam cups with bite marks. "Girls, go pick some berries for pancakes." We obediently disappeared into the shrubbery.

We followed the berries further and further into the dense thicket. Suddenly there came the sound of heavy steps in the underbrush, men whistling and swearing. We froze: too late to run away. And then came a curious sight. Two gray-uniformed soldiers stepped into view. They were sporting Civil War uniforms complete with sweat rings and intense BO. One man's sideburns clung like pork-chop puffs to cheeks that rolled methodically over chew. Being Mennonite, I had never even seen anybody smoking a cigarette, let alone issuing a brown stream of tobacco in an impressive arc. This man spat, and I knew, even at ten, that he really wanted to call attention to the gesture. The other soldier's chin was obscured by a dense beard that had taken over the south of his face, like kudzu. The spitter mopped his forehead with his sleeve, still holding his machete. The bearded soldier had a Wesson and

Leavitt Dragoon single-action revolver, though I was to learn this later.

"Missy," drawled the spitter. He touched his cap with the machete. "Kin you tell us wayer ta git uh drinka watuh?"

I pointed back to the campground, then trailed with my little sister at a safe distance. When we emerged from the olalla, the soldiers were already wowing our parents at the picnic table. My mother was ecstatic: she had lucked onto the teaching moment of a lifetime. Dad commanded us to draw up lawn chairs and give ear to these chaps. And many were the facts vis-à-vis the Battle of Shiloh, whose full-scale reenactment, complete with canons and corpses, was to commence later that same afternoon. Of the thousands of "living historians," some would have head lice. Some would play rousing military tunes upon a fife. Some would crouch in the grass and shout, "Permission to die, Sir! A ball has lodged in my shoulder!"

Or so I surmised. Our Confederate guests never once broke character, unless you count a polite request to borrow some sunscreen. They told us more than we ever wanted to know about abolition, secession, and death by bayonet. They overshared about dysentery, the "bloody flux." Eventually, winding it all up, my mother prodded each of us to ask the soldiers a question. My brothers asked about gunpowder and gangrene. My sister, who was five, asked if they had a kitty. I had already concluded that these guys were the last word in encyclopedic dorkdom—right, the irony!—so when it was my turn, I asked, "How come a bunch of grown-ups are playing soldier?"

The spitter twiddled his whiskers and said solemnly, "Missy, tell you whut. We need tuh live history in order tuh understand it."

Which brings us to the last kind of claim: the claim of solution and policy. Usually you can recognize a claim of solution and policy by the words *need, should,* or *ought.* Here is a thesis that advocates for a specific course of action. Sometimes it even purports to have the solution for a particular problem, typically when the author has weighed and rejected several other possible solutions for the same problem. A claim of solution and policy almost always affirms a position that the author strongly holds. More, it nudges the reader to take action. Reader, it suggests, you should adopt the position that I have taken, and I will be happy to tell you why I am right. Do this, change this, repeal this, fund this. Put your money where your mouth is. Get on board! If you want to understand history, you must walk a mile in another man's boots!

Being ten, I had no way of knowing that my instant objection to the soldier's logic was a textbook response to a typical claim of solution and policy. Up until that moment, preoccupied with cartwheels and recess, I had experienced a peaceful indifference to the idea of understanding history through reenactments of it. If you had forced my ten-year-old self to articulate a position, I would have shrugged. War encampments and pioneer villages: so what? If folks sought to perfect a historically accurate cornpone, well, it was a free world. Let them make pone. Let them double over in the grass with their imaginary diarrhea!

But something about the fellow's claim instantly called up an opinion where none had existed before. As soon as he said, "This is the way to understand history," I instantly thought, *No it's not.* I wasn't buying it. I secretly thought that a whole mess of grown-ups just wanted an excuse to play dress-up, like buxom wenches who go around exclaiming "Odd's bodkins!" at Renaissance fairs. How come nobody dresses up like a hobo and stands in a bread line? Do we need to re-create the Great Depression in order to understand it?

Please know that I was not a courageous child. Nor was I an intellectual maverick. So what made me jump to an opposing opinion so fast?

Human nature.

What the soldier actually said was

| *We need to live history in order to understand it.*

What the soldier did not say was

| *I have found a useful way to understand history.*

No, the soldier made it pretty clear that people could not understand history without historical enactments. If his way was the one and only effective course of action, that meant there wasn't room for another. An audience inevitably bristles rather than nods when people take such a position. More than any other, the claim of solution and policy seeks to persuade an audience to try a new position, so there's often a lot at stake.

And note that the desired audience isn't made up of people who already agree with the claim. It's made up of the ones who don't. Thus the solution-and-policy argument can come with something that smells a bit off, as when on a freeway you get a protracted afterwhiff of skunk. Sometimes the arguer has just the opposite effect of the one he intends, as indeed he would see if he would study the lingering effect of his argument on his audience.

Focused questions - Examining your purpose

Well, how do we avoid creating (or experiencing) such an afterwhiff? If you're the one preparing to lay out a solution-and-policy essay, try this. Examine your purpose *before* you begin to address an audience who does not already share your views. It's a good idea to ask some focused questions about purpose before launching a solution-and-policy argument.

 ▷ Why am I writing this essay? What do I want?
 ▷ Do I want to explain my position?
 ▷ Has anybody even asked me to explain it? Or do I just think they need to hear it?
 ▷ Do I want to convert my readers to my own position?
 ▷ Am I hoping to establish a solution that meets the needs of two opposing viewpoints? Am I looking for a solution that both sides will find acceptable?
 ▷ Have I already done the work of reading/listening to the opposing viewpoint?
 ▷ How have I demonstrated my intention to be fair, generous, and accurate as I describe the position that challenges my own?

Answering any one of these questions can dramatically change the shape of a solution-and-policy argument.

My Civil War soldier's motives were altruistic. He was taking time out of his Battle Day to educate four children he didn't even know. His position should have, could have, interested me. Too bad I was a self-absorbed little peanut, eh? However, he would have had me at hello if he had said something like this instead: "Missy, this ain't the only way to understand history. But actin' it all out like a big ol' goofus has helped me learn some surprisin' things. Know what happens when you survive for four days on hardtack and creek water?" Which is all to say, if that Confederate fellow and his sidekick had given me a good reason to nibble moldy crackers and ingest tadpoles, I surely would have been willing to give it a go.

In hindsight, it was my mother who had the better response, one that seems practical to writers trying to work their claims of solution and policy today. My parents are Mennonite, a Protestant group that bases their faith on a theology of pacifism. They do not believe in war. Historically the Mennonites have been conscientious objectors, peaceful protestors, the very last people on earth who might invite a drop-in Civil War soldier to teach their kids about guns and bayonets. Yet that's exactly what my mother did. She herself would rather forfeit her life than commit any act of violence against another human being. But instead of preaching her pacifism at the soldiers, she listened to what they had to say. She asked questions. She made sure we understood where they were coming from. In short, she modeled civil discourse for her four kids.

The main thrust of a solution-and-policy claim is to urge the reader to do something or think something. The dissenting reader, by definition, will never be an easy sell. But the dissenting reader will always be more receptive if the writer has created a climate of respect. Conversely, if it is the *reader* who practices respect, even a one-sided claim of solution and policy can function as a useful information exchange. Respect is never just an attitude or a mind-set. It is a verb. It is something you do on purpose as you write or read. And because it is something you do, it comes with results you can literally point to on the page. Respect is my mother, inviting a Confederate soldier to demonstrate the brass trigger guard of a Wesson and Leavitt Dragoon single-action revolver, there on the picnic table. The practice of respect makes it a habit to acknowledge the opposing position, using the other's own language if possible.

Sometimes a claim of solution and policy seems to be two mints in one. That is, it seems to be two kinds of claims twined together. It is indisputably a claim of solution and policy, because it is calling for action in no uncertain terms. (You should walk a mile in Confederate boots! You must relive history!) Yet the directive might also be simultaneously drawing on the logic of cause and effect. (Participation in Civil War reenactments produces a fresh understanding of history). When this double-claim thing happens, the emphasis leans to the more aggressive claim, which is the call to action. This is because a call to get up off your butt is more likely to produce a measurable outcome than a call to sit around and think about something.

A mandate to action doesn't necessarily make a better thesis. It depends on you, the writer. It depends on what you believe an author is ultimately arguing. Fact, cause and effect, and solution and policy can all make a great thesis statement.

None is preferable to the others, though freshmen often tell me that they get the most bang for their buck with cause and effect. For me it makes sense to take my cue from the kind of text I'm writing about. Sometimes a text makes me personally want to implement immediate action, especially when I already happen to share the author's opinions or beliefs. But some authors want to provoke thought, not action. And our job as thoughtful writers is to figure out what the author wants us to see, do, and believe.

To recap, all four kinds of claims are useful, but each ushers in a different kind of writing and a different goal. If you want to assert an opinion without argumentative evidence, stick to the value claims of casual personal writing. If you want to prove a statement using academic resources, craft a statement of fact. If you want to explore a relationship between two things, try to hook up cause and effect. And if you want to persuade the reader to adopt a certain policy or take measurable action, use solution and policy.

Hot Topics

Whip out a piece of scratch paper. Quickly and anonymously jot down three hot-button things that are being discussed in American media right now. The repealing of Obamacare! The controversy about *13 Reasons*! Tensions with North Korea! Cyber-bullying!

Your instructor will collect, shuffle, and redistribute. Choose one of the three topics that you receive. *Without labeling what kind of claims you are writing*, in random order, craft a claim of value, fact, cause and effect, and solution and policy for your hot topic of choice. Your instructor will shuffle and swap one more time.

Now read all four of the claims written by an anonymous classmate.

▷ Can you identify what kinds of claims they represent?

▷ Assuming you are not tempted by the claim of value, which of the remaining three claims would you pick to front an essay on this topic?

6 How to Know What a Text Is Arguing

6.1 How to Find the Central Argument

Is there an easy way to figure out the central argument of a reading assignment?

The short answer is yes, there's an easy way. But first, some useful guidelines.

Make sure that your central argument actually expresses a full thought.

Imagine how you would react if a casual acquaintance came running up to you and said with enthusiasm but no preamble, "T-REX!" This actually does happen to me and my husband on a regular basis. Most Sunday mornings an energetic toddler, Asher, sprints over to us—us specifically, even though we are not related to him in any way. Although this occurs in a church sanctuary, he uses his outdoor voice to shout, "T-REX!" Sometimes he follows it up with an ambiguous little dance, as if twerking. Sometimes he just runs away.

Rhoda & Mitch: Good morning, Asher.

Asher: T-REX!

We interpret the overture as follows:

Asher: Good morning, large adult friends! I need to find a restroom.

At age two, this child is right on schedule, and I look forward to hearing more of his thoughts on the late Cretaceous Period after he is potty-trained. But Asher's approach would not work for a college-level central argument. You might be thinking, Puh-lease, nobody in college would do that. Oh yes. Yes, they do. Allow me to present a central argument that shouts, "T-REX!" and then runs away.

> The central argument of William Faulkner's short story "A Rose for Emily" is the corruption of old values.

Take away the drumroll at the front, and here's what you have left:

> The corruption of old values.

The corruption of old values.

Like a dinosaur with shriveled little arms, this so-called central argument presents an image but not a complete thought. It's just a thing, a phrase, a T-REX. Economic marginalization. Corndog on a stick. The inhumanity of war. The corruption of old values.

If you're like many new college students, you're a little tentative in the area of the takeaway. In school up until now it may have been enough to prove that you actually put your eyes on every page of the text, that you read the whole enchilada like a responsible student. You took quiz after quiz on reading assignments. You wrote summaries and reflections. You discussed stories and essays together as a class and in small groups. You saw the movie/documentary/dance production with jazz hands.

Too bad none of that guarantees that you have done the single most necessary piece of intellectual work, the thing that is a must for every college assignment. You can do all of the above, see, without committing to a central argument. And now it's time to get confident in this necessary skill.

6.2   Working to Understand a Text

Tip: Write a central argument for every reading assignment *before* you go to the class where you'll be discussing it.

I am happy to report that you can totally change your mind about what the text means later. In fact, you probably *will* change your mind. I hope so! That often happens when you hear what other readers and your instructor have to say. They may have noticed different but eye-opening things, or they may bring special knowledge that will expand and deepen your own reading.

The reason I'm urging you to do this important bit of intellectual work before class is that you need to get in the habit of knowing and trusting what you think. These two skills are mighty important to critical inquiry, every bit as important as the flexibility you will develop as you seek to grow your intellect by reading other authors. But in order to experience change, you need to know where you are at the start. That's why writing down a preliminary (okay, tentative) central argument is so important. It helps you flesh out your sense of what the text means. Thus you need to start practicing immediately. And the only way to do that is to write down, with actual words, on an actual screen or piece of old-fashioned paper, a clear, substantive takeaway for the whole text.

It's downright easy when the author spells it all out for you. But you can't count on an essayist who hands you her main point up front in the first paragraph. Unlike you, the published essayist is no longer in college, and she can do whatever she wants. Maybe she wants to announce her thesis matter-of-factly, there in a helpful abstract. Maybe she wants you to figure out that her essay is written in a kind of dialogue, a response to other critics or essayists. Or maybe your reading assignment is one of those cryptic braided creative nonfiction pieces, where the author is skipping around with three separate narratives that don't seem to have anything to do with each other. What if it's a poem or a short story where you're left feeling clueless? Let's be frank: some undergraduate classics seem designed to mess with your mind. Allusions to stuff you haven't read, pedantic vocabulary, ambiguous endings, fuzzy symbols—Hey, I've been teaching a long time. I recognize the Kafka-inspired groan and its inevitable follow-up: "Why can't the author just SAY what he means?"

He *is* saying what he means.

If your family celebrated Easter, think back to when you were little and your parents hid Easter eggs for you. Notice that your parents didn't hide the Easter eggs *from* you. They hid them *for* you, with the full expectation that you would find them. If you were a busy toddler, no doubt you shrieked with joy when you detected a neon-pink plastic candy-filled egg next to the sprinkler, in full sight on the lawn. Your parents hid the eggs according to where you would be most likely to find them, yes? Recall that as you got older, the eggs got harder and harder to find. At no time in your childhood did the whole Easter Egg Hunt seem like a bummer, a duty, a chore. It was supposed to delight you—hidden chocolate, yay! Marshmallow peeps, tell your friends!

Doing the work of finding the eggs yourself somehow made it better than if your mom had merely said, "Sweetie, wanna chocolate bunny?" Same thing is happening in college reading assignments. The reward is in the discovery of interesting complexities that are not hidden in plain sight by the sprinkler on the lawn.

> **Q**: What's better than candy?
> **A**: *Finding* candy.

> **Q**: What's better than understanding a text?
> **A**: *Working* to understand a text.

6.3 Choosing Binary Pairs

If you're nervous about the process of grasping hidden complexities, I have another useful trick for you. Plus this trick works no matter what kind of reading assignment you get, whether essay, op-ed piece, play, story, poem, journal article, even *Moby Dick*.

After you've read the text, make a list of binary pairs that the text features, this versus that. For example, say you read all the way through William Faulkner's short story "**A Rose for Emily**," which is taught in so many college courses that it's a safe bet you'll be asked to read it before you graduate. A southern belle murders her boyfriend, Homer Barron, and then (spoiler alert) sleeps with his decaying body in her bed for forty years. If I were to scribble down a quick list of binary pairs in this text, I'd go with

dead vs. living	married vs. unmarried
North vs. South	sane vs. insane
man vs. woman	power vs. submission
rich vs. poor	bloated vs. slender
black vs. white	now vs. then
old vs. new	public vs. private
stasis vs. change	dusty vs. clean
gay vs. straight	victim vs. rebel
townsfolk vs. Emily	slavery vs. freedom

When it starts getting challenging to think of new pairs, don't sweat it. Just move on to the next step.

Now skim over your list and pick the pair that seems to be the main concern of the text. Go with your gut; there's no one right answer. Different readers might be drawn to different pairs. Of the ones that I came up with above, I'm inclined to think that *dead vs. living* is the most important.

Last part, and easiest. You've got two things at opposite ends of a spectrum. Of the two options, which one does the text seem to frown on? I'd say it frowns on dead stuff. Faulkner's descriptions of Emily get progressively ickier as Emily moves toward literal death, both her own and her lover's. When she is a young woman, Emily presents as pretty, good, and pure: a "slender figure in white" with hair cut short like a girl or an angel (171). But by the time the aldermen come to call on her, she looks like a corpse: "She looked bloated, like a body long submerged in motionless water, and of that pallid hue" (169). Any time something comes in on two levels—part of the literal plot and part of the metaphoric language used to describe it—it's always a big deal. Here we've got four people literally dying in six pages, and also a living person being compared to a dead one. I'd say death is a very big deal in this story, wouldn't you?

Bit of a caution. The text does seem to be frowning at one element in the pair you have selected as important. Yet that doesn't mean the other element is getting a thumbs-up from the author. Since the Old Guard is dying and dead, and since Miss Emily is the last representative of the Old Guard, it's reasonable to infer that Faulkner equates Old Guard values (the arrogance, the aristocracy, the entitlement) with death. But Faulkner is pretty mean to some of the living people, too. Those townsfolk can't wait to get up in other people's business. They gossip and judge. They lack compassion. When Emily appears suicidal, they mention it to each other but offer no help. So this method of choosing a binary pair for emphasis doesn't mean you have to set up an either/or argument. You don't.

In four quick steps, here is an easy, reasonable way to approach the task of forming a central argument.

1. Make a list of binary pairs.
2. Pick the main pair.
3. Ask: "Which side of the pair does the text favor?"
4. Use that side as the basis for your central argument.

Maybe before you made the list, you had only a hazy idea of the text and its issues. Maybe before you made the list, you would have run up to me like young Mr. Asher and shouted, "Corruption and death!" Now, though, having made your list, you are gathering a sense of possible direction. Faulkner is criticizing the Old South for having failed to bury its dead ideology of classist superiority, and you can say so explicitly:

> In "A Rose for Emily," Faulkner urges southern white supremacists to let go of their historical entitlement, hypocrisy, and false sense of superiority.

Totally doable as a central argument. It's a claim of solution and policy, too, so it's the kind of strong claim that demands action. You know it's a workable central argument if you can use the central event of the text to prove it. In this case, the central event of the text is Emily's decision to hang on to a rotting corpse. If we say that Emily, heiress of rich white Mr. Grierson, represents Southern Privilege, then her refusal to bury Dead Guy represents an unhealthy, deadly refusal to let go of the past. The implication is that some folks are hanging onto dead ideas *on purpose*.

Let's say, though, that you pick a different binary pair. Let's say that you're going with an incest reading, and you picked *power vs. submission*. Can you do that? Sure. You can pick any binary pair **as long as you can show its importance to all the main events of the text**. Mr. Grierson, Emily's father, insisted on a role of absolute power over his daughter. In accordance with his demand for absolutism, she was absolutely submissive while he was alive. "None of the young men were quite good enough for Miss Emily and such," remember the narrators. Maybe in *your* reading the reason Emily's father kept chasing away perfectly appropriate suitors—cracking the leather of a bullwhip, no less—was because Mr. Grierson wanted his daughter all to himself. And maybe that's why Emily couldn't bear to part with her father's dead body (171). The relationship with her father, whatever it was, was the only one he had allowed her to have.

But in the *power vs. submission* pair, who is powerful, and who is submissive? Couldn't you make the argument that Emily manages a power-grab of her own after her controlling dad dies? When he was alive, he was the one cracking a leather bullwhip, a distinctly southern symbol of white power. But it's the putatively powerless Miss Emily who inherits the mantle of sexual transgression. She responds by cracking some leather of her own: "When the Negro opened the blinds of one window, [the aldermen] could see that the leather was cracked" (169). It's almost as if she's answering his cracked leather with more of the same, like a conversation in which both parties are speaking Cracked Leather. And just like her sexually transgressive father, Emily forces sex on an unwilling partner. Both incest and necrophilia violate taboos we normally revere: the sanctity of the parent-child bond and the honor due to the dead. Therefore both kinds of sexual assault illustrate the dangers of power at its ugliest and most perverse. And in a story set in the Deep South, it is pointedly in the house of Caucasian privilege where rape happens, where consent is violated.

What's interesting in this *power vs. submission* reading is that the story charts *Emily's* movement from powerless to powerful. She becomes a rapist like her dad. In fact Faulkner goes out of his way to compare her elsewhere to a man: "Up to the day of her death at seventy-four, [her hair] was still that vigorous iron-gray, like the hair of an active man" (174). An active *man*? Why wouldn't Faulkner say, an active *woman*? Because the gender comparison accents Emily's movement to a position of power, that's why.

So if I had picked the binary pair *power vs. submission*, I might have come up with a different sort of central argument:

> In "A Rose for Emily," Faulkner warns readers that an inappropriate use of power perpetuates a cycle of violence, compromises awareness, and prevents growth.

Notice that this time my central argument is cause and effect. Can we prove that the abused becomes the abuser? Absolutely. Emily one-ups her dad by becoming both rapist and murderer. Can we prove that Emily's power-grab has compromised her level of awareness? Yup: girl doesn't even know that Colonel Sartoris is dead, and, p.s., that was a *decade* ago. She thinks she owes no taxes, for heaven's sake. Can we prove that her particular movement to power has prevented her growth? For sure. She ages but does not grow. She grays but does not mature. She not only avoids change; she actively *resists* change.

Here is a woman with artistic talent. We don't know conclusively that she was the artist who drew the pencil portrait of her father displayed in the parlor (169), but it's a reasonable inference, given that she could draw well enough to teach china-painting lessons. As china painting went out of style, did she adapt her talent to a more viable aesthetic medium? No, she did not: "The front door closed upon the last [china-painting pupil] and remained closed for good" (174). We can easily prove that Miss Emily makes it a point to Just Say No to change. Faulkner provides abundant textual details such as her refusal of a mailbox or house numbers. We can argue that stasis, rigidity, and lack of inquiry have all contributed to her premature decay.

In sum, you don't have to choose the binary pair your teacher picks. Pick what you think is the main focus, for starters, and, unlike poor Miss Emily, you will be open to change later. Choosing a nice binary pair is like wedging your foot in the door. You still have to write a central argument, but now it's a lot easier to get in.

7. On Beginnings and Endings

7.1 Creating Your Introduction: A Two-Step Process

"I am certainly eager to write this entire essay two weeks before it is due," said nobody, ever.

Thank goodness there's an easy way to get in. However, even the easy way involves some steps, a strategy. A character in an E. M. Forster novel asked, "How can I tell you what I think till I see what I say?" I'm a big fan of this approach because it allows us to break down the process of writing the introduction into two manageable steps, with the first being downright easy. As we all know, getting started is the hardest part. Thus it is helpful to begin with the easiest thing.

The first step is to write a bad introduction for your eyes only. The sole purpose of this piece of writing is to let you know what you think. You're not going to share it with anybody, so the pressure's off. Attention, procrastinators! At this stage there's nothing at all to dread, so procrastination is technically a waste of time!

What's hard about writing a bad introduction? Not a thing. In fact, many students find it a bit of a relief to give themselves permission to let go, to write quickly, to use the act of writing as a form of discovery. It's like cranking the music when no one's around. Go ahead, shake your thang. Feel free to experiment to find out what strategy works for you—brainstorming, mind-mapping, clustering, list-making, and so on. Some writers even swear by drawing out their ideas as pictures, sketching as a kind of visual writing. These activities are terrific not just because they get you started but because they often take you in cool new directions where you wouldn't otherwise go.

The second step is to craft the version that you're going to use as a hook to hang the essay on. The game changes now. You are no longer writing to discover. You are writing to *share* what you've discovered. Step two, obviously, makes more sense if you have already completed step one. Freewriting activities are supposed to function like warm-up stretches before you exercise. We have all learned that warm-up stretches aren't supposed to take the *place* of the actual exercise, and neither will the freeform introduction take the place of the well-crafted one. Know that you will almost certainly make many changes to the introduction before you are ready to share the essay with others, and that's okay. Tweaking is your right and privilege up to the moment you turn the thing in. And in a composition class you often get another shot at it afterward, too.

By the time you get around to writing the actual essay, you need to know what you think. Don't make the mistake of using the essay itself as a vehicle to discover what you think. That's putting the cart before the horse. If you fail to use prewriting to articulate what you think *in advance,* you run the real risk of filling your essay with irrelevant crap, as when you go into one of those stores filled with unicorn paperweights and whimsical doodads, and you're, like, "Why is this store even here?"

Crafting the introduction that you share

If an assignment asks for a short essay (fewer than twenty pages), I recommend an introduction that is crisp and to the point. One paragraph will usually suffice. Of course there are times when writers have reason to change it up a bit. For example, a longer introduction can build tension or provide necessary background. It can set the stage for something the author will circle back to later. It can use images or data or even anecdotal evidence to make the reader care about the issue at hand. Those are all perfectly viable writing strategies.

Whether you choose to comply with writing conventions or depart from them, it's a good idea to get in the habit of asking, *Why did I make that particular choice? How will a long introduction help my paper?* Craft, by definition, is intentional. I would no more expect my students to make the same choices than I would expect them to look alike. Your professors aren't looking for a cookie-cutter stamp that accommodates all the rules of college writing. No, they are looking for textual evidence that your writing is intentional and self-aware. If a student writer delays the thesis until the second page, she's asking me to wait for it ... wait for it ... wait for it! Will I? Sure. If she has done her job right, the wait will be worth it. I will be able to nod at a deliberate strategy that makes me appreciate the delay.

So if long introductions are okay, why am I recommending the one-paragraph version to new college students? I have a no-frills reason. The shortie is easier to craft. This is because of two things. One, the delay tactics you need to pull off a longer introduction are harder to manage. Two, sometimes a longer introduction accidentally creates the wrong effect, as if the author doesn't know his or her own point and is hoping to find it somewhere over the rainbow. A long intro might also make it look as if you are trying to pad your paper for length, or as if you are hoping that the thesis will appear after you knock on enough doors. You don't want to be like Cinderella's Prince, searching for a foot.

Your argument will not arise gradually and organically, by some natural force, like a majestic stalagmite. You have to build it, starting from the first sentence. And that first sentence can't be purely decorative. It actually needs to do something. What is your subject's immediate context, decade, or sphere of influence? Start there. In other words, try to focus your discussion in the first couple of sentences. That's why it's a good idea to avoid these yawners:

| Since the dawn of time ...

| Throughout human history ...

The introduction isn't the place to trace the larger connections between your topic and the ins and outs of human history. That's what the *conclusion* is for: tracing implications. For now, at the start, it's a good idea to get in and get down to business.

7.2 Can I Begin My Introduction with a Dictionary Definition?

The ol' standby. Starting your essay with a dictionary definition is like displaying a gnome with whimsical fanny crack in your yard. Technically it is your right to do it, and I can't stop you. But why would you want to? The dictionary definition, like the fanny-crack gnome, adds nothing substantial. It's often distracting. An introduction is not the time for cute or gimmicky.

If you must sprinkle your college writing assignments with dictionary definitions, do yourself a favor and cite the *Oxford English Dictionary*, which is available to you for free on your college library database. The *OED* is the granddaddy of dictionaries, the scholar's choice because it is rich with useful etymology as well as denotative aha moments. Sometimes you will find a

The *Oxford English Dictionary*, 2ⁿᵈ Edition

tidbit about a word's history that produces a cool lightbulb insight. Let's say that you're wondering why nobody uses the word *plague* anymore. We all know what it means, but nobody actually says it, right? These days people say *epidemic* instead. Why is that? When you look up the etymology of *plague* in the *OED*, you realize that it comes from a Latin word, *plāga*, the sort of bodily affliction associated with divine punishment. Today when we're talking about contagious diseases, most of us do not want to suggest that God is inflicting an epic punishment on human badness.

Sometimes a dictionary definition does add some cool new angle. I'd consider using a dictionary definition in any of the following three cases, all of which seem justified to me.

1) The history of your word (etymology) sheds new light on your larger argument.

Once I was looking up the old-fashioned word dot, to better understand nineteenth-century conventions surrounding the etiquette of the dowry, or what they used to call the bride's "portion." The bride's father or elder male relative would enter into negotiation with the groom. What sort of hard assets would the groom receive as a dot? Maybe a chunk of cash, livestock, land, jewelry? I found out that the word dot was etymologically connected to the word dotage, the "second childhood" of seniors who need memory care. Suddenly I saw that the etymology of the word dot was really useful to me, because both dot and dotage position someone as utterly dependent and helpless. That worked great with my argument about how nineteenth-century upper-crust young ladies were taught to seek the very thing that limited them.

2) The dictionary denotation is different from the connotation.

In other words, the actual meaning is different from how we usually use the word. The dictionary definition therefore presents a welcome moment of "Hey, look at that! Who knew?" For example, I had always thought that the word *volatile* meant *flighty* or *explosive*. In general we use the term with a negative connotation. We say that things are volatile when we mean, "Uh-oh, this situation has the potential to take a seriously wrong turn." When I looked up *volatile*, though, I realized that it's not necessarily a negative term. It means, merely, *subject to change*. So sometimes a dictionary definition can help correct a common but limited usage.

3) The dictionary definition reveals a useful surprise.

Once I looked up *braggadocio*. I knew the word referred to a certain type of funny cockiness or over-the-top swag, as when Kanye compared himself to God. My idea was to see how *braggadocio* was different from garden-variety *bragging*. Then I noticed something curious. All the quotations in the *OED*, from Walpole to Carlyle, listed literary examples of *men* who were guilty of braggadocio. Where were all the bragging *women*? Suddenly I thought of the word as gendered, not unlike *cock*iness itself. Interesting.

If your dictionary definition involves any of the three

situations above, green light. However, I recommend tucking the dictionary definition into a body paragraph, not the introduction itself. It will look contrived and effortful in the intro.

Too bad I don't see the cool new dictionary angle very often. What I usually see is a student who can't think of any other way to get started. Here's my advice. Go ahead and use the dictionary definition to get yourself going, if you find it helpful. Just don't forget to go back and edit it out. A dictionary definition in the intro feels plastic and decorative, like the fanny-crack gnome.

7.3 The Trick to Focusing the First Sentence

I have an easy-peasy trick for that. Just use your hand to cover up the rest of what you've written. Read that first sentence out loud all by itself. Now ask, "Would any reader be able to tell from this one sentence what my exact topic is? Does this one sentence rule out the possibility of other related topics?" It should.

Let's say you're getting busy with a three- to five-page essay assignment for a freshman composition course. You're now using your hand to cover up the four sentences you've already written, and you read your first sentence out loud:

> From the recent Black Lives Matter movement to Boko Haram's abduction of the 300 Chibok Nigerian schoolgirls, vigilante justice has always been a part of society.

You're keenly aware that there's a lot you could say about vigilante justice. You could write about mob violence, the 2015

2015 Black Lives Matter protest

Baltimore riots, acts of political terrorism, America's history of lynchings, and on and on. Before you started writing the introduction, you probably jotted down some of these possibilities, and a bunch of others. But now, reading it out loud, you realize that your first sentence invites your reader to expect a paper that explores the relationship between vigilante justice and race. Why? Because you start out by mentioning the Black Lives Matter movement and the kidnapped Nigerians.

If that's where you want to go with your paper, bravo. But what if you feel that vigilante justice isn't *always* an outcropping of race relations? Maybe you can think of plenty of cases when people have taken the law into their own hands, cases that aren't necessarily related to race issues at all.

This first sentence has three problems. One, it suggests that you will be connecting vigilante justice to racism in contemporary American culture [*Black Lives Matter*]. That could be a great paper, but if it's not your direction of choice, then that doesn't do you much good. Two, your first sentence promises to hook up vigilante justice to political acts of global terrorism [*Chibok kidnappings*]. If that's not part of the plan, then that's not your ideal first sentence. And three, uh-oh, you're doing that thing with the Dawn of Time again [*always been a part of human society*].

So you write a new opening sentence.

> A favorite Hollywood hero is the figure of the strong but desperate maverick who takes the law into his own hands to single-handedly save his family, nation, or even the world.

What kind of a focus would you expect now? It's clear that the essay will be about vigilante justice. But now your first sentence is misleading in another way. It promises a discussion about *fictional* movie heroes. An essay that focuses on Hollywood stereotypes of the stock indie hero would be okay too, since Hollywood's action genre offers some intriguing cultural commentary. However, in this case, you feel that the stock Hollywood hero is actually a bit off topic.

Dirty Harry, John McClane, and Batman are lone rangers who undermine the power they represent. But all of them experience the law as tragically inept. Therefore, if they are to uphold the power paradigm, they are *morally obligated* to wop the evildoers. In the Hollywood formula, the vigilante is forced to act because the law has failed to do its job. This sets up a black-and-white morality that doesn't take into account the complexity of moral decision making in the real world. The sexy-action-cool movies often make it seem as if the vigilante hero has no moral choice. What interests you, though, is the real, nonfictional vigilante who does have a choice. You want to write about the vigilante who chooses to circumvent the law not because the law is inept but because the delivery of personalized justice is more appealing. Back to the drawing board.

> Despite access to many legal forms of crisis resolution—911, police presence, small claims court—some Americans choose to take the law into their own hands.

Given your particular interest, this is a better opening sentence because it signals the topic that you actually have in mind, not some other cool topic that is slightly tangential to the one you were thinking of.

7.4 Three Things Your Introduction Needs to Do

Many college essay assignments share similar expectations for the all-important first paragraph. While there's plenty of wiggle room for creativity, it's a good idea to consider the usual expectations for an introduction.

Three things your introduction needs to do:

1. signal your topic right up front
2. promise a methodology (strategy)
3. include a thesis (a one-sentence statement of your essay's main point)

The first sentence of the introductory paragraph has already signaled your topic. And the last sentence usually takes care of the methodology and the thesis.

Here's a practical tip. The second sentence of the introduction is often even better and more focused than the first, so get ready to press DELETE. After I have been writing for a while, I find it helpful to go have a snack, call a friend, then come back with fresh eyes to ask, "Which is better, the first sentence or the second?" If those two sentences are versions of the same thing, pick the stronger sentence and omit the other.

Methodology

Methodology is a ten-dollar word for *strategy*. And you need to know what yours is. The trick in determining your methodology is to look at the language of the last sentence of your first paragraph. The last sentence is typically the thesis, the most important sentence in your whole paper. The thesis goes by a couple of names. Some instructors call it the *main idea* or the *central argument*. Whatever you call it, it's the whammy sentence that tells the reader what your paper is going to achieve in the space of three to five pages. The thesis is also the sentence by which the efficacy of your paper will be judged. Your instructor will grade your work based not only on the insight of this all-important sentence but on whether the paper actually does what the thesis says it will do.

Signal phrases

Signal phrases are those little bits that are supposed to aid in transition and digestion, like Alka-Seltzer. We all use them, both in our speech and in our writing:

| First

| Second

- Having said that

- In sum

- To begin with

- On the other hand

- In conclusion

Signal phrases are supposed to help us smooth things out, and they usually do. But here's why they can seem high-schoolish, especially when placed at the very beginning of a paragraph. Sometimes writers over-rely on them by using them as a substitute *for the intellectual work of transition-making.* You can't use a signal phrase *instead* of a transition in thought. You have to use it *in addition* to a transition in thought.

Oftentimes when writers are fresh out of high school the signal phrase falls on the reader's ear like a thud. It makes a loud declaration that isn't even necessary. I am reminded of my friend Amanda, who once decided it was time to connect with a guy she'd met online. She and the guy were meeting at an urban park for a half-hour walk on a gentle paved path, sociable and safe. The guy shows up kitted out in full survival gear, with a huge backpack, emergency flares, and, get this, a sun hat topped with a water bladder. That dude was *hydrating,* yessir! He sipped his water via an attached plastic straw that came down to his mouth like a little headphone. His gear announced what didn't need announcing. Amanda couldn't get out of there fast enough.

If you're gonna take a walk, you don't need a lot of fancy gear to announce that you plan on taking a walk. If you're gonna write an essay, you don't need a lot of fancy phrases that announce you are changing the direction or making a conclusion. Your logic should be so clear that the thinking *itself* does the job for you.

I'm not going to lobby for us all to stop using signal phrases such as *First* and *Second*. But I'd like to suggest that you ditch the signal phrase *In conclusion*. Reading an essay is not like listening to one of those classical pieces at the symphony, where sometimes people mistakenly start to applaud before the piece is over. Everybody feels bad for the premature clappers, because if you don't know the piece, it might truly seem like the end. For most readers, the essay is visual, not aural. Every sighted reader will be able to see that you have reached the conclusion. You can trust that the reader of your college writing assignment, usually a professor or a competent TA, has the ability to smell a conclusion coming.

Tip: Read your conclusion out loud, all by itself, before you turn in the assignment.

Think about how you respond at the end of a movie when you're seeing a film in the theater. At the end of a sucky movie, you turn to your friend and say, "You up for falafel?" But when you see a good movie, you can barely wait for the credits to roll before you start discussing it. Does your conclusion make anybody want to discuss anything? It should.

Scaffolding: When to take it down

One last tip for setting up a strong introduction. In high school many of you learned to announce your plan of action for the essay:

> **In this essay, I intend to argue that** identity formation in a social context is influenced by cultural environment, by subjective interpretations of formative cultural experiences, and by role models in the identity group.

> **The purpose of this essay is to** demonstrate that Rebecca Skloot's *The Immortal Life of Henrietta Lacks* should not be read merely as an exploration of scientific ethics but as a clear statement of the effect of racism on scientific ethics.

Phrases that announce the game plan function like scaffolding. You build them up just outside the walls of your real argument so that you can *get* to your argument. Climbing up on them helps you see everything clearly.

Here's the deal with those scaffolding phrases. They're there to help *you*, not your reader. The reader, probably your instructor or your peer, doesn't actually need them. If you craft a good thesis, the reader will be able to spot it. Trust your reader! By the placement as the last sentence of the first paragraph, by the tone, by the language of the claim, by the heightened attention to craft—by all these things, the reader will recognize that your thesis is your thesis. That's why you don't even need those scaffolding phrases. Check it out:

> Identity formation in a social context is influenced by one's cultural environment, one's subjective interpretations of formative cultural experiences, and one's role models in the identity group.

> Rebecca Skloot's *The Immortal Life of Henrietta Lacks* should not be read merely as an exploration of scientific ethics but as a clear statement of the effect of racism on scientific ethics.

These are cleaner and stronger without the prop, right?

Scaffolding is handy if you get when to use it, and when not to. Builders use scaffolding in the construction phase, not for the finished structure. They remove it at project's end. The reader can see that the document is an essay, so you don't need to say that. The reader can see that it's written by you, so you don't need to say *I intend*. And the reader can see by virtue of the language that follows that this is an argument, so you don't need to say that either.

7.5   Crafting a No-Yawn Conclusion

I don't know anybody who writes the conclusion before coming to the end of the paper. Yet I have often noticed that before I dive into the main points and textual support, it's helpful to think briefly about where I want to end up. At Target the other day I smiled at a little chap smitten with somebody's service dog, a Golden Retriever making brisk progress in the other direction. Distracted, the boy caught a corner of a display fixture. Down he went, one arm shooting up to sow a wide arc of Legos, like Johnny Appleseed. I bent down to help pick them up, so I heard the dad saying quietly but firmly into the boy's neck, "Gotta look where you're going, Son, not where you've been!" Same principle. Sometimes it pays to look ahead.

Please do not be mad at your high school English teacher. She was merely teaching you the lesson you were ready to learn at the time. She probably told you that the job of a conclusion is to *sum things up*. She may have even advised you to repeat what you had already said earlier in the body of the paper.

It's time to take it to the next level. You have learned a dear but limited application of the formulaic Aristotelian, five-paragraph essay (intro, three body paragraphs, conclusion). Imagine the familiar high school outline organized according to this model:

Dinner at My House

I. Introduction
   I will now invite you to dinner at my house.

II. Body
   A. Please come to my house
   B. For dinner
   C. On Friday

III. Conclusion
   I have just invited you over for dinner.

If it would be weird to sum up what you've just said in a regular conversation, why wouldn't it be equally weird to do it in your college writing?

The conclusion is not the time to repeat yourself. If you're a repeater, go ahead and text eighteen versions of the same thing to your best friend. Your friend will still love you. But the expectations change in academic writing, where, if you need to repeat something within the span of a very short essay, it means you didn't say it very well the first time. If that's the case, go back and fix it. But don't restate it, especially not in the conclusion.

Some composition textbooks suggest that you use the conclusion to make connections to your personal experience, so that the conclusion becomes a mini form of the personal essay. I would advise against this. The idea is that at paper's end you should open the discussion up, not shrink it down. Writing about your personal experience *can* be a great way to connect the reader to larger ideas. However, the crafting of meaning from personal experience represents a methodology that we usually study as its own genre, in personal essay, memoir, and creative writing. I wouldn't risk personal experience in your conclusion if an academic essay assignment is asking for research, critical thinking, or argument. Read the prompt carefully. If the assignment wants memoir strategies from you, it will ask for it. You'll see phrases like "personal reflection" and "personal experience."

The conclusion is not a cul-de-sac. Your argument is not supposed to come to a dead end where there is NO OUTLET. This would make the reader walk away from your paper and forget having read it. You want to give the reader an opportunity to *make some connections.* Thus the conclusion is more like one of those turnouts for a scenic overlook. From its vantage point, it is totally possible to look back and see the road you've been traveling. But that's not the main point of a scenic overlook. The main point of the scenic overlook is to alert readers to the lay of the land that lies *beyond* the overlook. It shows readers just how far they can see from here. All they have to do is turn their gaze to the direction in which your conclusion is pointing, helpful-like.

What you want to do is usher your argument right up to the far edge of the overlook. In other words, you want to *trace the implications* of what you've said earlier in the body of the paper. Then you invite the reader to look beyond because, wow, this issue is bigger than it seems. Even before you begin to write the actual conclusion, you might want to ask questions like these, to get the ball rolling:

▷ What larger truth does my essay imply about _____?
   [our world today, democratic ideals, families, religion, human nature, the desire to conform, the desire to be distinct, systems of moral or political governance, etc.]
▷ How does this stuff apply to what we believe today?
▷ If what I have said in this essay is true, what else might be true?
▷ Does X have implications for Y? (Does my argument apply to race, class, gender?)
▷ What current events are mirroring this issue right now?
▷ Why should my outlook be encouraging? Or discour-

aging?

▷ What's a solution to the problem I have talked about in this paper?

▷ Is there some kind of negative consequence if we fail to fix this problem?

▷ If this essay were to result in change, what would that change look like?

▷ If you are writing about something abstract—an idea, a made-up poem or piece of fiction, a theory—where in real life do you see this idea being played out?

▷ If you are writing about a historical event, where in real life do you see these same issues today?

▷ Have the issues changed over time? If yes, you could talk about the forces that have made the changes or that have complicated them.

▷ Or are they still the same old issues? If yes, you could talk about why they have resisted change. Maybe they point to some universal cultural behavior, or even a trait inherent in the human condition.

Let's say that you are in the process of wrapping up an essay called "Dragons in Fantasy Literature: Totem, Terror, and Greed." You love your topic, but you don't know how to conclude. So you naturally procrastinate by posting a Facebook picture of a dead weasel the cat dragged in because, sheesh, you have never even seen a weasel and had to look it up online. You sort some laundry, you make popcorn. Okay, ready. You now tentatively try out a couple of the questions listed above. "What larger truth does my essay imply about *dragons*?"

Dead weasel/love totem presented by Ace the cat.

Ridiculous question, right? Dragons are make-believe. They have zero application in contemporary American society, except that people *think you're a dork* if you're into them.

You stare into space, thinking. Hmmmm: people think you're a dork if you're into dragons. Why do we associate dragon love with dorkdom? Because any gesture toward the power of myth adverts to inquiry in the supernatural. Myth speaks to the human *spirit*, never the intellect. It narrates the human quest for meaning by tapping into the larger spiritual themes of good and evil. When people confess that they attend *LOTR* fantasy reenactments, or when they name their kids Elfin and Percival, people are *forced* to roll their eyes in pity and embarrassment. If they didn't, they would have to admit that myth might actually be speaking to larger realities. Embarrassment is a familiar response of modern hipsters when they see a froofy needlepoint pillow that says, I BELIEVE IN ANGELS. In short, the religious folks and the dragon crowd may be *the same people*. (In this excursus the dragon crowd implicitly includes conspiracy theorists, people abducted by aliens, online gamers who call themselves Ravyn, and Star Trek enthusiasts who dress up as Count Spocula.) All are believers in the purest sense. They insist on the validity of an unseen, unprovable reality.

To intellectuals who privilege demonstrable evidence,

this insistence on a mythic reality is troubling. It is troubling not because belief subsumes critical inquiry. It's troubling because the paradigm is actually a little too close to home. Scholars know that human history is full of unseen realities that everybody once made fun of because they used to embarrass the bejesus out of dominant culture. I BELIEVE IN GERMS. Later on science proved these unseen realities to be verifiable phenomena—for instance, malaria, atoms, global warming, the subconscious mind. So for the ratiocinative majority, mockery of any unseen reality functions as a knee-jerk form of Nietzschean *ressentiment*. Mockery of dragon dorkdom is a useful tool to privilege the human mind over the human spirit.

You should have absolutely no trouble connecting dragons to a larger idea, seems to me.

Not that I have ever been tempted to write about dragons. I should probably mention that I am not a dragon fan. Like the guy in *Green Eggs and Ham*,

I do not like
them diced or whole;
I do not like
their mythic role.

The dragon cannot
make amends
with cute and
chewy vitamins.

I do not like this dragon lit.
For God's sake please
stop writing it.

That said, the beauty of being a modern college student is that you no longer have to care what your professor doesn't like. Therefore, I cordially invite you to keep reading those YA fantasies that feature an accursed sword trapped in stone. And if there is also a slender lady, gently bred, who carries within her womb the One who shall save the Earth, thereby fulfilling an ancient prophecy that was discovered on runic shards beneath Darghouth-Säer, perhaps next time you can write about wombs. Because there aren't enough wombs in literature.

8

How to Craft a Solid Paragraph

8.1 The Purpose of a Paragraph

Delivering the main point of your essay up front is the main job of the introduction, but it's also the job, on a smaller scale, of the first sentences of each of the paragraphs in your essay.

Some student writers never give any thought to the purpose of a paragraph, and it is certainly possible to keep stringing paragraphs together until the paper meets the length requirement. When you're writing an essay, it's tempting to think exclusively of your *content*, not your structure. I don't recommend this approach, however. Until you've mastered the art of crafting a good solid paragraph, you might want to direct at least some attention to it. Paragraphs are important. They are the primary vehicle that allows you to organize your thoughts. And your essay's organization will certainly contribute to, or detract from, the grade you earn.

In academic writing the punch line of a paragraph almost always comes up front, though I've seen brave rebels who sometimes tuck it at the end of a paragraph for a powerful caboose effect. But it's generally safer to learn the conventions before we choose to defy them. That's why I recommend this strategy for all new college students. Consider the first sentence as a mini thesis of the whole paragraph. **Whatever it promises, the paragraph must deliver.**

Because so many students have never learned the difference between topic and idea, professors often see something that makes them wince: a paragraph that begins with a fact of plot or some other tidbit of unarguable information from a text. If your paragraphs start with sentences like the ones that follow, I am sorry to report that you are just asking for a mediocre grade.

> The story opens with a newlywed going to stay in a house in the country.

> Today many people choose to get tattoos.

> Kenji Yoshino's book *Covering: The Hidden Assault on Our Civil Rights* (2006) foregrounds biographical narratives.

> In *The End of Faith* (2004), cognitive neuroscientist Sam Harris critiques organized religion.

These sentences are all topic: ouch, no idea. That's bad. And it actually gets worse. When the first sentence of a paragraph says nothing arguable, the material that follows in the interior of the paragraph is doomed to spin its wheels. It will take up space without actually saying anything. So if you want your paragraphs to have traction, you need to get beyond a lackluster opener that merely sums stuff up.

The idea is that each paragraph needs to **advance** the argument. Imagine a staircase, with the paragraphs as ascending steps, each one necessary to get you to the next. Each paragraph needs to add something so important that without it, the reader would be unable to arrive at the conclusion. Obviously this means that each body paragraph needs to be ordered carefully. If you can shuffle your body paragraphs around in no particular order, you are again inviting the mediocre grade, this time for weak organization and lack of momentum. Pacing is a big deal. There's no Big Bang theory of essays, where paragraphs explode into being in perfect order. If there is order, it's because you have created it on purpose.

Most college composition assignments involve writing in response to a textual prompt (an article, an essay, a film, a story, a poem, artwork, or indeed any other text that the class has considered together). I've got a surefire way to prevent a crappy first sentence when you are writing in response to another text. For every paragraph you write, read the first sentence out loud. Then ask this question: "Would everyone on the planet who has read this text agree with this sentence?"

If the answer is *yes*, you have just produced a dud of a first sentence. Everyone who reads Charlotte Perkins Gilman's short story "The Yellow Wallpaper" will agree that, yes, the newlywed *does* go to stay in a house in the country. It says so right there on the first page of the story. And yes, right, lots of folks choose to get tattoos. "Winona Forever!" Further, you will be unsurprised to learn that the legal scholar Kenji Yoshino does include lots of biographical narrative in his book *Covering*. And Sam Harris? He flat-out critiques religion in *The End of Faith*. The title sort of gives it away. Who would dispute these things?

No one, because they are not arguable. What I'm saying is, if the first sentence of your paragraph repeats an unarguable fact of plot, heave ho. The first sentence needs to be arguable. That sounds abstract, but it's actually easy to tell the difference between an arguable and an unarguable first sentence. All you have to do is ask, "Does the first sentence of this paragraph **do more** than repeat a factoid of plot?"

8.2 How Do I Set Up a Topic Sentence?

These first sentences of body paragraphs are universally called **topic sentences**. This label doesn't make much sense to me, because we require topic sentences to do so much more than state a topic. Sadly, no one asked me to name them, and I have had to make my peace with it. Let's say that a student is writing an essay that responds to a reading assignment in Susan Bordo's book-length study about the role of the female body in advertising, *Unbearable Weight: Feminism, Western Culture, and the Body* (1993).[1] The class has read an excerpt, a chap-

---

1   Susan Bordo, "Hunger as Ideology," in *Unbearable Weight: Feminism, Western Culture, and the Body*. (Berkeley: University of California Press, 1993), 99-134.

ter called "Hunger as Ideology," in which Bordo says some provocative things about the social construction of women's bodies in print media. Check out a weak topic sentence. (I actually made this one up, but over the years I have seen plenty just like it in real student essays.)

> In Susan Bordo's chapter called "Hunger as Ideology" a trend in contemporary advertising is to use sexual language in dessert ads.

"Hunger as Ideology" looks at a bunch of real ads that all use sexualized language to sell a dessert. That's the text's *methodology*. By this I mean that's the action plan that Bordo uses to get from A to B. It's how the text operates, and, as such, that's not arguable. Everyone who reads "Hunger as Ideology" will agree: yes, yes, Bordo is examining sexual language in dessert ads. Therefore the paragraph's topic sentence is weak on the grounds that it doesn't say anything arguable. When Bordo wrote this provocative book back in 1993, she was laying down an argument of noteworthy impact because she was making connections that a lot of people hadn't considered. But my imaginary writer above is merely reporting a fact. Yup, the text says this. Once you prove it with a quotation, where's the paragraph going to go from there? In sum, if you come up with a topic sentence that requires no *development*, try again.

Second try:

> When advertisers use the language of sexual taboo to sell desserts, they are suggesting that women should feel guilt for enjoying their food.

That's better. The revision illustrates a reliable shortcut you can use to boost the oomph of a sentence that twiddles its thumbs. The shortcut is to adapt your own sentence to a tried-and-true formula:

▷   When X happens in the text, it means Y.

A reasonable person will follow right along if you can show your reader why X doesn't just mean X but also Y. An ad sexed up with naughty female behavior doesn't only mean that advertisers have chosen to eroticize the dessert experience. It means that the naughtiness is being transferred, morally speaking, to the woman's body. Oh, you tramp, you! It's sinful to enjoy your food. Your natural appetite is a form of moral transgression. In fact, the reason it is sinful to eat is because *the culture wants you thin.* See it? X might look like an obvious X, but it's really a Y. And that's arguable. You can go ahead and quote the chapter to prove that there is really an X happening, there on page 110, but with this better topic sentence, your paragraph will actually have somewhere to go *after* you include the quote. This is because your first sentence has made a promise to the reader. After the quote you're still going to have to prove that the X has a larger meaning, a different implication. X points to some other thing. We must interpret it as Y.

Now let's kick it up a notch. Here's another trick that

will up the ante further still. Don't start by focusing on X, the thing stated in the text, the thing you want to write the paragraph about. Instead, start by focusing *on the author*. Think about the author's position, attitude, or motivation. How does *the author* feel about X? If you're not sure, start with the basics. Does the author seem to be pro or con? Why is the author trying to call our attention to X in the first place? The trick is to hook up X (the thing you want to write about) to some argument you feel the author is making. Like this:

▷ Author uses X in order to suggest Y.
▷ Author analyzes X in order to attack Y.
▷ Author undercuts X in order to imply Y.
▷ Author connects X and Y in order to conclude Z.

If you're having a tough time crafting topic sentences for your body paragraphs, this is a good way to get started. This is also a useful method to scoot average writing in the direction of excellence. If you've been getting Cs on your college assignments, try this strategy to push through to the next level. (Don't forget to pick the low-hanging fruit. If you haven't been advancing, do the easiest and most obvious thing first. Present yourself during office hours and simply *ask* your professor or TA for counsel on how to advance. Can't hurt to ask, right? Who knows, you might get some valuable help! You would be amazed at how many students fail to take advantage of a service that they have already paid for.)

The more you write, the less you rely on formulas like the ones offered above. They're sort of like training wheels on a bike. Once you're up and rolling, you don't need the training wheels anymore. Maybe you start with the formula, clean up the language, tweak as needed—then *voilà*! Look, Ma, no hands! Once you get in the habit of deepening the scope, crisp topic sentences come naturally. For now, just know that the formula nudges your topic sentence toward excellence because it encourages you to think about the textual details as part of the author's overall message, which we usually assume to be intentional. What does this author want us to think, say, or believe about the world? Well then, how is X, the thing you want to write about, a part of that overall vision?

▷ **Author analyzes X in order to attack Y.**

> **Bordo** analyzes **sexy dessert ads** in order to attack **advertisers who make women feel guilty about their bodies.**

Almost there! Now all you have to do is tighten it up:

> Bordo attacks dessert ads that suggest it is a sin for the female body to eat dessert.

This last topic sentence is the strongest version of the three because it makes a clear promise to the reader that the paragraph can and will deliver: "Hey reader! Not only will I prove that Bordo is making an attack, but I will use her text to show you exactly what is being attacked, and why this attack is invidious and effective!" It's going to take a whole paragraph to do that; your topic sentence can't be proven by turning to one easy obvious page. When you involve the author by name, you still have room to talk about the content of the reading material (individual dessert ads, this cake brand or that pudding cup.) But now you, like Bordo, are making a powerful argument. You're talking about way more than *oohlala* and *can't say no*.

Which brings me to the main difference between the writing you did in high school and the writing you are now doing in college. In high school your writing assignments were frequently designed to establish *that you had read an assignment.* ("Do your homework! Eat your peas!") In college, not very many assignments do that. Why? Because we're already assuming you have read the material. We don't want to know *that* you've read it. We want to know *how* you've read it.

Thus in college, the purpose of your academic writing has changed. Now you are attempting to pull a larger argument out of your reading. And this is the part where you get a lot of leeway. You may hook the text up to any argument you think the text will support. That's your prerogative. But you have to use the text to prove whatever argument you pick. That's your job.

8.3   Troubleshooting a Paragraph

What if my paragraph is too long? Or too short?

If you ever write a paragraph that takes the scenic route, diddling here, musing there, and it goes on for longer than a page, this is a sign to you. My counsel will be exactly the same if you have produced a confused nub of a paragraph, too short at three or four lines. These two structural gaffes are flip sides of the same coin, and they require the same fix. This is because they originate in the same problem. It's not that the assignment is wobbly or the professor difficult. It's only that you haven't set the paragraph up right.

Both the gumby and the peewee have an easy fix. The first sentence is the culprit. If you go back and focus that first sentence, the paragraph will behave. Troubleshooting a paragraph is easy if you are trained to see the source of the problem, just as, when driving, you know to pull over when your temperature gauge starts overheating. If you find yourself asking or saying any of the following things, it's time to pull over.

- ▷ Is this paragraph talking about too many things?
- ▷ Is this paragraph using too many quotes?
- ▷ Is this paragraph too loose, too vague?
- ▷ Does this paragraph sound like a bunch of BS?
- ▷ Yikes, I'm only halfway through this paragraph, and I can't think of anything else to say.

All these moments of uncertainty lead to one conclusion: go back and fix that first sentence. First sentences crave clarity. Paragraphs want to be told what to do. And it is your job to tell this paragraph what its expectations are. If you don't tell it, no one else will.

When you can't think of how to develop a paragraph, the problem lies, once again, in the topic sentence. *It* is limited; *you* are not. Just go back and deepen the scope. It is likely that you have not hooked up the thing you're writing about to a larger idea. Have you tried rewriting the first sentence with the author's name, declaring what you perceive to be the author's position on this topic? Do that. The system works. Trust it. The flaw isn't you. It's the first sentence.

When can I start a new paragraph?

When your current paragraph has delivered what it promises.

What if my paragraph only sort of delivers what it promises?

Then you can expect a sort-of good grade, probably in the B range. If a boss hires you to work an eight-hour shift, how would you feel if you got paid for the first seven hours only? You'd be irate, maybe even outraged. "She SAID eight hours, I heard her!" You might pitch a hissy, give two weeks' notice, even call the Better Business Bureau. That's because the entire culture operates under the assumption that *we must deliver what we promise.* So it is with paragraphs. If a paragraph's topic sentence says that it will demonstrate a robust change, it needs to document robust change, not just a sliver of change.

And you can write the most brilliant first sentence of all time, but if the paragraph starts talking about something *else* halfway through, get ready for the C you have earned. Academic writing doesn't stray off topic.

Isn't that kind of uptight?

Hey, I didn't invent it. Personally, I would rather sit around discussing what kind of a bobblehead historical figure you would have on your dashboard, if somebody forced you to have a bobblehead in your car.

What kind of a person would force somebody to drive around with a historical bobblehead in their car?

Let's just say.

(Long pause.) I'm gonna go with Sor Juana Inés de la Cruz, Nun and Activist.

Nice choice!

Speaking of off topic, what if I'm halfway through the paragraph and I think of a cool thing that I'd like to add that's sort of related to the topic, unlike bobbleheads?

Hold that thought. The time is coming when you can say whatever you want, whenever you want. You will be in the middle of a professional craft talk on the difference between anagnorisis and epiphany, and, if the mood strikes, you will be able to interrupt yourself with a story about how once at a cocktail party you accidentally lobbed a cube of pepper jack at the famous philosopher Jacques Derrida. Derrida was not a tall man, and I was wearing my highest heels. So I had to lean over to hear what he was saying. Jacques Derrida, I tell you! In the flesh! Making small talk about alligators! The pepper jack jumped out of my hand and beaned him directly in the forehead.

A Jacques Derrida bobblehead would make a nice stocking stuffer!

I am ignoring you right now.

If you want to break the rules fruitfully and to smart effect, first you have to learn them. By all means, wander off topic! I bless you in this endeavor! But you might want to wait until you have proven that you can stick the rigors of academic writing first. Then, later when you choose to stray off subject, everybody will know that you're *doing it on purpose*. You don't want to go changing the subject while there is a possibility that your reader might interpret your sporty high jinks as ignorance or underexposure. What you do with conventions can make or break your writing. So graduate or get famous, whichever comes first. Then you can break rules willy-nilly, and maybe even get paid for it.

Let us agree: in your academic college writing, your paragraph should not send the content scuttling off, crabwise. Just stick to the plan you laid out in the first sentence of the paragraph. Can't go wrong with that.

What if I'm talking about two different authors in the same paragraph, and then by the time I get to the second thing, it feels like a massive subject change? Is it okay to begin a new paragraph for the second thing?

This organizational error happens a lot when you are setting up an essay that asks you to trace parallels or juxtapositions between two separate texts. The assignment asks you to discuss two things, essays, authors, or ideas. Seems like a no-brainer, right? You craft a topic sentence that mentions both things. You say everything you need to say about the first thing. Then when you're ready to transition to the second thing, suddenly it seems like an abrupt subject change. So you start a new paragraph. Good, you should. But don't forget to go back and adjust the first topic sentence so that it promises to discuss only the first thing. Write a new topic sentence for the second thing.

What if I want to use the last sentence of one paragraph as a bridge to the next paragraph?

To show you this mistake in its plainest form, here is a made-up paragraph about summer camp activities.

> Camp Eagle Rock presented a whole new series of threats to our physical safety. Although the activities were fun, they were not without real risk. In the swift currents, for example, our kayaks might unexpectedly capsize at any submerged log. The river's undertow was strong enough to take down even an experienced swimmer. At night we uneasily became aware of our position on the food chain when, tossing and turning in our sleeping bags, we heard the eerie yip of coyotes. It wasn't uncommon on the trails to come across bear scat. And the deer ticks were so bad this year that every evening before bed we had to strip down for Tick Check. When I feel unsafe in Chicago, it is usually be-

| cause of people.

This paragraph asks us to imagine a series of rustic threats that make a camp experience seem risky and exciting. I don't know about you, but after the turbulent river and the roaming predators I am ready for some s'mores around the campfire. What I am not ready for is a libidinous commuter exposing himself on the El.

But the next paragraph is going to be about Chicago! I was trying to make a transition.

Fine, okay, make one. But put it in the right place. Don't use the last sentence to transition into the next paragraph. That is not how you create good flow in an essay. Every single sentence in a paragraph, including the last one, must support the topic sentence of that same paragraph. By all means, talk about urban risk in Chicago! Throw in a couple of pickpockets, some road rage, and cables that snap on the 49th floor! Thing is, do it in a paragraph about Chicago.

Caution: this may seem easy, even reductive, when we're talking about concrete things. But structural integrity is what it is, whether you're talking about ticks or transcendentalism.

9

How to Handle Quotes

9.1 Demonstrating Evidence

Whether you are writing a longer research paper or a shorter piece that responds to one or two reading assignments, the goal is to integrate quotations from the reading into your essay. If you fail to include textual citation, your essay will skate the surface. And your grade will swan dive, often below a C-. The only paragraphs of your essay that are off the hook for including citation are the first and last, the introduction and the conclusion. Please do not cite an outside source in either the introduction or conclusion. Those paragraphs are not meant to showcase your careful reading. They are for something else. They are there to showcase your careful thinking.

Here is why quotation in academic writing is not optional. Do you remember in middle school when you had to write a book report to show that you had read a book? Perhaps you had an urgent foosball commitment in the basement. Rather than actually reading the assigned book, you may have opted for the time-honored tradition of flipping to the back cover for a description of the plot and then timing how long you could suspend a licorice whip from one mighty nostril. "Check it out, Twig, a personal best of thirty-eight seconds!" Self-improvement, as we know, is important.

Quotation is a surefire way to demonstrate the degree to which you have engaged with the text and with other authors who have written about your topic. If you haven't read the material at all, you will not quote it. If you have read the material in a shallow skimming hurry, your quotation will be shallow, skimming, and hurried. Hopefully that does not come as a surprise. If, on the other hand, you have read the material in a thoughtful and alert way, your quotation will be thoughtful and alert. It's pretty simple.

Quotation is the only way to present demonstrable evidence that your ideas are in dialogue with the ideas of published scholars. It is never enough to talk *about* an author in your paper or to describe what the author is known for. Anybody with access to a smartphone can talk *about* an author. That's why there is no substitution for knowing and citing the author's work.

When you are writing an assignment that asks you to read several secondary sources or critics, you'll be expected to quote every text you consult or refer to it in such a way as to signal your thoroughgoing readership. If you spend time chasing after a secondary source and you don't find anything that you can use, out it goes. Don't even include it on your

Works Cited list. The Works Cited list is there to document the published sources that have actually played a shaping role in your argument.

Some students arrive in college having learned only one reason to quote. If that's you, branch out a bit! There are plenty of good reasons to include quotations. Mix-n-match, for the sake of variety and depth. You can quote in order to

▷ prove a point
▷ extend a point
▷ side with or against an expert in the field
▷ document the variety of perspectives from which other scholars are coming
▷ put scholars in dialogue with each other (What would this expert say to that one?)

Usually when you begin your first college-level composition class, the instructor gets to decide what kind of print or visual material you will read. You will be quoting from that. Later, as your scholarship skills mature, you will get to make the yummier decisions yourself. You will craft not just your topic and takeaway but also what kind of secondary sources to consult, and how many. It gets much harder when the professor shifts the responsibility to you, because you have to make informed decisions regarding the appropriateness of your secondary sources.

The bar will be raised like this quite soon, no doubt in your first semester or term. This is because the whole point of college is to get you to think critically on your own. Independent critical thought is exactly what the professor is looking for when you get the, deep breath, Big Research Paper Assignment. In a research paper, *you* have to find the sources. *You* have to decide which ones to quote. That's a lot more responsibility. And a lot more work. But it is a skill that will come naturally to you, if you have already been integrating quotation in order to strengthen an argument.

9.2   The Nonquote

Can't I just refer to a text? Do I have to quote it verbatim?

Before we talk about the ins and outs of quotations, I'd like to take this opportunity to introduce a particularly useful strategy that I like to call the **nonquote**. It's a good idea to get in the habit of crisp, competent documentation, and the nonquote will help you get in that habit. The idea is to include parenthetical page numbers that document the precise textual moment you're referring to *so that you can sidestep an actual quotation*. I use this strategy not instead of actual quotation, but in addition to it, for balance and variety. It's pretty darn useful for three reasons:

1. It demonstrates a superb level of engagement with the text.
2. It gives the reader a shortcut to the passage you're talking about.
3. It provides proof when you need to document a pattern that involves reference to multiple events on different pages.

The nonquote applies to all kinds of college writing assignments. In the first year or two of college you write essays that respond to prompts or questions. Later, when you are a junior or a senior, your professors may expect *you* to write the prompts or questions. Check out this discussion question that Hope College senior Tristan Engel wrote for a class presentation. Engel was presenting on *Take This Man*, a memoir by Brando Skyhorse (2015).

> Brando appears to read his grandmother's final written words to him as cruel and bitter (216–17). It *does* seem to come out of left field. But is it possible that June's words were instead facetious and sardonic, which would better match her character? If we admit that possibility, what does that say about Brando's reliability as narrator?

See how Engel handles the citation? He doesn't want to stop to quote the granny's final words, so he *tells the reader where to go*. (Which is what the cranky granny does, come to think of it!) This question was one of twenty great ones that Engel prepared for class discussion. If he had included textual passages in each of them, his handout would have been unmanageably bulky, way longer than a page. Engel wanted to get us *talking*, not reading. So instead he sprinkled in page numbers as needed, so that we could grab a quick textual pick-me-up along the way. I, the professor, noted a quality preparation. Who wouldn't? Engel's questions carefully engaged with details and patterns. Anybody could see that he hadn't knocked out a couple of generalized vagaries half an hour before class.

Alert pagination signals excellence.

The nonquote as textual proof

What happens when you apply the nonquote to an academic essay, as opposed to discussion questions? Let's look at a paragraph about America's very first best-selling novel, a weepy tearjerker by Susanna Haswell Rowson. *Charlotte Temple* was published in 1791, so you may be unsurprised to learn that the heroine's hobbies are languishing, crying, and fainting. I hereby nominate Miss Charlotte's heaving breasts in the category of Best Quivering Bosom. An unsympathetic modern scholar might like to cuff poor Charlotte smartly upside the head. A more compassionate reader would surely consider a donation to a GoFundMe, so that we could get that gal a 5-barbell high-impact sports bra and maybe some pepper spray.

While breasts rise and fall like empires, the more interesting character is actually the naughty seductress, La Rue, who lures Charlotte and her breasts from the path of moral virtue. Here's how you can cite with the nonquote:

> Rowson would say that the most immoral form of female badness is a lack of transparency. Rowson therefore is careful to establish a pattern of furtive manipulation for her female villain. *La Rue* means "the street" in French, but it is not the suggestion of streetwalking that demotes La Rue's character from fallen woman to sneaky villain. Rather, it is her dishonesty. Earlier in the text La Rue finds a sponsor by pretending penitence for various sexual sins (26). Next she postures as a good

girl who faithfully attends church, when in reality she is meeting men under clandestine circumstances (27). Later, aboard ship, La Rue attracts Colonel Crayton by telling him a poignant victim story (58).[1] The truth, of course, is that La Rue is the victimizer, not the victim.

Careful pagination lets you hop around in the text, identifying patterns and the like. Note that in the paragraph above, you're not just saying that these events are happening (unarguable). You're saying *why* they are happening (arguable). You are connecting three instances of dodgy behavior so that you can make an assertion about one of the author's strategies. And you have been careful to name that very strategy up at the top of the paragraph, before you use the text to establish a pattern.

9.3 Quoting a Textual Passage to Prove or Extend a Point

Quoting a textual passage to prove a point

You can quote to prove a point. This is what they teach you in high school, and, as far as it goes, it's great. However, if you were taught to think that the sole reason to include quotation is to prove a point, then you may have some work ahead. Let go of some stuff, learn some stuff.

    Here is journalist and former soldier A. J. Somerset,

---

1   Susanna Haswell Rowson, *Charlotte Temple* (New York: Oxford University Press, 1986).

writing a nonfiction study called *Arms: The Culture and Credo of the Gun* (2015). Somerset is a scholar, gun owner, and marksman who has conflicted feelings about gun control, as you will doubtless infer from the sarcastic tone of this paragraph, from a chapter called "A Nation of Riflemen":

> In the late-nineteenth century, rifle shooting was held to promote all kinds of martial and manly virtues, by the same dubious logic that gave us *mens sana in corpore sano* [a healthy mind in a healthy body]. "A marksman is already more than half a soldier," as the *New York Times* explained in promoting the NRA's new range at Creedmoor: "He has developed those qualities of quickness, precision, self-reliance, and coolness which are most valuable to the soldier, and without which all the drilling in the world will make but an indifferent imitation."[2] Behold the benefits gained by lying on the cold ground, shooting at distant targets![3]

Somerset's first sentence makes a claim of cause and effect that invites proof. The first sentence does demand a quotation, because the claim isn't perfectly obvious. You can't just look up "late nineteenth-century rifle shooting" on Wikipedia and scoop up a clean little quotation that announces that A caused B, rifle shooting promoted manliness. No, you have

---

2   "Police Rifleman," *New York Times*, June 8, 1873.

3   A. J. Somerset, *Arms: The Culture and Credo of the Gun* (Windsor, Ontario: Biblioasis, 2015), 11.

to go out and find a source that will provide support.

Somerset does so. Because he's talking about the late nineteenth century, he logically looks around for a source written in the late nineteenth century. And he finds one: an article from the *New York Times*, circa 1873. Somerset makes fun of the idea he's documenting, but he's documenting it, sure enough. He proves his point that in the late nineteenth century, Americans thought that rifle shooting did more than improve marksmanship. They thought it improved manliness and moral character, too.

Did you notice the bit that bracketed a translation of Somerset's Latin phrase? I did that, not Somerset. Somerset was probably assuming that his readers had read the Roman poet Juvenal, who first said *mens sana in corpore sano*. Or maybe Somerset was assuming that his midlife readers would remember enough high school Latin to figure out the thing about the healthy mind in a healthy body. Dude was right about it. I'm a midlife reader, and I was able to figure out the Latin. But these days it's increasingly rare to find freshman students who have studied Latin. So I thought you might appreciate a freebie translation. Like mints at a wedding: nice but not necessary.

My decision just now to privilege what would work best for you, the probable non–Latin scholar, illustrates an important writing principle. Namely, it's on you, the author, to **clarify things that need clarifying**. Sometimes an event in a quotation will seem unclear because it has been taken out of its original context. Sometimes a quotation creates a moment of confusion with pronouns, and the reader doesn't know what or to whom the quote is referring. Sometimes the verb tense in a quote seems wonky with the verb tense that you would like to use in your own sentence. When these things happen, give the reader a mint. Smooth things over; clear up the confusion. Do this by presenting the original quotation verbatim. Then add your clarification in brackets. Use brackets, not parentheses. The brackets tell the reader that you are interrupting the quote, but only for a second, so as to forestall confusion. It's good manners, and your reader will thank you.

Now let's use a textual passage to prove a point when we are writing about a primary text rather than researching a secondary source. Let's say that you're writing about the chilling 1899 Charlotte Perkins Gilman story "**The Yellow Wallpaper.**"[4] Professors like to teach this one in intro

Charlotte Perkins Gilman ca. 1900

writing courses because it offers a super-useful model for how to assess whether a first-person narrator is credible. (Spoiler alert: not credible.) The text is the diary of a young wife who spirals into insanity. The scenario is: you're already past the introduction and thesis, you're now well into the body. You want to argue that John, the doctor husband, infantilizes his wife.

---

4   Visit link: goo.gl/i4Hrou

This would be one of those moments that require textual proof. Why? Because the wife does not come right out with an explicit announcement: "Help, my husband is infantilizing me!" Plus it is clear that *John* thinks he's a fantastic husband—tender, supportive, solicitous. Maybe there are readers who think so too, especially since throughout the text, from first to last page, John does display unarguable, overwhelming evidence of hands-on care. He cares so much about his wife's well-being that he's 100 percent involved in the teensiest activities of her day, such as telling her when she can eat and why she shouldn't keep a journal. So now would be the perfect time to quote the text. We will use the text's own words and phrases to prove a point that may not be altogether obvious to every reader.

Gilman links the wife's mental illness to the infantilization of women in nineteenth-century American culture. Although John cares for his wife, he refers to her as a "little girl" (71). Moreover, this wife expects to be laughed at by her husband (64), a view that suggests a model of marriage in which the wife's role is to amuse her husband. John refers to his wife as a "blessed little goose" (67). This manner of speaking usually signals an endearment, but what John is really saying is that his wife's presence is insignificant (little) and her wit lacking (goose). And this little goose is fortunate to have a husband like him (blessed). An endearment between romantic partners acts as a declaration of affection, but this one functions more like a scold from father to daughter. In fact, we learn that John exerts a control over his wife that prefigures the contemporary figure of a helicopter parent: John "hardly lets me stir without special direction" (65).[5]

Did you notice you don't need to include long block quotes in order to prove your point? You can do that, of course. Somerset, the gun author, did that in the quotation from the *New York Times*. But you can also change it up by quoting useful little words and phrases, as in the paragraph above. When trying to prove a point, **a good writer switches back and forth between nonquotes and verbatim quotation.**

Quoting a textual passage to extend a point

Quoting to *extend* a point is even better than quoting to prove it. This is because quoting to extend squeezes all the juice out of your quote. In the infantilization paragraph above, the quotations matter-of-factly support the point about how John infantilizes his wife. They also show why the infantilization is important to the author's overall message. But why settle for mere proof when you can actually use quotation to turn up the heat? Quotes can *advance* an argument. Make the quotation say something new! Make it *add* something to the argument, not merely prove it!

This practice of turning up the heat under your quotation is called **close analysis**. I'm gonna go ahead and say it:

---

5   Charlotte Perkins Gilman, "The Yellow Wallpaper," in Janet E. Gardner et al., *Literature: A Portable Anthology* (New York: Bedford St. Martin's, 2017), 64–77.

you can't become an excellent academic writer without developing this skill. In fact, close analysis is one of the most valuable skills you can have in life, let alone college. And I'm not just talking about the writerly life. Basically, when you learn how to read the details in any text, you add value to your professional marketability for the rest of your life. Whether you decide to become a barrister or a barista, you need to be able to read people, to read their words, their moves, their choices. Practicing close analysis now helps you do that later.

The best way to show you the difference between using quotation to prove versus quotation to extend is to take the same infantilization paragraph and rewrite it so that this time we use the quotation to push the argument to a new level. We're going for the same vibe, the same overall argument. But this time let's saddle up those quotes and make 'em *work*!

> Gilman links the wife's mental illness to the infantilization of women in nineteenth-century American culture. Although John cares for his wife, he refers to her as a "little girl" (71). John also calls his wife a "blessed little goose" (67). His manner suggests an endearment, but what he is really saying is that her presence is insignificant (little) and her wit lacking (goose). This little goose is fortunate to have a husband like him (blessed). An endearment between romantic partners acts as a declaration of affection, but this one functions more like a scold from father to daughter. John speaks to his wife as to a child: "*Bless* her heart, she shall be as sick as she pleases!" (71, emphasis added). Here the third person recalls a condescending father indulging a stub-

> born toddler, and again John invokes the language of *blessing*. Part of the problem, suggests Gilman, is that women are supposed to feel blessed by male behavior that consistently undercuts their abilities, freedoms, and cognitive functions.

See the difference? In the second version, we spot a detail that might otherwise fly under the radar. Two of the quotes use the same word: *bless*. By connecting the repeated words, we can use our quotations to advance the argument.

In our two separate infantilization paragraphs, we see that the quotations are used with two different goals in mind. The first one uses quotation in order to prove that nineteenth-century husbands (as represented in this story) treated their wives like children. The second one uses quotation to suggest not only that nineteenth-century husbands treated their wives like children but that wives were *supposed to be grateful for it*. That second part adds a little *je ne sais quoi*. It takes the argument to a new level. Henry James would say it's another turn of the screw.

9.4   FAQs about Quotes

How do I know what parts of a text to quote?

The good news is that you have total freedom to quote anything at all. You can cherry-pick any word, phrase, or passage that will serve your argument, as long as you don't take the quote out of context so that you *mis*represent what the author is really saying.

Here's a short list of the sorts of things college students quote:

▷ a sentence that sums up the author's point or approach
▷ a distinctive word or phrase that an expert has coined
▷ a passage that really supports what you're trying to say
▷ a passage that you think is missing the mark somehow
▷ a passage that reveals the author's underlying assumptions
▷ a passage that another one of your sources would take issue with
▷ a series of words or phrases that reveal an important pattern
▷ a textual moment that's notable because it interrupts a pattern

Do I always need a follow-up for a quote?

Yes. If you think the quote is perfectly obvious and needs no commentary, then you haven't picked the right quote. And if you think the quote says everything that needs to be said, then, um, guess what? You're not reading very deeply.

But the good news is that reading deeply, like fluency in a foreign language, is something you can learn. And just like learning a non-native language, your skill set develops clout in proportion to your practice time. We all know that a lucky few get the chance to learn a foreign language by immersion in a cross-cultural setting. It is perfectly true that those privileged folks may eventually learn to speak the language just by living in the different culture. You might have already recognized this comparison's version of the privileged minority: they are the lucky kids who never seemed to struggle in school because, turns out, their parents were professors and they were living this stuff at home the whole time. No wonder they always seemed to have a leg up—they were learning by immersion.

Yet isn't it curious that no matter how you learn it, fluency is fluency? It's an asset no matter how you get it. Its value doesn't change by virtue of how you got it. The good news is *anybody* can learn to read deeply, even if your home of origin did not offer any encouragement to read at all. You don't have to be an English major or a smarty-pants professor's kid to read deeply and to write well.

So first things first. It is *your* job, not your reader's job, to connect the quote to the argument. This is not optional, like the mints at the wedding. This is necessary. If you fail to hook up your quote to your argument, if you leave the quote hanging there all by itself, it's like saying, "Hi there, Professor! Would you mind doing the intellectual work so I don't have to?"

What if I want to end my conclusion with a great quote?

I'm going to suggest that you don't do that. It makes your writing look high-schoolish. When you feel a need to borrow the language of a great orator or famous saying, it's as if you're dodging the task, relying on someone else to write your conclusion for you. It's *your* paper. Write your own conclusion. It does not matter that Abraham Lincoln said it better, or that Mother Teresa warms the cockles of your heart. Don't quote *anybody* for the last words of an academic essay, even if that person did devote her life to working with lepers. Let the lepers go, my friend, and Godspeed. Your conclusion needs to end with your own words. Polish them as best you are able.

How about starting a paragraph with a quote?

I can see *some*body's a fan of uplifting cursive wall decals such as

Cherish yesterday, dream tomorrow, live today!!!

Look, I do get it that prefab sayings often have a ring of eloquence or a memorable zing. Like everybody else, I tear up at Dr. King's "I have a dream" speech. And I do not dispute that the language itself can deliver a tasty wow factor. Later in this book I'll talk about style and voice.

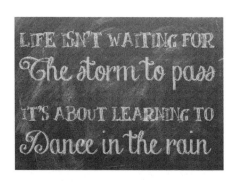

But the job of a paragraph's first sentence is not to sound all speechy. Please do not use your topic sentence to inspire a feeling of patriotism, altruism, or gratitude. The job of the first sentence is to deliver an analytical, arguable promise that *this* paragraph, and only this paragraph, can prove. If you lead the parade with someone else's language, you are using your paragraph's most valuable sentence to say, "Hey, I really like what this other guy says, and I wish I could say something that well myself!" I suggest that you put your quotes inside the paragraph. That way you can connect them to your argument, and your first sentence can do what it is supposed to do. After you turn in the essay, you will have plenty of time to

live love laugh!!!!

How do I introduce a quote?

Never let a quote come drifting in all by itself, sad and alone, like a child lost at the mall. All quotes need to be tethered securely in or to your own sentences, even the little phrases and one-word wonders. This is actually pretty easy. All you do is plug the quote into the flow of one of your own in-progress sentences:

> Mrs. Child, author of *The American Frugal Housewife* (1833), identifies the best use of saved earwax as a successful home remedy for those "who are troubled with cracked lips."[6]

When you're using a li'l peanut of a quote, just a wee snippet, like Mrs. Child's phrase *who are troubled with cracked lips*, tuck it safely into your own sentence so that the reader won't trip over it. Take your earwax suggestion and plop it whole into

---

6   Mrs. Child, *The American Frugal Housewife*, 12th ed. (Boston: Carter, Hendee, and Company, 1833), 116.

the sentence you were already writing. All you have to do is adjust your own sentence so that it makes sense with the quote inside it. Use quotation marks to show that it's a quote. You want the reader to keep rolling, even though somebody has just made the serious suggestion that we harvest wax from our ears and rub it on our chapped lips. Thank you, Madame! I, for one, will keep reading to see what you have to say about secondary saliva!

The game changes when the quote is longish, maybe a whole sentence. Now you have to use punctuation to hook the quote to one of your own host sentences. Here you have two choices. Both are perfectly respectable. Most scholars switch back and forth between these two choices, for variety.

The first choice involves a signal phrase, a nice hospitable tidbit, like this:

> Wormser observes, "One day someone says, 'Hot diggety dog.' The phrase throws [de Kooning] into a paroxysm of confused delight. He doesn't understand it, but he intuits the excitement."[7]

When you've chosen to use a signal phrase, you need a comma.

Tip: Here's how to tell if you need the comma. Say the signal phrase out loud all by itself:

---

7   Baron Wormser, "Legend: William de Kooning," in John Jeremiah Sullivan, ed., *Best American Essays* (New York: Houghton Mifflin, 2014), 207.

| "Wormser observes."

| "Omi contends."

| "In his analysis of string theory Kaku states."

| "At the outset Chakravorty notes."

Now ask this question: Is the signal phrase a stand-alone sentence? If it doesn't sound right all by itself, you need a comma.

The other option is to craft a whole stand-alone sentence as a way to introduce the quotation. When you take this route, you always use a specific piece of punctuation: a colon. The colon leashes the quote to your own stand-alone host sentence, as when, at the museum, you see an energetic group of kindergartners tethered to their teacher. In this comparison your own sentence is the teacher, large and in charge. The quotations are the tethered tots who will surely run off to admire the T-REX unless you recapture their focus. "Look, kids! A tiny prehistoric bee, trapped in shale!"

> Wormser suggests that on de Kooning's arrival in New York City, the artist's inability to speak English was more titillating than humiliating: "One day someone says, 'Hot diggety dog.' The phrase throws [de Kooning] into a paroxysm of confused delight. He doesn't understand it, but he intuits the excitement."

Note that in this second example, the introduction to the quote can indeed function as a complete sentence on its own.

If your intro to the quote can be a lone ranger, you need the colon.

Here's what you do not need when the intro is a stand-alone. A comma. I know what you're thinking. The difference between a teensy comma and a colon seems too small, too minor, to react to, like the fossilized bee. I am sad to report, however, that the difference is a big deal. If you use a comma to connect two complete sentences, even if one of them is a quotation, then you have just made one of the three worst usage errors in the English language. More on that later.

What is close analysis? Do I have to include it?

When you are in college, **close analysis** is the skill you use to craft a good follow-up for your quote. Post-college, close analysis is the skill that will get you promoted at your job. For now it means you zoom up close and personal, scrutinizing the chunk you have just quoted in order to deepen the level of analysis that you're offering the reader. You do this by picking out a couple of words or details in the quoted chunk, and then you show how those specific words or details help advance the argument you are trying to make.

Most freshmen arrive in college already knowing that you have to follow up your quote. You can't just leave it hanging there and then move on to the next thing. Good writing requires that you, the writer, perform the labor of hooking up every quote to the logic of the paragraph. But although everybody knows that you do need a follow-up, not everybody has learned how to craft a good one.

Let's start with a crappy follow-up. A weak follow-up

will merely paraphrase the quote. That is, it will repeat the gist of the quote in the writer's own words.

Let's say that you're writing a paragraph about an abusive husband, Sykes, who tries to murder his wife by planting a rattlesnake in her laundry basket. (Is it just me, or is American literature replete with mean husbands?) Sykes gets bitten by the snake instead, and now he's thrashing around in the dark. I'm starting in the middle of the paragraph, just as a real student writer introduces a quote.

> Delia describes the rattlesnake as she listens: "His whir sounds to the right, to the left, straight ahead, behind, close underfoot—everywhere but where it is" (147). In this passage, the wife is listening outside as her abuser realizes that the rattlesnake is loose in the same room with him.

This is a crappy follow-up because it merely restates what is happening in the quote. It doesn't add any analysis. It doesn't tell you what the quotation means to the argument that the writer is making.

Fortunately the scholar who actually wrote this paragraph, freshman Rebecca Stanton, would never have dreamed of a follow-up so crappy! I wrote that myself, to show you what a bad one looks like. Here is Stanton's excellent follow-up for the same quote:

> Delia describes the rattlesnake as she listens: "His whir sounds to the right, to the left, straight ahead, behind, close underfoot—everywhere but where it is" (147). This

> can symbolize two things. The first can be a darkness much like that which Sykes inflicts on Delia, coming at her from her weakest sides, surrounding her with criticism and violence. However, the snake can also represent God. He sounds all around, and you cannot know where He is or what his plans are for you. Like God, in this moment the snake has an all-powerful hold over Sykes. Choosing to represent God as a snake, something that is closely tied to fear and evil, can be an argument that God is not just a provider and a lover, but also a punisher.

Wow! Stanton won a seriously competitive award for this essay, and this particular follow-up demonstrates her skill in action. Notice that Stanton plucks a detail from the quote—the fact that the snake's whir seems to come from all sides—in order to *advance* her argument. She manages to equate that snake with the abusive husband *and* the Almighty! It's not an intellectual stretch to connect a violent cheaterpants of a husband to a snake, right? But Stanton is also trying to show that the author, Zora Neale Hurston, identifies *God* as a punitive entity. God, like this monster rattlesnake, is both omnipresent and punishing. Stanton's follow-up is all the more original because snakes, as she points out, are closely tied to fear and evil, qualities that are the very *opposite* of God in many religious traditions.

The quality of your close analysis determines the quality of your grade.

Here is a short list of things that are fair game for close analysis when you are crafting your follow-ups. These are all things that you can potentially pluck out of a quote to analyze in the follow-up:

- **details**
  (*His* whir? Why is this snake being described as male?)

- **objects** that are repeated and/or symbolic
  (Does the snake represent evil or good, human nastiness or cosmic justice?)

- the significance of the **setting or context**
  (Does literal darkness signal moral darkness?)

- the meaning of **gestures or actions**, like the fact that Sykes repeatedly uses real or fake snakes to scare his wife

- the relevance of **name imagery** or the withholding of names
  (If you know what the river *Jordan* means, for example, your understanding of the whole text deepens abruptly. *Jordan* comes from a Hebrew word meaning *descend* or *flow down*. Something's flowing down from the Almighty, and it ain't water!)

- the language of **similes and metaphors**, as when Sykes's girlfriend is described as a *hunk uh liver wid* *hair*

▷ the meaning of **verbs** that keep coming up, like *sweat* or *pray*

▷ the meaning of **tone**, as when the narrator interrupts all the southern idiom to speak in educated, eloquent standard English

(The contrast makes us ask immediately, "Why is the author spotlighting these eloquent high-toned passages that interrupt the pattern?")

▷ the importance of **structure**: how long or short the sentences are; style; vocabulary

(In "Sweat," we interestingly shift back and forth between past tense and present tense. Why is that? What's the author up to?)

▷ references or **allusions** to mythology, the Bible, or other widely known texts

(You could connect the rattlesnake to the serpent in the Garden of Eden, for example.)

▷ how a passage **foreshadows** something that will happen later in the text, as when Sykes steals all of his wife's matches for his girlfriend

(This foreshadows the literal and moral darkness to come.)

▷ how this passage **recalls** an important thing that

happened earlier, as when we hear from the townsfolk that Sykes has actually been cheating on his wife all along, with lots of women

All of these components of close analysis are viable with any kind of text, even visual texts such as ads, films, paintings, and graphic novels. If an author has produced a piece of visual artwork rather than an academic essay, she is still making intentional choices about vocabulary, tone, syntax, structure, content, and data. How do her choices affect the overall message? When you are deciding which passages to include as quotations in your work, you might want to choose with an eye to detail. Which passages will invite the best close analysis? Those are the ones to pick as quotations.

10 How to Explain Something

10.1 Analysis, Function, Antonym, Example, and Analogy

Writing to explain is the bread and butter of college assignments. It is called **explication**, which is **saying what something means in a clear and detailed way**. You are called to incorporate this skill in most college writing assignments.

There are five classic forms of explication, see. Here are the five biggies:

1. **analysis**   You say what something is.
   "A romantic partner is trustworthy and kind."

2. **function**   You say what something *does*.
   "A girlfriend shows physical affection."

3. **example**   You provide an illustration.

"My boyfriend, Santiago, was cool about taking my nephew to the emergency room when he got a pinto bean stuck up his nose."

4. **antonym**   You say what the thing is not, or what it does not do.

"A boyfriend does not break up with you because you come back from a trip to Honduras with your eye grotesquely swollen shut. It is NOT YOUR FAULT that you got Chagas!"

5. **analogy**   You make a useful comparison.

See below, because I want to focus on this one.

Practicing Explication

Grab a piece of paper and don't overthink it. If you are attracted to men, define *boyfriend*. If you are attracted to women, define *girlfriend*. If you are attracted to both men and women or identify as asexual, define *romantic partner*.

Write for ten minutes, just a paragraph. Your instructor might want to run this as a class activity, collecting the anonymous definitions at the end of ten minutes. The instructor can read a couple random definitions out loud, sentence by sentence, while the class tells the instructor which explication strategy each sentence is using. The instructor puts the following list on the board, and keeps tally.

This exercise proves something interesting. Curiously, most student writers take advantage of only two of the five explication strategies, as you will likely discover for yourself when you try your hand at this activity.

10.2 Analogy

Of the five explication strategies, analogy is the hardest to pull off, which might be why it is underused in college writing. Too bad: analogy is often the most compelling and the most memorable. For many incoming freshmen, using analogy in academic writing is a new strategy. And when you're new at this skill, it's easy to come up with a comparison that's sort of meh. It's not enough to say that this one thing has something in common with that other thing. Your comparison should *add* something to the discussion, not just restate it. You need to be able to say exactly what the comparison is adding, and how. If you are unable to articulate this to yourself, know that you are asking your reader to do what you have not done yourself.

The following analogy makes sense, but it's meh. I wouldn't choose it even though it does provide a solid semantic comparison for the term *romantic partner.*

> You could say that a romantic partner is like salt because it flavors all the food on your plate.

Use what you have been given: your common sense. If you've already heard a comparison, perhaps from a familiar cultural text, or if you've ever seen it in print, find another. We've all heard the one about how salt is basic but necessary. In case you don't have time to get a friend to give you some savvy critical feedback on the freshness of your analogy, here's how to check for cliché. Scan your mental files for mention of this comparison in familiar cultural documents. Maybe you first heard it in a snippet from a popular song, a memorable movie moment, a TV classic?

I recognize the salt analogy from one of *Grimm's Fairy Tales*, a story in which a king's daughter offends His Royal Highness by comparing her love for him to salt.[1] Apparently this King has more power than insight, and he's deeply insulted by the salt comparison. (Severe plot twist! The King finally ends up tasting unsalted food! He has an aha moment, hugs his daughter, orders a pizza, and everybody lives saltily ever after.)

Extended analogy

Don't be afraid to pick an analogy that comes from your own unique experience or sensibility, even if the comparison is surprising or quirky. As long as you can explain how your subject is like the thing you're comparing it to, it's a go. Here is an excerpt from an essay by college freshman Samantha Mattingly, undeclared but probable music major, tasked with ex-

---

1   Visit link: https://goo.gl/4R8Mnt

plaining her view of a college liberal arts education. Mattingly titled the piece "Yellow Hats and Curiosity: The Vehicle of the Liberal Arts Education."

I wasn't the professor who assigned the essay, and Mattingly isn't my own student. At this moment, I'm just a regular reader, like you. Perhaps you share my first response to the title, which is, What does a yellow hat have to do with a liberal arts education? Because I have no clue, I'm curious enough to keep reading. Take it away, Sam.

"Yellow Hats and Curiosity: The Vehicle of the Liberal Arts Education"
By Samantha Mattingly

How is the liberal arts education like a certain yellow hat? In order to answer this question, I must compare my current academic situation to my younger self's favorite character. The story begins as follows:

This is George.
He lived in Africa.
He was a good little monkey and always very curious. (Rey 4)

In the initial pages of H. A. Rey's 1941 classic, Curious George spends his days in the jungle munching on bananas, playing with the other animals, and swinging from tree to tree. Then a yellow hat enters his life. George's curiosity, coupled with this intriguing yellow hat, takes him out of the jungle, onto a ship, and ultimately to a big city where his inquiring mind is nurtured and given ample opportunity to grow. If not for George's curiosity, he would have a very different identity; perhaps we would be reading—or not reading—books about "Apathetic George." Without that yellow hat, though, we would potentially know George as a curious monkey in a small jungle with a hardly exciting life. Just as the yellow hat freed George from the jungle, so the liberal arts free us from the confines of our narrow views. In this way, both the yellow hat and the liberal arts education act as vehicles; they cause movement in the forward direction. Metaphorically speaking, the same two ingredients that are essential to George's story are also essential to mine.

Mattingly bases a whole essay on the explication strategy of analogy. Of course, drawing out the comparison (**extended analogy**) is not necessary to make smart use of the analogy tool, though Mattingly's essay does it to creative effect throughout. Her choice to build an extended analogy illustrates something important. When you build an effective analogy, you are layering one cake on top of another, doing twice the intellectual work that the assignment has asked you to do. The first layer is Mattingly explaining her view of a liberal arts education. The second layer is Mattingly explaining her chosen analogy to the reader. A fresh analogy in the hands of a competent writer has a rich payoff. Mattingly has doubly proved that she can explicate. Plus, side bonus: I'm guessing that her professor, who gave her an A+ on this essay, found the whole thing to be memorable. "Oh yeah, Sam Mattingly. She's the one who wrote about Curious George." Who else in the whole freshman class did that? Again, an educated guess:

nobody. Sam Mattingly, like the farmer's cheese, stands alone.

A successful analogy requires a bit of swag. You have to have the confidence, the brio, to pick an unexpected comparison. At Mattingly's age, would I have had the chops to reference a kindergarten story in a college class? No way. But then, I was the one hiding a meatball in my purse. And anyway, back in the day professors were more likely to resemble the matcha guy, with a fairly narrow definition of what constituted culture. George Steiner, George Berkeley, George Santayana—those Georges would have shown up in my college classes. Curious George, not so much. No matter that Mattingly's comparison devolves from books we haven't read since we were five. She's using her reference resourcefully because she's not actually talking about Curious George the Kiddie Lit Monkey. She's talking about Curious George the Exemplar of Intellectual Inquiry.

Constructing your analogy with care

Swag isn't the only thing that comes in handy with analogy. May I also suggest a spot of sensitivity? You might want to skate carefully where the ice is thin, as Mattingly does. Curious George, published in 1941, would almost certainly not be published today. Mattingly knows this. Never mind the jaunty references to booze, tobacco, and guns in a children's book. I'm talking about the man in the yellow hat who kidnaps George from the jungles of Africa. That man could be, and has been, read as The Man, symbol of colonial conquest. One scholar sums up the voyage of Curious George as "eerily rem-

"Please join me in a short meditation on cultural hegemony and its relationship to the history of colonialism, which America tends to both deny and romanticize!"

iniscent of Middle Passage slave narratives."[2] Another notes that George's story is not even told in his own voice but the voice of the Master who is "always warning, often scolding, and forever superior."[3] Yikes.

Do the troubling implications of the story mean that Mattingly should not deploy it as part of a college explication assignment? Not at all. Mattingly clearly understands the cultural implications. She gets it that you could write a very different essay about this feel-good childhood story.

---

2   Daniel Greenstone, "Frightened George: How the Pediatric-Educational Complex Ruined the Curious George Series," *Journal of Social History* 39.1 (Autumn 2005): 221.

3   June Cummins, "The Resisting Monkey: 'Curious George,' Slave Captivity Narratives, and the Postcolonial Condition," *Review of International English Literature* 28.1 (1997): 69.

Mattingly constructs her analogy with care. She is obviously aware that any interpretation is tenable if you can support it with material from the text. And she does that. She intentionally interprets Curious George's ocean voyage as a metaphoric passage to self-discovery rather than as a representation of a morally problematic captivity narrative. Mattingly does not choose to read the man with the yellow hat as a representation of cultural hegemony. In her analogy he is a helpful professor or mentor. Her extended analogy connects an open mind and an adventurous spirit to intellectual risk-taking. Please note that Mattingly's positive analogy doesn't deny the historically problematic evocations that *I* would probably focus on, if I were the one writing about this children's tale. The upbeat analogy means, merely, that the essay's author is exercising her right to choose her focus—a focus that she uses the text to support. Yay: you can do that in college. A moment of silence, please, for academic freedom.

Mattingly's essay focuses instead on Curious George's willingness to try out new skills, such as the part where George, inspired by seagulls flying overhead, tries to fly himself. Alas, George has no natural talent for flying. In case you missed the Curious George series when you were a child, George is a literal monkey. (Did you know that there is an ongoing scholarly dispute over whether George is a Barbary macaque or an ape? Let us hope that this intriguing debate may attract future scholars to the field!) In Mattingly's analogy, George's failure to fly codes Mattingly's own success. The extended analogy connects the liberal arts education to *intellectual* flight. Mattingly reveals that she has purposely tried out a variety of academic subjects: "As a person of many interests,

I appreciate the option to take Intro to Psychology, Digital Photography, and Poetry, and therefore satisfy some of my curiosities while discovering new ones. Although I may find myself, like George, lacking in natural talent in some areas, I can freely experiment with all that the liberal arts education has to offer." Do you see how Mattingly is adroitly guiding our reading? For her the issue is not *whether* George can fly. The issue is that *he tries to.*

10.3   Skittles and Sensitivity

In your shoes I would want to know what it looks like when the sensitivity component is missing. That does happen sometimes in student essays, which is why I am mentioning it here. But I couldn't find a college student with the chutzpah to contribute an insensitive analogy, not even my own niece, who has admitted that she is now embarrassed by some of the essays she wrote in her freshman year. When I tried to bribe her to let me have one for this book, she laughed and said, "You wish!"

Fortunately I have located an alternative. Perhaps you recall a certain controversial Twitter posting from September 19, 2016, in which Syrian refugees were compared to a bowl of poisoned Skittles? The author of the tweet is a well-known political figure. His analogy prompted a swift media backlash. Why? Insofar as analogies go, this one was certainly original. I had heard U.S. immigrants compared to salads and melting pots but never to Skittles.

The donor of the Skittles comment was advocating a course of caution in U.S. immigration policy. In his candy-bowl analogy, the great majority of Skittles (nonthreatening Syrian refugees) are depicted as desirable and wholesome, if you can call a Skittle wholesome. Then the analogy asks us to imagine our response if we were to learn that the bowl might also include a few poisonous Skittles (terrorists). Would we be as eager to accept a handful? The analogy implies that the United States should not be admitting terrorists willy-nilly. Few would disagree. True enough.

So why were folks so upset? The *New York Times* observed that the Skittles analogy "appeared to suggest that the nation was faced with a blind selection process in which a few potentially poisoned pieces would be lurking among the thousands of Syrians fleeing a brutal five-year-old civil war." This response from the *New York Times*[4] neatly locates two of the reasons why many readers objected to the Skittles analogy as insensitive. One, since all Skittles look alike, the comparison implies that government officials have *no way of knowing* who is and who is not a terrorist ("blind selection process"). Homeland Security implements a policy that is a tad more complex than blind selection, however. Two, the *New York Times* strongly suggests that the Skittles analogy lacks compassion for the many Syrian refugees fleeing a "brutal five-year-old civil war."

Perhaps the analogy's greatest insensitivity lies in the demeaning nature of the comparison in the first place. Suffering, desperate people are being compared to something small, cheap, and consumable, like low-end, dime-store candy. The

---

4   Visit link: https://goo.gl/5rxo6P

analogy trivializes the refugees' suffering because candy itself is fundamentally trivial. Skittles, unlike Syrian refugees, have no problems. Skittles are not raped, displaced, bombed, or oppressed. The only reason Skittles exist is to be consumed. And the analogy asks Americans to imagine themselves in the role of the consumer. Would Syrian refugees exist without Americans to consume them? Maybe we should ask them.

I'd like to think that the Skittles analogy, a tweet, was posted quickly, as a part of an ongoing political conversation, without much careful thought, though I happen to know that another politician proudly claimed to have said it first. Take it, dude. You can have it. With social media it is all too easy to go on written record with comments we might like to delete later, no matter our political affiliation. The Skittles comment is merely one in a sea of online bergs we might get stuck on, and I don't mean to suggest that it's as epic as the one that took down the *Titanic*. In fact, the only reason I've cited it here is because it got so much media attention that you are likely to remember it. Even the *maker* of Skittles objected to the analogy.

My point is that an analogy must be thought through if it's going to be effective. One practical tip is to think about the writer's/author's role in the analogy. Sam Mattingly, the freshman, was comparing *herself* to Curious George. The author of the Syrian refugee tweet was comparing *other people* to Skittles. Generally speaking, you have more leeway when you are speaking from your own experience than when you are thrusting a metaphoric identity on someone else. Doing the latter might be a bit risky. Does that mean you can't compare other people to stuff? No, not at all. Just remember to think it through. A little sensitivity at the front end may prevent a reading you don't intend.

Let's wrap it up

If you have been using only one or two explication strategies to define your term of choice, then it may be time to branch out. I encourage you to be intentional about incorporating the others. Doing so shows your breadth and spices things up for the reader.

Literalize This!

Incoming freshmen are often intimidated by analogy, which seems risky for so many reasons. But it's important to practice it, since so many college assignments are the better for it. Here's a pleasant classroom activity that gives you a leg up.

Divide into small groups. Together answer this question: What *object* in our contemporary culture best represents the following abstractions? In your answers, don't use any person or part of the human body.

1. gratitude

2. deceit

3. beauty

4. violence

---

5. racial conflict

6. doubt

7. stupidity

8. excellence

9. relaxation

10. memory

11. innocence

12. creepiness

13. starting over

14. style

15. conformity

16. individuality

17. ambition

18. creativity

19. permanence

20. depression

Analogy Assignment

Time for a tribute to Sam Mattingly and her yellow hat. Write a three-page essay that compares a familiar practice or value to an extended analogy. How was growing up in a commune like glass-making? How is playing college volleyball like the board game *Clue*? How is amateur entomology like reality TV? Surprise us!

11 How to Write from Personal Experience

11.1 The Personal Essay

If you haven't yet been asked to produce a personal essay in college, buckle up. The skill of drawing insight from your own personal experience is so in demand that you will probably get a separate essay assignment asking you to do nothing but that—no library research, no critical reading, no integration of outside sources. You, you, you! All you, all the time!

The good news is that this essay is easy and fun to write. The bad news is that in college classes you probably should not draw from your personal experience unless you are specifically tasked to do so, as Sam Mattingly was in the Curious George piece. It's a bit of a mind-bender. On the one hand, you hear the consistent message that your personal experience is valuable to academic writing. On the other, there's a time and place for all things under the sun, and too much personal writing would mean less writing about what others think. The time for personal writing does not include research papers, lab reports, or an assignment that asks you to compare this author's work with that author's work.

However, it's a pretty sure bet that you will have to write some **personal essays**, also sometimes called **reflections**, while you are in college. The personal essay is one of the distinctive features of American higher education, which consistently teaches that one of the signs of cultural literacy is the ability to integrate our personal experience into a developing worldview. In some European universities, you might never be asked to write a personal essay. Stateside, in the land of Rugged Individualism, you will undoubtedly be asked to connect what you have learned in your head to what you have lived in your life.

Phillip Lopate, one of our best-known anthologists of personal essays, points out that the hallmark of the personal essay is intimacy. He describes it like this: "The writer seems to be speaking directly into your ear, confiding everything from gossip to wisdom."[1] The kind of intimacy Lopate is talking about can be achieved by making careful structural choices in style and tone. I am doing that right now as I craft this very nontraditional textbook. Conventional academic writing and casual, intimate writing have historically practiced different brands of writerly etiquette. Sometimes it is fruitful to explore the intersections thereof. If your tone is chatty, and

---

1   Phillip Lopate, *The Art of the Personal Essay* (New York: Anchor, 1994), xxiii.

your prose stylish, even a study on the moral roots of conservatives and liberals can seem intimate, as demonstrated in a popular TED talk by social psychologist Jonathan Haidt. The obvious advantage of writing about intellectual content in a casual way is accessibility. The obvious disadvantage is that it is challenging to learn a whole new skill set.

You, the student writer, will be invited to try your hand at this skill set by starting on the ground floor, which is the production of Lopate's intimate tone through choices in your content (not structure). This kind of essay usually draws stories from the writer's personal experience or from the experience of those near and dear to the writer. And it is this kind of personal essay that you will probably be asked to write in a freshman composition class.

Memoir vs. Autobiography

The personal essay is a subset of creative nonfiction essays in general, but because its special purview is intimacy, it has more in common with its cousin, the **memoir**. Since you will be crafting your personal essay with real-life experience— something that you didn't make up, something that actually happened to you—you do need to know a couple of basics about the parent company, the genre we call memoir. Everything I say here about memoir also applies to the personal essay.

For starters, let's get our terms straight. *Memoir* is not the same thing as *autobiography*, even though both genres focus on the centrality of personal experience. When you are asked by a college instructor to write a personal essay, you do not want to submit an autobiography. Both genres take as their subject something that has happened to the author. Yet there are important differences.

Sometimes uninformed readers pardonably get these two things confused. I'm not arguing that we can't tack back and forth between the conventions of memoir and autobiography in the same piece of creative nonfiction. Rules, after all, were made to be broken. I can think of several contemporary authors who blur the lines on purpose, and to interesting effect. But let's start with the basic differences before we get all creative and try to smoosh them together.

11.2   Time as We Know It: Chronos and Kairos

Autobiography and memoir represent the difference between two completely different understandings of time. If you don't understand the difference, you will write a lousy personal essay. These two understandings of time are not just different. They are direct opposites, hence the importance of knowing the distinction. Our mother tongue has pretty much one word for *time*. Time to brush our teeth! Bed time, play time, old-time, time capsule. We had the time of our life. Time flies. Time's running out. Do you have enough time to stay late? Speakers of English have slim pickins: all we got is time, 24/7. Therefore let us turn to our friends the ancient Greeks, who helpfully had different words for the two separate kinds of time that make memoir and autobiography so different from one another: *chronos* and *kairos*.

Autobiography is grounded in the reality of *chronos*, the Western understanding of time as linear. This is the idea of time that is embodied in our many Western methods of measurement, such as eons, eras, millennia, centuries, decades, months, weeks, minutes, seconds, and so on. We have chosen to define our time by finitude, according to a straight-line Western scale, start date here, end date here. (Think milk cartons, tombstones.) Calendars and watches are all about chronos. So is autobiography.

An author embarks on an autobiography often in the twilight years, after a full life of exciting or unusual activity that is interesting precisely because it connects the author to a certain chronos time frame. I had an affair with Harrison Ford! I hung out with Jimi Hendrix at Woodstock! I survived a concentration camp! I went undercover during the Cold War! If we read the story of these autobiographies, we also read the story of an era. Since the autobiographer is writing on the other side of these events, the chapter is closed now, but it's still mighty interesting. Think about the device we use for keeping linear time, the *chronograph*, or the word *chronicle*. *Chronos* implies

Chronograph watch

time as a line. An event, once it happens, is gone forever. Time keeps on ticking.

So an event happens, then it's done. Woolly mammoths live, thrive, evolve, die. On to the next era. As the autobiographer records her history, she is using this kind of time. She is asking a key question, the signature question of Western *chronos*, and of autobiography: **"What time**

is it?" In other words, What external event should I now be focusing on? Autobiography is the factual story of someone's life and times, a series of events and experiences that constitute the whole span of the writer's life up to the time the autobiography is written. What happened when is the main point. This, then this, then this, and so on, in a straight linear line until we come to the end.

Book-length memoir and the downscaled college assignment mini version, the personal essay, draw by contrast on the Greek concept of *kairos*, a word that we do not see in wide use in the English language. This is curious, given how important the concept is to America's pet genre, memoir.[2] *Kairos* means *a period of time with a designated purpose*. In memoir the writer is no longer asking, "What time is it?" He's asking, **"What is this time *for*?"** The model is not the Western image of the linear line but the Eastern notion of the circle. A circle implies cyclicity, eternality, recurrence. This is a familiar notion to many Eastern spiritual traditions, and even to the Western Judeo-Christian tradition. The idea is that if you miss an important opportunity or a lesson that the universe is trying to teach you—well, stay in peace, because that wheel will keep turning, and you will surely encounter the same opportunity (or test) again. Perhaps the next time you come across your dad simultaneously flossing while singing a Journey song (*"The wheel in the sky keeps on turnin'"*), you might nod with

---

2   Ben Yagoda documents a recent jaw-dropping uptick in memoir. In his study *Memoir: A History* (New York: Riverhead, 2010), Yagoda observes that in America, the number of published memoirs increased more than 400 percent between 2004 and 2008 (7).

recognition and compassion. It is not your dad's fault he sings Journey in the bathroom, and one day you, too, will be vaguely grossing your kids out with a stalwart combination of oral hygiene and Bruno Mars. What goes around, comes around.

It is here that we see the distinctive stamp of the personal essay. The author is doing two things simultaneously. One, he's telling the story of an event that really happened. Two, he's reflecting on its meaning. The personal event turns back like a circle in its retelling, when the writer understands what the experience was *for*.

Why is this difference so important? Because if we believe that our personal experience has a larger meaning, we must conclude that we should come to know this meaning and apply it to our lives. In short, memoir promises a practical application. This explains why you will be asked to write a personal essay in college. Because you can profit from it, see.

Typically the narrative arc of the autobiography is the full span of the subject's life and times. The autobiographer decides to write it when mortality's a-knockin' at the door. With memoir, though, the narrative arc is usually much shorter, focusing on a specific period of the subject's life, for a particular reason. Have you noticed that memoir often limits itself, as if on purpose, to a specific season of the memoirist's life? The author has so many experiences she could write about, a lifetime of them, but here she is, plucking these six months from all the rest. The reason is, she's asking, "What is *this* time for?"

For better or worse, writing from personal experience has become a college staple, even as reading *about* personal experience has become a national pastime. Yet not all American scholars endorse writing from personal experience. Some critics believe it doesn't belong in the college classroom at all. And there *are* risks with this kind of writing. In fact, you will be more likely to profit from the personal essay assignment if you understand the main arguments against it.

11.3 Three Complaints against Personal Writing

The naysayers do lay out some tasty food for thought. In January 2016 William Giraldi wrote in the *New Republic*, "The average memoir is at the fore of the kindergartening of American letters, wherein Emersonian self-reliance becomes salubrious self-expression."[3] Giraldi is suggesting that America's ever-intensifying flirtation with personal experience might be actively *regressing* our national literature. An intriguing suggestion, eh? Here are three objections to writing personal experience that I still occasionally hear from students and published authors alike.

Writing from personal experience is a form of solipsistic belly-gazing.

America believes less and less in the centrality of traditional external Subjects, systems of governance such as religion, patriotism, and fixed moral absolutes. Those systems of governance used to be the Subject of our collective lives. In our postmodern world many thinkers have demoted those ideas,

---

3   William Giraldi, "The Unforgiveable Half Truths of Memoir," *New Republic*, January 15, 2016.

positioning them as constructs of the human mind rather than as external absolutes. Demoting the old absolutes leaves a void. What can fill it? We need a Subject! Hey, we can be *our own subject*! And so we promote our own sense of agency to a position of new authority. We ourselves are the ultimate authority—look, we can create, re-create, remember, interpret! In other words, writing from personal experience is a form of solipsism. Interesting argument.

Making meaning from personal experience is a specious, slippery project.

Here the critics have another great point. Writers simply cannot remember whole conversations verbatim from forty years ago, and they often write as if they can. Who can remember every single detail? And then, too, some writers feel they need to change names, details, or timelines for ethical/legal reasons. Plus, where does one person's truth leave off and another person's deception begin? American readers have been scandalized by memoirs that purported to be true but later turned out to be made-up. Wool, meet eyes! My favorite fake memoir is Misha Defonseca's *Misha: A Mémoire of the Holocaust Years* (1997). I hereby nominate it in the category of Best Fraudulent Memoir with Wolves. Defonseca told a story of escaping a concentration camp and being raised by wolves—ferocious, yet nurturing; mangy, but kind! Turns out Defonseca *wasn't even Jewish*, sheesh. And when it all came out in the wash, she was forced to give $22.5 million back to her publisher. Slippery. You could say that.

Writing from personal experience is schmaltzy and sentimental.

I hear this one most often from students with science majors, particularly when their chosen field focuses on measureable outcomes rather than the self-report of personal writing. But I also see this objection from established authors and scholars. For many readers, popular book-length memoirs often seem as predictable as trade romances or murder mysteries. The argument is that memoir *by definition* lends itself to an artificially easy schema: "That was then, this is now." And for these critics, such a dichotomy is reductive and oversimplified, a form of black-and-white thinking that smells like formulaic triumph over adversity, where everybody gets a pat on the back and a round of applause just for opening their mouth to tell their story. "You go, Misha!"

First Memory

1. Step one of this activity happens in small groups during class. Divide into clusters of three or four. On a blank piece of paper write down the story of your earliest memory. Even if the memory seems sort of lame and undramatic, go with that. Note everything you can. Include people, place, textures, smells, even the details that you can't explain, the tangential ones that managed to lodge in your memory. Do you know how old you were? Jot down what

you do know, as well as all the hazy bits.

Then take turns narrating your first memory to your peers. Don't analyze it; simply report it. Remember Chapter 3, "Considering Your Audience"? Telling your first memory out loud to people who were not there when it happened forces you to take your audience into account. You will have to provide information, make adjustments, and foreground some facts so that your peers can make sense of your story. Pay attention to the changes you make for the sake of clarity.

2. The second step of this exercise happens at home. Even if your earliest memory represents a profoundly atypical moment, a rare rupture, or a huge emotion, there's still the matter of all the *other* big moments that did not stick as your first memory. Isn't it curious that this memory, and not some other, is your earliest recollection? Strange, right? Maybe we'll never know why that is, scientifically speaking. We're going to use your inexplicable first memory to illustrate the sort of work the personal essayist does and to practice the *kairos* understanding of time.

How did this early memory predict the person you would become? In other words, what was this time *for*?

11.4 Kairos and First Memories

We're going to use our inexplicable first memories to illustrate the sort of work the personal essayist does and to practice the *kairos* understanding of time. Here's my *kairos* version of my own first memory, by way of example.

According to my mom, I am two. She has just cut my hair into a very short bang, like a surrey with a fringe on top.  We are in Saskatchewan, visiting her sister Agnes in an old-fashioned farmhouse with a pump on the kitchen sink. I love this pump. The handle holds the warmth of the late afternoon sun, and my aunt is carrying me down the stairs to the kitchen so that I can work the pump's handle. We are German-speaking Mennonites, but my mother has recently started speaking English around me. The Canadian relatives are more conservative than we are. On the stairs my mother's older sister expresses a hint of disapproval about the bangs. "Was sind diese?" What are these?

She cut them with Scotch tape and a ruler. And she admits this freely, almost proudly.

The English word for *bangs* is on the tip of my tongue—I know it, I know it, it sounds like an explosion, one syllable, starts with a B. I have it! And I say proudly, "Diese sind BOOMS!"

This little encounter on the threshold of an old-fashioned farmhouse kitchen is an analogue for the person I have become. Over the course of my life I have been in perpetual negotiation between my Mennonite and American identities. As on a stairway, that liminal position between two places, I still don't know where one identity ends and the other begins. Sometimes I struggle with language in all its forms, and though I have studied several, I am fluent in none. The language of heritage isn't enough. The language of critical inquiry isn't enough. And when language fails me, as it must, I find myself returning to the kitchen, the defining room in my life. If I stand in the place of preparation and prime the pump, from it flows all creativity. From it flows what my mother gave me: the gift of identifying that which is precious. Hey all y'all! You *wish* you had booms like these!

Perhaps I may never know the "real" reason this small moment has stuck with me into middle age. Aunt Agnes, deceased these past eight years, never remembered the incident. As far as I recall, the trip to Saskatchewan was otherwise uneventful. Mom: "Not uneventful! You urped up in the car and I had to remove my dress and hang it out the window! For a couple of hours, I sat there in a bra and slip, in front of Vern and Carol Heidebrecht!" Much as I enjoy the visual, I don't remember either the projectile vomiting or the astonished Reverend Heidebrecht, there in the back seat. Memory is weirdly selective. All I know is that, when challenged by faint disapproval about those worldly bangs, I fired right up in defense of the one who had authored them. And I tried my best to utter *her* word.

Do you see how it works? It doesn't matter if all this meaning really inhered in the bangs incident back when it happened in 1965. The point is that the meaning inheres *now*, now that I am capable of hindsight. Hindsight is **insight that implies action**. If you guess that I take my mom to Barbados every chance I get, if you sense that I let her cheat at Scrabble and photograph her wrapped in the picnic tablecloth, you'd be right about it. Would I have had the insight to appreciate my mother had I not exercised my capacity to make meaning from personal experience? I think so. But the appreciation has grown in proportion to the hindsight that has studied her choices over time. In other words, **personal writing results in growth**. That's a darn good reason to do it in college.

So the point of personal essay isn't recording what happened. It's saying what it happened *for*. Writing from experience is the genre that most honors the process of radical, saltatory change. (*Saltatory*: very cool word. From the Latin *saltare*, meaning *to hop* or *leap*.) Thus the personal essay implies that in the telling of our own stories, we learn things about ourselves that will jump us to a new place in consciousness. In other words, an experience has changed us forever, and it is only through writing and thinking about it that we come to a full awareness of its meaning in our lives.

When you were a kid, did your parents ever give you a big fat time-out where the point was to go to your room and contemplate the full implications of your naughty behavior? The reason that never worked was because you, being six, had not yet arrived at the cognitive stage where contemplation is an option. Six-year-olds are still in the developmental stage psychologists call Light Your Little Sister's Barbie on Fire and Shoot Her Out of a Homemade Cannon. But I am delighted to report that you are now much more likely to profit from a contemplative time-out. It's called the personal essay.

Epiphany

This genre of writing insists on the importance of **epiphany**. You probably are already familiar with this word, but it has a specific use as a structural term when we're talking about writing. Epiphany comes to us from the ancient Greek work *epiphaneia*, which means *a manifestation, a striking*. The word was originally used in a religious sense, to mean a manifestation of God. But when we use this term to talk about writing today, we intend it to mean *a sudden insight that changes everything*. Even now, though, the term *epiphany* still crackles and flickers with a religious energy. This is because when it comes, the astonishing flash of inspiration seems somehow *otherworldly*. That is, it seems to come from outside the self, a movement from an exterior reality to the interior landscape of consciousness.

The epiphanies people write about are not the major outside events that change us on the outside, though of course external events can bring abrupt and lasting change to our bodies. I know a young man who came away from a diving accident paralyzed from the waist down. Certainly the change that his body experienced demanded his utter and total attention, especially in the aftermath of the initial hospitalization. This change to his body had a lasting effect on his career plans, too. It eventually led to a whole new life as a badass wheelchair tennis player. But if my friend were asked to identify the part of himself where the biggest change happened, he wouldn't say his legs. He'd say, "My mind."

▷ Jot down a couple of sentences about the greatest physical pain you have ever been in. How painful was it? Did you pass out or throw up? How long did the physical agony last?

▷ Now jot down a couple of sentences about the greatest

psychological pain you have ever been in. How painful was it? What were the results of this pain? How long did it last?

Here's the interesting part. If you were forced to experience one of these hurts all over again, would you rather relive the physical pain or the psychic anguish?

See what I'm saying? Interior pain is often larger, more terrifying, more consequential. Matt, the wheelchair tennis player, said the surgeries and therapy and retraining were a walk in the park compared to the pit of depression he had to climb out of first.

No matter what's happening on the outside, the epiphanic change that is important to personal writing is caused by the internal event of interpretation. Change comes from insight, gradual or sudden, that makes us nod. Something is now different. A causes B, which demands C. Circumstance produces insight, which demands change. Our lives will never be the same.

Yet in this style of writing, you don't spell it all out for the reader. In most kinds of academic writing, you do, which is why I made a big deal about setting up a strong thesis in Chapter 5. In the majority of college assignments, it's on you, the author, to articulate exactly what the argument is. You can't just imply one. If you want a good grade, there's no whiffling: either you have an argument or you don't. In most academic writing you can't just gesture toward a thesis with loosey-goosey language. Not only do you tell your reader directly what the argument is; you show your reader how you came up with it, using persuasive evidence from the text or by citing experts in a relevant field.

In the personal essay, however, you're shooting for a different kind of relationship with the reader. You're no longer trying to get the reader to think as you think. Now you're trying to get the reader to experience the same epiphany that you experienced. Fact is, when you experience one, if you see writing on the wall, it's metaphoric writing and on an imaginary wall. How do you get a reader on the outside to follow an epiphany you had on the inside? The answer is simple—and by *simple*, I mean *complex*. You invite the reader to take the same journey you took (simple!). You do this by re-creating the journey (complex!). Since an epiphany, unlike a thesis, is subtle, the personal essay must tell its story so that the reader *gradually figures out how you changed*. Because that is how you figured it out. Gradually. Although an epiphany in writing seems to arrive abruptly, like a bolt from the blue, you can see in its wake that you have been gradually figuring something out all along.

11.5   Student Personal Essay

Here is a terrific personal essay written by Jourdan Lamse when she was an English major in her junior year. After college she snagged a cool internship with a publishing company, and she has written lots of things since. But I wanted to include an essay she wrote while she was actually enrolled in college. The essay is strong for many reasons. One that I really like is the surprise factor. Nobody ever expects a demon, is what I always say! The essay compares learning how to write with Lamse's negotiation of a conservative community of origin.

"Instructions for Pretentious Pentecostals, or, The Long Way to Becoming an Empathetic Writer"

by Jourdan Lamse

Bend your knees in your bedroom when no one sees. Put your face into the white shag carpet and stay there. Sing and be still. Sing and be still. Wait. Wait because you want to. Wait because the wait becomes worth it the moment you feel the Holy Spirit's presence in the room with you. This is where you learn to flow under the anointing and lead Never Enough Youth Church in spontaneous and prophetic worship. Here is where you've learned that God is your Defender, Refuge, Healer, Comforter, Lover of your soul. While you wait, sing words like "in love with you," "no cost," "turn my back on every other lover," and "take your name."

Approach writing the same way you approach life and worship. Those who hunger are filled, and if you do the right things, good things ensue. Write as a means of evangelism. Write in allegory. Think Aslan. Write from this lofty plane of existence and from the paradigm that if you love God deeply, He will shelter you with his arms and under his wings you will find refuge. Paint pictures of Heavenly bliss with stipulations. Write stories about men who give everything for the women they love, fighting, bleeding for and rescuing, stories that make your like-minded friends cry.

For your first writing workshop in college, submit a nonfiction essay comparing your cousin's spike-heeled-boot, garter-throwing, drunk-guy-falling-into-the-DJ-booth wedding with your best friend's Christian music, barefoot, father-of-the-bride-bawling, you-know-it-will-be-their-first-time-tonight sacred union before God. English majors study your essay with their eyelids drooped halfway down. The class feminists don't appreciate your simplistic ideas of womanhood. Some guy tells you not to "shit on somebody's wedding just because the bride had a kid." Until then you had no idea you were shitting on anything. Re-think your ideas. Realize that no one is waiting for you to lead them to a place of worship and undoing here. No women waving multi-colored banners from the blue platform in the sanctuary. No one dances through the halls.

Nowadays, you spend your time in colorless classrooms, discussing stories of people degenerating into insanity, necrophilia, illicit sex, murder, depression. Professors want to know what you think the author is getting at. But all you can imagine is Raymond Carver hunched over, pointing a wide finger at you and droning, "Life is hell; God is dead. Life is hell; God is dead." Your professors tell you, "There's no wrong answer," which takes you and your pre-established right answer and makes it repellent, the mark of a simple-minded and stubborn non-thinker. You don't have much to say when your religion professor tries to cure you of your Pentecostalism. He uses that word, "cure." Your writing professor tells you to subvert your preconceived ideas. Question everything. Question the things you've been taught never to question.

Replace wedding essay with long, contemplative piece about the almost-dead opossum you have to step over on the way to class. "Half-sitting upright, barely supporting the dead weight of its upper back and dangling head by a skinny black arm like a soldier just trying to breathe ... blood dripping from between its teeth into a puddle." Your classmates comment, "Better. Good imagery and sensory details."

Agree to let the people at church try to cast a demon out of you once they learn about the violent nature of your depression. You know you have to do something because you'll never get through school this way. Without your absolutes and the things that made sense to you, you have no idea how to approach life, let alone a white sheet of paper. And since the nature of writing demands self-exploration, you're convinced that writing will surely tip you off your tightrope and into a chasm of emotional dysfunction. It feels like prodding the sleeping monster and just hoping that it won't wake up to impale you on a tooth or a claw. Writing is madness.

The soft-spoken, silver-haired woman whom you and your friends have always known as Ms. Deliverance welcomes you into the dimly lit church building after hours. You follow her to the offices and sit in a swivel chair across from her. Lean your elbows on a table that looks more suited to filling out paperwork than stirring up the supernatural. You wish she would play some music or something. She wants to know about the panic attacks and the night terrors you've been having. You tell her about the crying. The crying and crying, the violent crying, and how it hasn't stopped since you started school, and you think you're depressed. You repeat after her and repent of everything any twenty-year-old has ever gone through from lust, to fear, to not trusting God, to not honoring parents, to being selfish, to losing hope.

The woman takes your face in her hands, looks in your eyes. She doesn't say your name. She says, "Spirit of Fear." She waits, and addresses it again. She asks if you feel anything moving. You tell her you feel a little nervous. Nothing comes out, which means that you have a very stubborn demon, or that the demons are all just you, dear. Walk back out into the empty parking lot with nothing to blame but the tired weight of your skin.

Write what you know. Write from this place. Write carrying your pieces in your arms. Lay them out in front of you and take an inventory. Arrange them into a story.

You are equal parts:

1. Pain.
2. Craving a place you used to believe existed.
3. Life-conflicted, trying to decide between bravery and fear.

Congratulations, you are human. Now when people tell you their struggles, cry with them. Buy gifts and write cards. Listen. When you write, go back to the lowest point of your depression, in a garage keeled over the drain with muck running out of your eyes and mouth and nose, and gagging you. Write from down on your knees in the mess with those you claim to love; say "I know it hurts." Say, "Yes, you can still make it into the beautiful," and "We can get there together." Decide that writing stories may be the most loving thing that you will ever do.

11.6   Memoir as the Story of Our Change

America has historically loved the idea of self-reinvention. In fact our national identity is founded on it. "We don't like what we are in England," says an oppressed Puritan. "Let's move to America, where we can *become something else*. We don't like the conditions of oppression as they advert to our beliefs, ethnicity, or economic status. It is in America that we can stop, change direction, and become something else altogether." The American Dream's tastiest promise is the reinvented self, as illustrated by Lady Gaga, aka Stefani Joanne Angelina Germanotta, or by President Trump, formerly "The Donald."

America has always connected the possibility of the reinvented self to probity, creativity, hard work, and strength of character. In the 1860s America had a sweet tooth for the rags-to-riches stories of Horatio Alger, who loved a book so much that he wrote it a hundred times. It's best remembered as the 1868 tale *Ragged Dick*. I will now summarize this significant cultural achievement with a helpful haiku:

> Black those boots, my friend!
> You too can get some prime real
> estate and a girl!

You know the saying "raise yourself up by your bootstraps"? That's vintage Dick! Thanks to Horatio Alger, America's ongoing flirtation with self-reinvention helped shape a rigorous national work ethic. Now, 150 years post-Dick, you don't even need to love what you do, like Bill Gates. You don't even need amazing tenacity, like Oprah. You don't even need athletic prowess, like LeBron James. All you need to reinvent yourself is a single dollar, plus the kind of heroic optimism that gets its butt off the couch and over to the Speedway. There you may purchase your winning lottery ticket, self-reinvention at its most totemic ... and democratic.

This vision of intentionality and self-fashioning sums up our American national identity even as it adapts itself to every age, movement, and technology. Sock puppets! Identity theft! It is a vision that inheres in politics, music, sports, art. No wonder your college instructors want you to try the personal essay. They are sending you the same signal that all of America is sending you. Memoir is not, and has never been, the story of our circumstances. It's the story of our *change*.

Spot the lie

If your instructor doesn't assign the Details Don't Lie activity at the end of the chapter as a class exercise, see if you can spot the lie among the three paragraphs below. They were submitted by undeclared junior Anna Stafford.

Option #1

This was the first time I had sworn in front of an adult outside my family. I had recently turned 21, and I guess I thought that adult-on-adult swearing would be slightly more appropriate. I huddle down in my cube, the rain outside creating a comforting curtain for my workplace. "Dear Mr. P, although I appreciate the benefits of this assignment, I think LinkedIn is totally ass-kissing."

Option #2

I never got many awards. When my boobs and bitch group of friends came in, I lost a lot of motivation for studying. But somehow I scraped by with an attendance award. The girls all gave me a grateful round of applause, as if to thank me for giving our group a bit classier of a reputation, like a restaurant with one random star.

Option #3

> I hated sixth grade. The girls were mean and the itch of the uniform was meaner. I vowed to simply never say a word, a coping mechanism I guess. Mrs. N asked the class if anyone wanted to have a solo in the Christmas program. My hand lifted up like a spaceship into the air. Only NASA didn't know they built this one. What was I doing? I was showing the whole sixth grade who was boss, that's what.

Which paragraph did you pick as the lie? Why? What made the other two paragraphs seem true and persuasive? You may enjoy hearing that Anna Stafford stumped the entire class with her three paragraphs. Every single student picked Option #1 or Option #3 as the lie. We were duly impressed at Stafford's detail management. And we demanded to know: Had she really stopped studying when she grew into her curves and rebel friends? Yes, she had totally blown off school. Had she not gotten the attendance award? No, she *had* gotten the attendance award, just for showing up. Turns out that the lie was the round of applause. Ironically, Stafford finally did receive a genuine but tardy round of applause for something she had achieved in the classroom. I hope you'll agree that she's an effective writer!

Details Don't Lie

Here's a great exercise that you can do in class to set yourselves up to write strong personal essays. Fair warning: this activity takes a full hour.

In class, take about twenty minutes to write three anonymous paragraphs on one piece of paper, in random order. Each of the three paragraphs tells the story of a time when you were proud of yourself for something. The paragraphs don't need to be about an external award or competition, though of course they can be. Maybe you just want to tell the story of a time when you felt really good about yourself on the inside, without any external hoopla.

The catch is, one of the paragraphs is based on a lie. Something in this paragraph never happened. But it *could have happened.* (So don't write a paragraph about how you were obliged to turn down the Chicago Cubs when they begged you to pitch for them.) Write a lying paragraph that could seem true, given your life as you have lived it. Do not identify which are the true paragraphs and which is the lie.

After you're done writing, divide into small groups. Your instructor will collect the paragraphs and redistribute them so that no one in the group receives his or her own paper. Now, still in small groups, take turns reading all three paragraphs aloud. For each set, vote on the lie. Record your reasons. What exactly has tipped you off to the fact that *this* paragraph is the lie? If you have a split vote, say why. If someone in your group is sure of the lie, say why.

12 How to Discuss Two Texts in One Essay

12.1   More Than Just a Comparison/Contrast Essay

Lots of university courses will ask you to incorporate a writing strategy that was once frequently taught all by itself as its own genre. Educators called it the comparison/contrast essay. Today, though, we see the practice of drawing parallels or juxtapositions between texts as a technique that is central to many kinds of college assignments. Thus we don't want to send the signal that this sort of writing occupies a single stiff-sided box, like a pet carrier. Since we now see this technique as the basis for much of our thinking and writing in general, you will probably be encouraged to practice this skill across a wide variety of college assignments.

One of the main projects of college is to get you to make smart connections between different ideas, genres, texts, or sets of data. Professors really want you to do this because we have already learned what you are now learning, and we know firsthand how valuable it is. Intelligence isn't mastering a body of knowledge or memorizing a bunch of facts. It's hooking up the knowledge in a useful way to something else.

Which brings us to the de facto problem of writing an essay that is supposed to respond to two different texts. Many professors have been doing this stuff for so long that they just assume you know what this writing strategy is *for*. And then, because they are making the assumption that you already know, nobody tells you. I will. Its purpose is to *show the reader something new* that comes out of having considered two separate texts alongside each other.

If you receive an assignment that asks you to discuss two texts in the same essay, your instructor is not looking for a discussion of the first thing followed by a discussion of the second thing. Let's say that you point out the main ways in which the two texts are like each other. Then you follow up by pointing out the main differences. Doing all that is mere busywork if you have failed to offer your reader a good reason for why you have paired these texts together in the first place. If all you do is trace parallels and show differences, your essay will be doomed to sound like the assignment it is.

You do not want to sound assignmenty in college. The equivalent of sounding assignmenty in college would be phoning it in in the professional world—doing the bare minimum, a work performance strong on coffee breaks, sudoku, and online shopping. Careerwise, you would never want to seem as if you are phoning it in, right? If you want to excel, to stand out, to achieve distinction or notice, you must operate with a spirit of excellence, both in college and in the workplace. So if you want to sidestep the beige badge of mediocrity, here is the one thesis you must avoid when writing an essay that responds to two different texts:

▷ _X_ is similar to _Y_ , yet different.

This insipid thesis says to your reader, "I would much rather be playing Frisbee golf."

Try this thesis instead.

▷ _X_ and _Y_ share significant ideological SIMILARITIES/ DIFFERENCES, but, taken together, they suggest _Z_ .

This thesis says, "Although we all know this essay is a contrived assignment, I have actually done some intellectual work here, and I have come up with a persuasive reason why we should read these two texts in dialogue with each other."

In college you'll come across many kinds of writing assignments that ask you to make connections or distinctions between two texts. Sometimes this type of writing is merely one component in a larger essay. I should also mention that you will be expected to put two texts together in assignments across the disciplines, not just in writing classes. However, what the assignments often have in common is that you would probably never put these two texts together yourself.

Have you ever had an essay assignment whose entire structure must be organized on a model that devolves from separate readings of two texts? On the surface, the readings probably won't have very much in common. They might even be two chapters or two essays that track totally opposing viewpoints. Let's say that you are planning to juxtapose two frequent flyers on American college-level English syllabi, Anton Chekhov's **"The Lady with the Dog"** and Zora Neale Hurston's **"Sweat."**

Zora Neale Hurston (left) and Anton Chekhov (right)

In case you aren't in the mood to go read Chekhov's amazing short story "The Lady with the Dog,"[1] here is a Speedway summary in four sentences.

1. An older player, bit of a creep, games a pious young

---

1 Visit link: https://goo.gl/g7rpUD

lady on vacation.

2. Over time their casual affair deepens into something serious, which is a problem because they are both married to other people.

3. In imperial nineteenth-century Russia you can't just up and file for divorce.

4. Bummer for them.

It's sort of hard to tell if Chekhov is attacking the institution of marriage as an outcropping of a stifling society or if he's suggesting that romantic love is a distraction from the terminal meaningless of our lives. On the Debbie Downer Scale, one being Postnasal Drip and ten being Mutual Suicide Pact, this story's about a nine.

A nine on the same scale is what I'd also give Zora Neale Hurston's short story "Sweat"[2]:

1. Hardworking Delia Jones has an unhappy life as a laundress and abused wife.

2. Sykes, the abusive husband, would like to kill Delia to inherit her stuff, so he looses a rattlesnake in the house.

3. The snake bites the husband instead of the wife.

4. Delia, a church-going woman, has plenty of time to go for help, but she sits down and waits for her husband to die.

---

2   Visit link: https://goo.gl/x4DxTD

Another Debbie Downer. As with the Chekhov story, the Hurston text draws plenty of conflicting interpretations. Some of my students say that Hurston is making an argument chiefly about race and economic injustice. Some say she's laying down an Old Testament whammy in which snakelike/Satanlike evildoers reap what they sow. However you slice it, though, "Sweat" leaves you in the same depressed funk as does Chekhov's tale about the doomed couple.

Most readers do not finish reading "Sweat" only to exclaim, "Hey, wow, Hurston makes me feel like crap, just like Chekhov!" Noting a similar effect on mood is just the starting point. This is where your instructor comes in handy. Your instructor's job is to get you to make connections between authors, ideas, and movements that you might not ordinarily pair up. Thus you might see a prompt something like this as one of the options for a five- to seven-page essay:

> "The Lady with the Dog" and "Sweat" both feature a Christian woman partnered to a man whose belief system is very different from her own. What are Chekhov and Hurston ultimately arguing about faith? Christianity often presents as a comfort for the oppressed. Is it a comfort in these two texts? If not, why not? To what extent are Anna Sergeyevna and Delia Jones reliable indices of the beliefs of the authors?

Thanks to your alert reading, you are not tempted to create the following thesis:

> Anton Chekhov's "The Lady with the Dog" and Zora Ne-
> ale Hurston's "Sweat" both feature a Christian woman
> partnered to a man whose belief system is very differ-
> ent from her own, yet both stories are arguing some-
> thing very different about faith.

Put in other words:

▷ These texts are alike, but different.

Which is all to say:

▷ Dear Professor, please give me a C–.

Instead of a thesis that reads as contrived and ho-hum, you
spend some time thinking about what these two completely different stories really are implying about faith. And you
come up with something like this:

> Although these female protagonists both profess Chris-
> tianity, neither Chekhov nor Hurston finds faith useful
> for life. Indeed, taken together, these stories suggest
> not only that religion fails to comfort the oppressed but
> that it deepens unhappiness and blunts self-awareness.

See the difference? The first thesis says that the two stories
are making an argument about faith. But the second one comes
right out and says what that argument is. Notice, too, that you
don't have to agree with this interpretation of Chekhov's and
Hurston's stories. I'm not trying to talk you into thinking that

Chekhov was a terminal atheist and Hurston a disillusioned skeptic. In fact, you could turn around and argue that Christianity plays a salvific role in these stories. Check it out:

> In "The Lady with the Dog" and "Sweat," Chekhov and Hurston use the faith of their female protagonists to promote growth, movement, and change. In these stories, it is the Christian focus on good and evil that empowers women to risk action according to moral conscience.

You could use the texts to argue either one of these thesis options, and plenty of others as well. The important part is that you come up with a bona fide message that presents a whole idea. I often find it helpful to think of two texts in one of these assignments as having a chat with each other. One says this, the other answers this. When both stop talking, what's the ultimate takeaway?

12.2 The Two Basic Ways to Structure a Two-Text Discussion

As we all know, it's totally possible to write an essay the night before it is due, with no prewriting or outline, while watching *Game of Thrones* and eating leftover caramel straight from the pot. However, don't say I didn't warn you. This two-text essay is a bit harder to pull off without some intentional structuring. Students generally opt for one of two tried-and-true ways.

I recommend that you actually do choose one of these two ways instead of winging it. These two structural styles aren't designed to trap you in a rigid system—quite the opposite. They are designed to make your work easier. And they do simplify things. But if you hate inhabiting a structure, hey, it's a free world. Nobody's twisting your arm. The reason young scholars often like these formulas is that when you're tacking back and forth between two texts, it's easy to lose sight of the original plan, which is to give balanced essay space to *both* texts. Plus most scholars are secretly more interested in one of the texts than the other. Overinvesting in one can result in too much to say about the one and not enough about the other. Me, I'm not a stickler for an outline any more than I am for a grocery list. But some stuff you simply don't want to forget.

Added to that, most American colleges and universities are running at quite a clip, either on the quarter or semester system, which means that for most courses, the majority of undergraduate essay assignments tend to be fewer than ten pages. If the typical freshman or sophomore version of a two-text essay is five to seven pages, you don't have much space to support a tight argument involving not one but two texts. That's why it pays to be intentional about the choices you make at the front end. You want to maximize the space you do have.

Point-by-point

The first way to structure an assignment that discusses two texts is called **point-by-point**. We've already come up with our main idea. ("Thumbs down on faith.") Next we brainstorm three or four main "talking points" that occur in both our texts:

- ▷ religion offers zero comfort
- ▷ religion prevents self-awareness
- ▷ religion results in a focus on the bad instead of the good

For each main point, we will be creating two separate paragraphs, one for each text. So if our first point is that Christianity offers no comfort in these stories, we'll show that faith does not comfort Chekhov's Anna Sergeyevna; then we'll move to the next paragraph, which will show that faith does not comfort Hurston's Delia Jones either. It's kind of like call-and-response. We'll work down our outline one point at a time, cleanly discussing how the point in question emerges in both of our texts. And we won't mix-n-match. If we start out discussing Chekhov before Hurston, we'll stick to that order for every point, all the way through the paper. Finally, we'll wrap it up in one last paragraph, a conclusion that will apply to both texts. In outline form, the point-by-point structure looks like this:

Point-by-Point Method

I. **Intro and thesis**

An outline is like a grocery list. You do one so that you won't forget anything important. Nobody needs to see it but you.

II. **First point:** Christianity offers **no comfort to the unhappy or oppressed**
  A. Paragraph about Chekhov's Anna Sergeyevna
    - ▷ faith causes guilt, tears, self-hatred; invokes "Evil One"
    - ▷ faith prevents Anna from enjoying sex

> Anna's religion perpetuates misery by prevent-
ing divorce

> "so sad she seemed ill"

B. Paragraph about Hurston's Delia Jones

> church community provides no support

> church attendance source of contention and
mockery

> prayers unanswered

> sings "mournful key"; "Jurden water, black an'
col' chills de body"

III. **Second point:** Christianity **prevents self-awareness**

A. Paragraph about Chekhov's Anna Sergeyevna

B. Paragraph about Hurston's Delia Jones

IV. **Third point:** Christianity results in a **focus on the bad
instead of the good**

A. Paragraph about Chekhov's Anna Sergeyevna

B. Paragraph about Hurston's Delia Jones

V. **Conclusion**

Block

The other structure available for all your two-text needs is
called, simply, **block**. You can probably guess how it will be
organized. You craft two big superchunks, one for each text,
with each block containing a fixed number of paragraphs. Basically, you present everything you have to say about the first
text. If you plan on making three separate points about it, the

corresponding three paragraphs for those points would all follow one another, bambambam, all focusing on the first text. Then you transition to your second text. Lather, rinse, repeat.

Remember, you've still got the same idea for your essay. Nothing needs to change about what you want to prove. The only thing that's going to change here is how you choose to structure the argument on paper. So, to recap, we've got three main points to make about two stories:

1. Christianity offers no comfort to the unhappy or oppressed.
2. Christianity prevents self-awareness.
3. Christianity results in a focus on the bad instead of the good.

In the block method, the challenge is to stay parallel. You always present your three main points in the same order for both texts. That way you won't confuse your reader by jumping around. Your structure sends a nice reassuring signal so that the reader will know what to expect. What you prove in one text, you will also examine in the other.

Here is an example of the sort of outline you'd use to set up block. Same idea, different method.

Block Method

I. **Intro and thesis**

II. **Chekhov's "The Lady with the Dog"**
   A. Anna Sergeyevna experiences no comfort from her

Christianity

   B. Anna Sergeyevna's faith stops her from becoming self-aware

   C. Anna Sergeyevna's faith causes her to focus on the bad, not the good

III. Hurston's "Sweat"

   A. Delia Jones experiences no comfort from her Christianity

   B. Delia Jones's faith is the very thing that prevents her self-awareness

   C. Delia Jones's faith invites a focus on the bad instead of the good

IV. Conclusion

Both of these structural choices make good sense, and both do what the instructor is asking you to do. That is, both choices help you to put two texts together to produce a new meaning, one that is distinctly your own. Both strategies have their challenges. Point-by-point can give the reader mild whiplash, snapping back and forth, as in a formal debate. It can seem stiff and awkward if you don't pay close attention to the flow. On the other hand, block can make it too dang easy to wander off the path, like Goldilocks on her way to Grandmother's house. If you're still developing your style, you might well pull toward one of these structures. But you won't know which you prefer until you try them both.

12.3 Troubleshooting Wonky Paragraphs

There's no one right way to craft writing that seeks to discuss two texts. But there are plenty of wrong ways. You do have to stay on your toes. In this style of writing, two frequent structural mistakes can compromise the impact of your argument. The first error is a topic sentence that mentions both things you're writing about (texts, authors, movements, events, ideas, science experiments, etc.). There's nothing wrong with mentioning both things in the topic sentence if the paragraph does, in fact, go on to deliver a discussion of both. The mistake happens when the topic sentence promises to discuss both things, and instead the paragraph delivers on only one of them. Here's an example of this mistake:

Both Chekhov and Hurston create Christian characters who are preoccupied with the presence of evil but who are unable to see goodness. "Sweat" begins with the wash-woman Delia Jones surrounded by dirty laundry, sorting stained garments (175). Hurston thus establishes a governing metaphor for her protagonist's Christian outlook. Delia sees not the clean and the fresh but the sweat and the stains, a literalization of moral badness. Because Delia's laundry-sorting takes place on a

As far as topic sentences go, this one's pretty strong. But there's a structural problem. Notice that it promises to discuss both authors. Too bad the paragraph delivers only on Hurston.

Sunday after church, we are reminded that the business of sorting stains is an analogue for the making of moral judgments. Delia's *job* is to see stains. And her job has become synonymous with her entire Christian outlook. Indeed, Delia associates her faith with the unrewarding tasks of her marriage and the sweat business: "Ah been married to you fur fifteen years, and Ah been takin' in washin' fur fifteen years. Sweat, sweat, sweat! Work and sweat, cry and sweat, pray and sweat!" The fifteen-year marriage has exacted sweat, a symbol of toil with no reward. As with the laundry business, the marriage is a problem that Delia foregrounds in the Christian activity of prayer. Delia, preoccupied with her husband's mean-ness, sees nothing good in her marriage, nor does she ever take comfort in her well-established business, in her financial self-sufficiency, or in the faith itself.

This could be a great paragraph. It proves that Delia has a problem with negative vision, it hooks up Delia's negative vision to her Christianity, and it even establishes some positive things in Delia's life that she utterly fails to see. It's always cool when the writer of an academic essay is capable of seeing some important stuff that never gets mentioned in the text at all. That's all good news. The bad news is that there's a major disconnect between what the topic sentence promises and what it delivers.

Both Chekhov and Hurston create Christian characters who are preoccupied with the presence of evil but who are unable to see goodness.

Where's the part about Chekhov?

Now let's say that you love your Chekhov-Hurston topic sentence and you don't want to change it. You decide to fiddle with the paragraph so that it does indeed deliver on its topic sentence. But get out the looooong white beard, because here's what that would look like.

Both Chekhov and Hurston create Christian characters who are preoccupied with the presence of evil but who are unable to see goodness. When Chekhov's Anna Sergeyevna first invites Gurov to her hotel room, she looks "grave"; she "mused in a dejected attitude like 'the woman who was a sinner' in an old-fashioned picture" (65). Attaching Anna Sergeyevna in this way to death, sin, and damnation undermines notions of Christian peace, comfort, and salvation. Moreover, Anna Sergeyevna describes her sexual interlude with Gurov as "awful," believing that "the Evil One" has beguiled her (66). Her faith prevents her from enjoying the relationship with Gurov, both in Yalta and later in Moscow, when she has developed real feelings for her lover. Its chief effect is to bring her misery and guilt, and to make her feel cheap: she "continually urged [Gurov] to confess that he did not respect her, did not love her in the least, and thought of her as nothing but a common woman" (67). Obviously she would not be urging Gurov to make such a confession if she did not believe she had sinned against God. The Christian burden of guilt is so heavy that when Gurov surprises her at the theater, she responds "with horror" (72) and almost faints. Although Anna is a young, healthy newlywed, affluent enough to take month-long holidays in wealthy Yalta, she never acknowledges anything good or positive about her life. Faith-driven guilt skews her vision. Like Chekhov, Hurston creates a protagonist whose vision is grim. "Sweat" begins with the wash-woman Delia Jones surrounded by dirty laundry, sorting stained garments (175). Hurston thus establishes a governing metaphor for her protagonist's Christian outlook. Delia sees not the clean and the fresh but the sweat and the stains, a literalization of moral badness. Because Delia's laundry-sorting takes place on a Sunday after church, we are reminded that the business of sorting stains is an analogue for the making of moral judgments. Delia's *job* is to see stains. And her job has become synonymous with her entire Christian outlook. Indeed, Delia associates her faith with the unrewarding tasks of her marriage and the sweat business: "Ah been married to you fur fifteen years, and Ah been takin' in washin' fur fifteen years. Sweat, sweat, sweat! Work and sweat, cry and sweat, pray and sweat!" The fifteen-year marriage has exacted sweat, a representation of toil with no reward. As with the laundry business, the marriage is a problem that Delia foregrounds in the Christian activity of prayer. Delia, preoccupied with her husband's meanness, sees nothing good in her marriage, nor does she ever take comfort in her well-established business, in her financial self-sufficiency, or in the faith itself.

What you have just read reveals the second problem that can go wrong when you're writing about two texts in the same assignment. Even though the topic sentence in the above paragraph now makes good on its promise, and even though we've got a nice transition between Chekhov and Hurston, the paragraph is just too long. The better choice here would be to craft two separate topic sentences, one for each paragraph. That way you'll provide a smooth sense of continuity while still giving your reader a chance to take a big breath between paragraphs. Like this:

The only Chekhov character preoccupied with the presence of evil is also the only Christian. Chekhov uses Anna Sergeyevna's faith to suggest that Christianity tortures rather than comforts the unhappy. When Anna Sergeyevna first invites Gurov to her hotel room, she looks "grave"; she "mused in a dejected attitude like 'the woman who was a sinner' in an old-fashioned picture" (65) Attaching Anna Sergeyevna in this way to death, sin, and damnation undermines notions of Christian peace, comfort, and salvation. Moreover, Anna Sergeyevna describes her sexual interlude with Gurov as "awful," believing that "the Evil One" has beguiled her (66). Her faith prevents her from enjoying the relationship with Gurov, both in Yalta and later

Look, a nice transition. Makes you want to keep reading, to find out more about this character who is obsessed with doom-and-gloom.

And then right behind the transition, right up at the top of the paragraph, a smart topic sentence. Did you notice that this is the same formula we talked about earlier? "Author uses X to suggest Y."

Smart follow-up to the quotation.

in Moscow, when she has developed real feelings for her lover. Its chief effect is to bring her misery and guilt, and to make her feel cheap. She "continually urged [Gurov] to confess that he did not respect her, did not love her in the least, and thought of her as nothing but a common woman" (67). Obviously she would not be urging Gurov to make such a confession if she did not believe she had sinned against God. The Christian burden of guilt is so heavy that when Gurov surprises her at the theater, she responds "with horror" (72) and almost faints. Although Anna is a young, healthy newlywed, affluent enough to take month-long holidays at a luxurious Crimean resort, she never acknowledges anything good or positive about her life. Faith-driven guilt skews her vision.

Like Chekhov, Hurston creates a protagonist whose vision is grim because of, not in spite of, her Christianity. "Sweat" begins with the wash-woman Delia Jones surrounded by dirty laundry, sorting stained garments (175). Hurston thus establishes a governing metaphor for her protagonist's Christian outlook. Delia sees not the clean and the fresh

Notice that the follow-up explicitly says why the quote is important to the argument.

See how the paragraph is careful to deliver what it has promised? The topic sentence talks about the character not being able to see any good in her life, so the paragraph needs to list some good stuff that the character cannot seem to see.

Check it out, you don't even need a sentence-long transition between paragraphs. you can get away with a wee phrase. Saying "Like Chekhov," is a great way to signal that this paragraph will not be about but the sweat and the stains, a literalization of moral badness. Because Delia's laundry-sorting takes place on a Sunday after church, we are reminded that the business of sorting stains is an analogue for the making of moral judgments. Delia's *job* is to see stains. And her job has become synonymous with her entire Christian outlook. Indeed, Delia even associates her marriage with the sweat business: "Ah been married to you fur fifteen years, and Ah been takin' in washin' fur fifteen years. Sweat, sweat, sweat! Work and sweat, cry and sweat, pray and sweat!" The fifteen-year marriage is as arduous as her work as a washerwoman and no more gratifying. Delia, preoccupied with her husband's meanness, sees nothing good in her marriage, nor does she ever take comfort in her well-established business or her financial self-sufficiency.

Chekhov's story but about Hurston's. But it will be in the same vein, still on the same theme.

Also notice that this topic sentence takes the previous one a step further. The argument is tightening up, moving forward.

You'll probably be using a version of this skill in almost every assignment, pretty much every time you discuss how two sets of data, two ideas, two authors, or two texts are unlike one another. Imagine a college exam that asks you to define Darwin's most celebrated contribution to science scholarship. How can you possibly describe how Darwin's theory of natural selection made a splash in the science community without showing how it was different from everything that had gone before? Imagine trying to explain why a sonnet's iambic pentameter is important if you can't implicitly contrast a line of iambic pentameter to a line of unaccented free verse. You can't talk about its significance without also talking about its difference. We cannot arrive at an understanding of any idea or thing unless we get what that thing is not.

12.4 Student Essay

Because you are likely to receive so many assignments that ask you to hook up two texts, I thought it might be useful for you to see a solid student-written essay in its entirety. This one was written by a scholar who went on to become a French major, Kellyanne Fitzgerald. She wrote it as a freshman in a composition course that gives students a lot of practice in writing about different kinds of literature. Here's the assignment Fitzgerald was responding to:

> ▷ Pick any two stories [on the syllabus] that feature a Bad Guy (or Bad Gal), a character who functions as an antagonist. What causes the badness? In old-fashioned literary stereotypes, the figure of the villain is often irredeemable and unchanging—that is, badbadbad, from beginning to end. Do your antagonists become bad, or do they remain bad? Why? Often it is the other characters, or even the readers, who must respond memorably to the badness of a villain figure. What are we supposed to learn about human frailty from these two stories?

"Social Structure and Responsibility in 'A Rose for Emily' and 'The Yellow Wallpaper'"

by Kellyanne Fitzgerald

In "A Rose for Emily" by William Faulkner and "The Yellow Wallpaper" by Charlotte Perkins Gilman, the protagonists struggle with social norms and the abuse of authority. Both upper-class white women, Emily and Jane buck the stereotype of becoming meek and obedient wives, although both were most likely willing in the beginning of their stories to attempt such a life. Their mistreatment at the hands of the men in their lives drove them to psychological deviancy in the form of destructive self-discovery. The fault of their eventual demise did not lie with the structures in their society that attempted to save them but with the faulty execution of those structures.

Emily of "A Rose for Emily" is mistreated by her father, who misused the social structure that put him in authority over her. In this era, women of her class and race had no other options than to obey the male authority figure in their lives. She may have wished to marry, but her father drove away all of the suitors. Described as "a slender figure in white in the background, her father a spraddled silhouette in the foreground, his back to her and clutching a horsewhip" (171),

It's an interesting thesis, yes? Fitzgerald isn't getting ready to attack the rigid social structures of yesteryear. In fact, it looks unexpectedly as if she plans to defend them. This thesis implies that women who suffered at the hands of a socially coded patriarchy suffered not from the patriarchy itself but from operator error. Pretty radical, I'd say.

Check out how Fitzgerald sets up her topic sentence to be arguable, by hooking up an unarguable thing (the fact that Emily is mistreated by her father) to an arguable thing (the fact that the social structure that put Dad in authority had a better function or intention.)

Emily operates wholly as a background figure. Her father has the power, and therefore is entirely to blame for any confusion in her psyche. She obeyed her father according to the social hierarchy of the time, and her submission when he drove away her suitors indicates that she was either in accord with his actions and did not wish to marry any of them, that she had developed Stockholm syndrome—growing too attached to her abuser to be able to fall for another suitor—or that she was too frightened to say anything. None of these problems are her fault, but nor are they problems with the social system. Her father's abuse both of the structure that placed him in authority over her, and of her, his charge, was unconscionable, and her development was twisted as a result.

Jane of "The Yellow Wallpaper" is also mistreated by a man in authority over her. She begins her story ready to be the perfect woman, as Emily did. She listens to her husband and brother and believes them when they say that she needs to rest, and that the "rest cure" will help her. Throughout the story she attempts to be well, to rest, and to ignore her mounting suspicions that all is not well with the wallpaper. She is even willing to kill herself to keep from going insane, saying that "if that woman does get out and tries to get away, [she] can tie her!" (76). Her husband, John, realizes her men-

Many readers would disagree with Fitzgerald. They might argue that the dad's misuse of authority does indeed inhere in the social system, and that abuses of authority happen only when one person is given this kind of ultimate power over another. But Fitzgerald is making an interesting point. Nineteenth-century gender roles never advocated paternal abuse, even if they allowed for it.

A simple, one-word transition takes us to the next text. You don't need a lot of bells and whistles. Note again the arguability of the first sentence.

tal fragility from the start, keeping details from her that would only distress her further, such as the fact that she is not sleeping in a nursery but in an asylum-like cell. He does not realize that his deception, though not outrightly evident to her, causes her subconscious to mistrust him and not to obey him fully and wholeheartedly. When he tells her that she ought not to write, she writes in spite of him, and "takes pains to control [herself]—before him, at least" (65). She can sense that he is keeping something from her, and this does not let her participate fully in a treatment that might have kept her from insanity. It was John's fault that her psyche was further damaged, as he did not consider the effect his actions would have upon his wife.

Notice that here Fitzgerald locates the paragraph's main idea inside the paragraph rather than up front, as with a topic sentence. It's a bold choice—but, then, she's a bold writer.

Emily did not follow the rules of a system which would have protected her, should she have given it an opportunity to do so. After the death of her father, instead of marrying quickly, or moving to live with relatives, Emily defies the norm and lives by herself with only a manservant to keep the house. As she continues to be self-reliant, her appearance takes a turn for the worse. When she visits the druggist she has "cold, haughty black eyes ... [with] eye-sockets as you imagine a lighthouse-keeper's face ought to look" (172). She no longer follows the rules as she did in her youth, and so her appearance twists from the virginal figure in white

X means Y. Emily's nonconformity (X) argues that the system would have protected her if she had given it a chance (Y).

to something like a lighthouse-keeper: someone with a huge responsibility, someone all alone, and someone who does not ask for help. According to the social structure of the time period, she should not have been alone, and the only reason that her appearance declines so rapidly is because she has failed to follow the social system at a time when she most needed to.

See how Fitzgerald is responding to a specific detail in the passage she has quoted? That's good close analysis. She's using the image of Emily as a lighthouse-keeper to comment on Emily's self-imposed isolation.

Jane intended to follow the rules of the system which would have protected her, but her insanity and pride kept her from that which would have saved her. Her fixation on the wallpaper symbolizes the illusion of self-discovery and her actual need for a cure. At the beginning of the story, she realizes her need for a cure, and the wallpaper disgusts her. "I never saw a worse paper in my life," she says. It is "sprawling [and] flamboyant ... committing every artistic sin. It is dull enough to confuse the eye in following, pronounced enough to constantly irritate and provoke study, and when you follow the lame uncertain curves for a little distance they suddenly commit suicide—plunge off at outrageous angles, destroy themselves in unheard of contradictions" (66). She understands the limitations of the human mind, and the potential consequences of insanity, by suggesting that following the "lame uncertain curves for a little distance" leads to suicide. But as the sto-

Wow, intriguing and arguable topic sentence! Most of my students argue just the reverse, that the wallpaper fixation symbolizes the reality of self-discovery. Frequently readers argue that women should have altogether jettisoned the medical "care" available from the patriarchy. Here Fitzgerald suggests that the women should have sought it out.

ry progresses and her sanity deteriorates, she sees the wallpaper as more and more positive. She acknowledges guiltily that she is becoming fond of the room "perhaps because of the wallpaper" (64). She knows that she ought not to be fond of it, but does not mention her positive views on that which she had once abhorred to her husband, who might have realized that she ought to be moved to a different room. John constantly called her infantilizing names, like "little goose" and "little girl," and his endearments, instead of empowering her, make her afraid that he will see her views as only another flight of imaginative fancy. Too proud to let her new ideas be seen as fancies, or worse, ravings, she denies herself the opportunity to be well again.

The apathetic and observational attitude of the townspeople in "A Rose for Emily" also contributed to the apparent failure of the social system. At the death of her father, Emily cuts her hair short, which the townspeople noted made her "look like a girl, with a vague resemblance to those angels in colored church windows ... tragic and serene" (171). The townspeople pitied her for her situation, in suggesting that she looked like an angel. Many years after Emily and her husband have disappeared into her house, the townspeople finally muster the courage to ask her about the taxes: "[A] small, fat woman in

Here's a clear cause-and-effect topic sentence: A causes B, indifference contributes to failure.

black … her skeleton was small and spare… she looked bloated, like a body long submerged in motionless water" (169). She looks more like a corpse in life than she does in death, after years of perversion and solitude and the insidious dust all around her. But the townspeople only care about making sure that the taxes are paid. Throughout the story, nobody ever feels enough for Emily to actually do anything to help her. The refrain "Poor Emily" repeats, but it always appears in the responsibility-diffusing scenario of plurals, with the we form, or the they form. No one person feels more for her than the others, and if they do, they keep it to themselves. The narrator says that the whole town went to her funeral out of "a sort of respectful affection for a fallen monument … [and] curiosity to see the inside of her house" (174). Nobody really pitied her more than the perfunctory "Poor Emily." She did not let them close enough to feel sorrow for her personally, but social accountability, key in society at that time, demanded more from the townspeople than they gave. The entire story operates from the point of view of the people that failed her, and her status as the observed and never the observer in the story tells us that her failings were not her fault or the fault of the system that the townspeople did not execute properly.

Jane's husband, sister-in-law, and relatives

Fitzgerald is using a textual detail to prove the indifference of the townspeople by citing something that they did do.

And then she follows it up by citing something that they did not do—something that kinder, more compassionate people would have done.

do not offer her the proper support and encouragement that she needed in order to recover properly. John constantly stifles Jane's ideas and opinions, no doubt due to his belief that as she was mentally unstable, any of her ideas or opinions were suspect. But this behavior only causes her to feel that she cannot rely upon even her own husband. When she talks about how the house feels ghostly, John denies the validity of her thoughts, and she immediately afterward writes that she "[gets] unreasonably angry with John sometimes" (65). She also mentions how John knows that there is no reason that she should be suffering, and how he therefore assumes that any suffering she has is not real. Her husband does not do what is best for her, but not out of malice or lack of thought. In contrast to this, her relatives do not seem to offer her even the verbal sympathy and support that the townspeople of "A Rose for Emily" offer Emily. They are wholly absent. Her sister-in-law Jennie looks after the house and only interacts with her as a nurse of sorts. Jane describes Jennie as "a dear girl ... and so careful of me!" (68). Rather than interacting with her as a sister-in-law or a fellow person, Jennie treats her as a patient or an invalid. Jane's ideas are tinged with insanity even at the beginning of the story, but the people around her never acknowledge her mental agency, which causes her to mis-

Interesting assumption, right? Fitzgerald is assuming that Jane could have indeed recovered . . . if she had received better care. Are you already making the connection to contemporary American paradigms of mental illness? I am. What kind of care do mentally ill people receive today? Fitzgerald is hinting that we need to be asking this question.

Nice link between the two texts.

trust them for denying her this basic right and herself for being such that they would deny it to her. Rather than acting as a support system for Jane in order to help her get well sooner, the people around her are unwilling to engage with that which would make them uncomfortable: the acknowledgement of her ideas as valid.

Both Emily and Jane are the subjects of observation by those around them due to their abnormal behavior. In contrast with Emily, Jane observes right back. Her fixation on the wallpaper symbolizes her mounting insanity but also her growing self-awareness and self-discovery, as her insights about the wallpaper come to represent how she feels about herself. Emily fixates upon the bodies of the men in her life, which symbolize both the victimization of someone or something that cannot fight back and her attempts to escape the norm by breaking the pattern of that which was considered acceptable. Both women tried to escape their own norms through whatever routes were accessible to them, and their escapes led them into insanity. The problem did not lie with the standards and overarching rules of society which attempted to normalize them but with the failure of specific elements in their lives that could have prevented, if not their escape, at least their madness.

Here Fitzgerald is making parallel observations, tightening the net, as it were. She's drawing parallels between the two kinds of fixation and what they symbolize: fixation with wallpaper, fixation with male bodies.

I'm intrigued by Fitzgerald's suggestion that contemporary Americans are perhaps too quick to blame our problems on what she calls "standards and overarching rules of society." She doesn't come right out and say so, but the implication is that, taken together, these two stories invite us to take a look at the way we assign blame. Note that for Fitzgerald this story is not mainly about stifling gender roles. For many student readers and critics, it is. The takeaway is that you don't have to be "most readers." You can be you. You can write an effective, well-supported essay even if your reading differs from your peers' or your professor's.

13 Who's Speaking?

13.1 How to Generate Good Stuff to Write About

Cracked highway near Long Beach, 1933

In L.A. everyone had an earthquake story. Mine involved weathering so many seismic events that I finally figured out that a temblor over a 4.2 would dislodge the earthquake emergency kit stashed on top of the living room bookshelves. When the room began to shake, the basket would walk itself to the edge of the shelf, then somersault safely to the couch below. Presto, a flashlight, a whisk broom, and raisins, just when you needed them most!

Of course you might not be at home when the uneasiness began to gather beneath your feet. If you were in public, just as the floor began to destabilize, everybody tipped a bit. On the heels of the collective disequilibrium came the sensation of an elevator swiftly sinking, an iffiness that made you grab something, anything. It always took me a couple of seconds to get with the program. Was I experiencing an attack of random nausea or a temblor that would shatter windows and maybe skid cars right off the overpass?

When you are frozen in a doorway, or perhaps crouching nobly under the desk, you think, *Now what?* It's not a rhetorical question, either. You really don't know. Although something has happened to make you freeze or crouch, it is clear that still another thing might happen to dislodge you from this place of waiting. You are occupying an in-between space and it does not feel good.

The reason I bring up that vague sense of ick is that in college I often felt a similar feeling when, having been asked to write about a topic I wouldn't have picked, I occupied the same tentative space between having read and needing to write. I'm not pretending to speak for all college students, and maybe you're a lot more confident than I was, but that unstable place always skewed my balance. It's not that I had blown off the reading. No, I had read the material all the way through. I had highlighted things in yellow, and I may have even written myself notes in the margins. Yet somehow the thought of sitting down to produce the actual essay made me long to grab onto something. Once I was actually writing, I would be okay. But what sort of things was I supposed to be writing about?

With the help of good professors—and my own trial and error—I discovered a metaphoric earthquake emergency kit teetering on a helpful shelf. That is, there was a reliable starter kit available, an easy way to generate material. I realized that I could often ask the same few questions again and again, and that these questions would deliver the goods for nearly every kind of reading assignment I came across. And these questions were so engaging, so useful, that within minutes of asking them I'd stop thinking *essay assignment essay assignment* because I'd already be scribbling down ideas. The following five chapters demonstrate some useful questions that can fast-forward you through the indeterminacy of wondering what to write about. Like the flashlight in the earthquake kit, these five questions provide reliable illumination when the power cuts out.

13.2　Four Kinds of Point of View

At this point, please join me in a refreshing review of something you no doubt learned in high school: point of view. In high school you may have dismissed point of view as an arcane piece of trivia that applied only to stuff you didn't want to read anyhow. Now, however, I'd bet good money that you will suddenly see the tremendous relevance of point of view to your overall intellectual development. That's because this discussion adverts not just to how you read and write but to how you live.

No matter what kind of writing you are doing, even so-cial-media updates, you are using one of the four kinds of point of view:

First person

One person is speaking, saying "I." Everything that is said issues from this one person's perspective. Occasionally you get a whole group of people speaking, as in the preamble to the Constitution: We the People. When a first-person plural narrator (We) fires up, it adds a layer of doubt, because how can all these people possibly agree? Or do they? Is somebody being left out? Are some speakers taking it on themselves to speak for everybody, as if they all agree when in fact they don't?

Omniscient

The narrator seems to know everything, and I mean everything. This narrator freely describes both actions and *thoughts*. This narrator can magically go inside the hearts and minds of every person in the text. This particular point of view isn't around much anymore, because c'mon.

Limited omniscient

Exactly like the omniscient narrator, except that now there's a limitation. This narrator can go inside the heart and mind of only one character, and it's the writer's choice. The result is that the reader usually identifies with that one person, because everything in the text comes from that person's perspective. It's like getting only one side of a story, so readers need to be alert.

For an added li'l somethin', the writer often chooses to use the vocabulary, sentence style, and kinds of observations that would come from the mouth of this one person. This person is the one mind into which the author has decided to go. If you don't stop to see what's happening, limited omniscient can seem as if the one person is narrating the whole text. This subtle point of view sometimes gets mistaken for first person, because the text does seem to be emerging from the perspective of one person. Yet the author never says, "I think this" or "I did that." It's "He thought this" and "He thought that." The person into whose mind the author can go is called a **focalized consciousness**. It's a subtle trick of very intentional, well-crafted writing. The author gets to direct our sympathies without seeming to. Are we going to let our sympathies be directed? That's up to us.

Objective

Really rare in literature but often admired in news reporting and lab reports. Here the narrator is like a big camera, recording only what is visible, only what is documentable, only what is actually happening. The objective point of view may deliver actions, dialogue, and scenery. But not emotions or thoughts. The objective narrator does not go inside anybody's head to tell us what that person is thinking or feeling.

This choice presents a structural challenge for the author. Hey, author! How do you plan on getting your readers to sympathize with the characters if you refuse to describe what's going on in their hearts and minds? Why should we care about these people? We want thoughts, we want emotions! The objective narrator tells us in a roundabout way, using behaviors or gestures that allow us to *infer* how the character is feeling.

> ▷ **Objective**: "Kyung-he crossed her legs, drumming her fingers on the desk."

> ▷ **Not objective**: "Kyung-he was dreading the disclosure she was about to make."

Note that both statements are shooting for the same awkward tension, but the objective one achieves it through exterior body actions, not interior thoughts.

13.3 It's All in the Craft

Since good writing is the product of intentional craft, it's easy to see the implications here. Obviously as a writer, you need to make a choice about your point of view. Then you need to stick to it. The only way you would switch it up on purpose would be if you were creating separate sections in a larger document, for instance, chapters in a novel that present stories from the perspectives of different characters. But if one essay or story accidentally shifts its point of view midway through, then you've got a major structural problem on your hands.

Consider the difficulty, for example, of trying to tell the story of real historical people who lived a hundred years ago. You're doing historical research for a work of nonfiction, meaning that the contents must be factual. You've got documentation to prove that a historical group really lived and did xyz, but how on earth can you make the reader sympathize with them if you have no record of the interior lives of these people? How can you make the writing come alive?

It's all in the craft, in the careful structural choices made by you, the author. Here's how one writer handles this point-of-view challenge, a shared bugaboo for authors who are trying to write readable history. The author, scholar Anna-Lisa Cox, is writing about a little schoolhouse in Covert, Michigan, circa 1870:

> A family of hogs had taken up residence beneath the floor of one of the schools, seeking the cool earth and shade there. Mostly, the children and the teacher had become accustomed to the sounds and smells of the schoolhouse swine, but, still, sometimes the pigs caused trouble. Once, class had been disrupted when an older student grabbed a pig's tail as it poked between the wide gaps of the floorboards, making the animal scream in fear and fury.

Ah, every class has a kid like that! At my grade school he was a highly esteemed desktop farter. He got mad when I said so in print, so I won't name him again here. But the legend lives on.

In the piggy passage Cox narrates a schoolhouse prank that happened 150 years ago. But she is able to tell the story in a published work of historical research only because she can document it. And she does document it. Apparently somebody in that schoolhouse remembered the pig incident and wrote it down. The eyewitness account ended up in Covert's county museum, where Cox came across it in her research.[1]

Cox has chosen limited omniscient for her point of view. This is a good, solid pick for her project. Limited omniscient makes you identify with one character, and Cox really wants her readers to like and respect a specific historical guy, a landowner named William Frank Connor. So far, so good. But what about when Cox wants us to get *inside* William Frank Connor's head? Check out what she does:

> The [African American] suffrage amendment was not uncontested—sixty voted for the amendment, and ten voted against it. Even so, William and all the other black people in Covert must have been grateful for the outcome.

William Frank Connor and all the other black residents *must have been grateful.* Cox cannot assert that all black residents of this town *were* grateful. This is because she has no proof of gratitude, an emotion that describes an interior state. Yet Cox really wants her readers to experience what must have been profound relief and thanksgiving that this piece of legislation passed. So she chooses her words very, very carefully. She cannot use a straight-up past tense (he was grateful) because she cannot document William Frank Connor's gratitude. So she uses a hypothetical tense (must have been grateful) to

---

1   Anna-Lisa Cox, *A Stronger Kinship* (Boston: Little, Brown, 2006), 95, 96, 239.

safeguard her integrity as a scholar.

Shifting point of view

Point of view, then, is a big deal. An author's choice in point of view adverts to everything from professional competence to the level of engagement that readers experience. One of the hallmarks of weak writing is an accidentally dithering point of view. One craft mistake can seriously derail a piece of writing. Imagine if an author has asked us to identify with one person's interior thoughts (limited omniscient) and then suddenly the author starts talking about what *another* character is thinking.

I sometimes teach a tasty novella, Willa Cather's *A Lost Lady*, in which the focalized consciousness lands on an upper-crust young man, Niel. Because the author is skillfully manipulating a limited omniscient point of view, readers latch onto this young man. Niel can't decide if he loves or hates an older married woman, Marion. The author's craft in setting up this limited omniscient point of view is structurally solid. Until it suddenly isn't. There's one jarring moment that makes every class suddenly change direction, and with no help from me. It's a moment when Niel is not present for a scene that would interest him (and us) very much. Niel's crush, Marion, is having a secret affair. Without Niel's observing eye, though, how are we going to know about it?

Marion and her lover sneak off into the woods to do the deed out in the open, on a buffalo robe spread under pine boughs. Remember, since the author has picked limited omniscient, all content must attach to a focalized consciousness.

Willa Cather ca. 1912

So if we're going to witness hot sex on a blanket, somebody has to be present to observe it. Suddenly the author makes a bizarre choice. She abruptly shifts the focalized consciousness from Niel to a *very* minor character. Along comes Adolph Blum. He's out rabbit hunting in the woods, see. When he spots the lovers' pony, he hides like a pervy but polite voyeur in the underbrush. Finally, a witness! Now somebody can observe Marion's deepest secret.

Well, what's the problem with that? What's not to love about a passionate interlude on a blanket? So you'd think. But every single time I've taught this book, the entire class gets stuck on this one scene. Before Adolph Blum gets his brief promotion to focalized consciousness, the class would have been puzzled at any mention of Adolph Blum's name. Adolph Who? The minor character who sells fish door to door? In the space of one weird paragraph everybody moves to the edge of their seat. "Riiiiiiight, Adolph Blum! Why didn't we notice him before!" Students begin urgently asking each other about his hopes, his dreams, his fish. The class combs the text backward and forward for every mention of Adolph Blum. "Why is this kid so important? What does he *mean*? And the fish, what do the fish represent?"

When the writer shifts the point of view, not only are readers pulled down a literal rabbit trail of divided interest;

readers have less sympathy for the person with whom they're *supposed* to identify. If you, the writer, want your reader to identify with one person, it doesn't make sense to wishbone the reader's sympathies.

13.4   Is the Author Credible?

Please take a moment to memorize this all-important question. No matter what sort of reading you have been assigned, it is critical to ask this question: "Who's speaking?" By this I mean, "Can I trust this voice talking in my ear?" Likewise, if you're the author of a personal essay, make sure you remember to ask, "What have I done to make my reader trust me?" If you haven't built trust on purpose, your reader will not trust you. In writing, just as in life, trust does not happen automatically. It has to be earned. An author's credibility is *structural*, a matter of craft. It's not so much what you believe in your heart. It's what you do on the page.

When you see something written in the first-person narrative, whether it's an essay or a poem or a story, your first move should be, "Okay, do I trust this speaker? Is he credible?" If you're reading an article or an essay, you ask things like:

▷   What credentials does this author have? Why should I be listening to him?

▷   Will this guy profit personally from what he wants me to read? What does he want from me? My money, my vote, my time?

▷   What kind of a venue published this guy—was it a

peer-reviewed publication, a respected journal, an established press? Or is this guy some hotdog blogger off the streets? No reason we can't learn things from all comers, but if somebody is presenting as an authority, he should have an expert's credentials if you plan to cite his work in an academic paper.

It would be naive to skate over the issue of credibility with a shrug. "Oh, I got an okay vibe from the speaker, that's good enough." Remember that your okay vibe is the sum total of some structural choices the author has made on purpose. You will be able to look back through the text and pinpoint a couple of moments where the okay vibe started happening. Again, the speaker's credibility is something that has been chosen and produced, like a TV show. But the producer is the author himself. **Credibility is an inside job as well as an outside achievement.**

If you believe a speaker's story, what makes you believe it? What makes you willing to play on a speaker's team? Maybe the speaker seems culturally literate, competent in the very area under discussion? Maybe the speaker gives equal time to both sides of an issue, and so comes across as level and impartial? Maybe the speaker has decades of relevant experience and a medical degree from Harvard? Maybe this speaker has the wisdom and humility to admit some areas of personal fault?

13.5 Is the Narrator Credible?

Narrator credibility is a writing term that gets thrown around a lot. If you're reading or writing a first-person essay, this term will surely come up once people start talking about the essay. In college you will get lots of practice at establishing your own credibility. You will also get lots of practice analyzing the level of credibility of authors and first-person narrators in things you read.

Answering the *Who's speaking?* question sometimes seems more challenging when the first-person narrator is a made-up character as opposed to a real person. In the last exercise we used inductive logic (making lots of small separate observations) to come to a general conclusion about an author's credibility. But did you know that we can flip the process on its head and start with the conclusion? You still have to identify the textual moments that drive your conclusion, but it's sort of fun to work backward. If this appeals to you, feel free to use my handy shortcut. "Would I like to have lunch with this narrator?"

No, no. Not Applebee's. An upscale local bistro with delicious fennel-crab cakes, served with a tangy citrus-garlic aioli. The first-person narrator is picking up the tab, naturally.

Robert Browning ca. 1888

Let's take a look at narrator credibility in one of the most anthologized dramatic monologues in Western literary history, Robert Browning's "My Last Duchess." This is a poem written in the nineteenth century, which means that many of you are probably already feeling panicky, especially if you just had the crab cakes. Not to worry. I have a home remedy for that too. If poetry gives you the severe willies, just take a deep breath and translate the poem into normal everyday English. This is sort of like sprinkling salt on a slug. The scariness shrinks up a bit and becomes more manageable.

My Last Duchess[2]

by Robert Browning

> That's my last Duchess painted on the wall,
> Looking as if she were alive. I call
> That piece a wonder, now: Frà Pandolf's hands
> Worked busily a day, and there she stands.
> Will't please you sit and look at her? I said
> "Frà Pandolf" by design, for never read
> Strangers like you that pictured countenance,
> The depth and passion of its earnest glance,
> But to myself they turned (since none puts by
> The curtain I have drawn for you, but I)
> And seemed as they would ask me, if they durst,
> How such a glance came there; so, not the first
> Are you to turn and ask thus. Sir, 'twas not
> Her husband's presence only, called that spot
> Of joy into the Duchess' cheek: perhaps
> Frà Pandolf chanced to say, "Her mantle laps

---

2   "My Last Duchess" is in the public domain.

Over my lady's wrist too much," or "Paint
Must never hope to reproduce the faint
Half-flush that dies along her throat": such stuff
Was courtesy, she thought, and cause enough
For calling up that spot of joy. She had
A heart—how shall I say?—too soon made glad,
Too easily impressed; she liked whate'er
She looked on, and her looks went everywhere.
Sir, 'twas all one! My favour at her breast,
The dropping of the daylight in the West,
The bough of cherries some officious fool
Broke in the orchard for her, the white mule
She rode with round the terrace—all and each
Would draw from her alike the approving speech,
Or blush, at least. She thanked men,—good! but thanked
Somehow—I know not how—as if she ranked
My gift of a nine-hundred-years-old name
With anybody's gift. Who'd stoop to blame
This sort of trifling? Even had you skill
In speech—(which I have not)—to make your will
Quite clear to such an one, and say, "Just this
Or that in you disgusts me; here you miss,
Or there exceed the mark"—and if she let
Herself be lessoned so, nor plainly set
Her wits to yours, forsooth, and made excuse,
—E'en then would be some stooping; and I choose
Never to stoop. Oh, sir, she smiled, no doubt,
Whene'er I passed her; but who passed without
Much the same smile? This grew; I gave commands;
Then all smiles stopped together. There she stands
As if alive. Will't please you rise? We'll meet
The company below then. I repeat,

The Count your master's known munificence
Is ample warrant that no just pretense
Of mine for dowry will be disallowed;
Though his fair daughter's self, as I avowed
At starting, is my object. Nay, we'll go
Together down, sir. Notice Neptune, though,
Taming a sea-horse, thought a rarity,
Which Claus of Innsbruck cast in bronze for me!

If you need a loose paraphrase translated into normal everyday English, read below:

My Deceased Duchess, or, Depending on How You Read It, My Most Recent Duchess

Have a seat to check out this painting of my late wife. BTW, I dropped the artist's name on purpose to impress you.

Viewers always ask the same thing. (And they have to ask me because nobody else can show the painting. I keep it behind a curtain.) Everybody asks, "Why was your wife always in such a good mood?"

But I wasn't the only one who made her happy. For instance, the artist would kiss up with some lame compliment, "Don't let your sleeve cover up your pretty wrist!" Or maybe, "I wish I could capture that lovely flush!" Jeez. My wife fell for all that drivel. How shall I say this? Girl had a low bar. She liked everyone indiscriminately, if you get what I mean. She was too easily impressed. This woman liked whatever she looked at. And her looks went everywhere.

She couldn't distinguish between my gift of a pricey necklace, a ho-hum sunset, some meh cherries, a pet mule. To all these she responded with approval, exactly as if they all had equal value. She always said, "thank you." But she'd thank a bottom-feeder exactly as she'd thank a Duke with a nine-hundred-year-old name!

Who would stoop to care? Imagine for a moment that I have no skill in speech. (Heh heh, I really do, we're just pretending.) Imagine that I lacked the ability to spell it out. Imagine that I could have conveyed my disgust. "You, madam, are a lousy wife."

Even if my wife had humbly received my counsel, I still would have been stooping. And a man in my position chooses never to stoop. Oh, I'm not saying she didn't smile when I walked by. Thing is, she'd smile at anybody.

She continued to fail in her duty to kiss my royal dukey. I gave some commands. Then her smiles stopped altogether. The painting makes her look alive even though she's dead now. She's dead, see. What I mean is, she's dead. Got it? If so, we can go downstairs and join the others.

Your employer, the Count, is generous and rich. Therefore I expect a big fat payoff if I agree to marry his daughter. Sir, don't even think of going down alone! We'll go down together. But do notice this other sculpture as you leave. It's Neptune, taming a sea horse. Not to name-drop, but I am rich enough to commission even the most famous artists. Did I mention that I am a Duke?

Note that the speaker in the Robert Browning poem seems culturally literate. After all, he's an art collector with deep pockets. He has the knowledge and the money to be a major player in the art world. If his main goal were to impress us with a fabulous sculpture (Neptune taming a sea horse) and an amazing portrait (painting of the Duchess), I might think, Yeah, the Duke probably knows what he's talking about.

However, careful reading alerts us to the fact that the Duke has a different agenda. He's far more interested *in showing somebody his late wife's flaws* than he is in making insightful observations about great art. At no time does he suggest that he, too, might have flaws. In fact, the further you read, the more this monologue seems like some kind of creepy warning: "Unless the Count's daughter is prepared to acknowledge that I am Lord of the Universe, she can expect to die like my last wife. So don't waste my time." By the end of the poem it's clear that this speaker is some kind of Bluebeard who has murdered at least one wife, maybe more. Moreover, he is deliberately using fear tactics to control yet another woman, a future Duchess he hasn't even married yet.

When you get an insight like that, I strongly urge you to get in the habit of asking, "At what point in this text did I become suspicious of the speaker's credibility?" Go back and note the place, the word, the moment. Say why this line tipped you off. If you can hook up all your insights to specific moments in the text, you will have plenty to write about.

But your job doesn't stop with the credibility decision. When you're thinking about the credibility of a made-up character, you also have to make the equally important decision of **whether the character is intended to function as the mouthpiece of the author**. In many nonfiction narratives, academic essays, and poems, the speaker's opinions and ideas may well represent the author's own agenda. Indeed, the author may not have intended the first-person speaker to be anything other than his own sweet self. An author's got something to say. He wants to persuade you to agree with his opinion, so he's taking the opportunity to direct your thinking. In some kinds of writing, there's no distance at all between author and reader.

But in "My Last Duchess" is the Duke speaking on behalf of poet Robert Browning? In some stories, plays, and poems, the author may have created a first-person speaker precisely so that we will doubt him. Maybe the author is *attacking* people with views like the Duke's. Maybe the author wants the reader to be savvy enough to join in on the mockery. Nudge, nudge, wink, wink: Can you even believe this gashouse palooka?

Maybe we will take the author's position, maybe we won't. It's our choice. Fortunately we don't have to do what the author wants us to do. We have an amazingly powerful role in the interpretative process. The reader's position is every bit as mighty as the author's. And when the reader becomes a writer too, that's when we kick it up a notch. When readers get ready to write about what we have read—well, ours is the most powerful position of all. We are building on and adding to what the first author has done. We are developing our own interpretation. We are creating a document that will produce an independent application to a situation the author may never have even considered. Thus the author's text becomes our footstool.

In the case of "My Last Duchess," the author, Robert Browning, wants us to question the Duke's motivation. I say this because the poem is filled with clues that make us sympathetic to the dead wife in spite of (and because of) the fact that the Duke is cranking on her. The Duke is asking us to *dis*like his deceased wife. Sorry, dude. The Duchess was nice to her pet, she was kind to the servants, she knew how to take a compliment! What's not to like?

So the reader experiences a curious gap between what the speaker wants and what the author wants. The Duke wants us to raise our eyebrows at his wife's inappropriate behavior. The author is smiling because he wants us to raise our eyebrows at the *Duke's* inappropriate behavior. Here is a confident, powerful Duke who gets away with murder just because he has a nine-hundred-year-old name. Well, we can exercise our powerful authorship too. Robert Browning, being both British and dead, could not have known the ins and outs of the contemporary American political process circa 2018 when he wrote this poem in 1842. But we can take Browning's poem and use it to ask if there are any powerful figures in our own society who are getting away with immoral behavior because they are protected by money and power.

Let's wrap it up

▷ In a nonliterary text, examine the point of view for clues about the author's reliability and credibility. The things you find that contribute to (or detract from) the author's credibility will provide great material to write about.

▷ In a literary text, don't assume that a first-person narrator is the author.

▷ The text will always provide a trail of breadcrumbs for your convenience. If the first-person narrator seems credible, you will be able to point to a series of textual details that establish credibility. If the first-person narrator is creepy, dishonest, or mentally ill, you will be able to point to a series of textual details that compromise the narrator's credibility.

▷ If the speaker you are considering is a made-up character, don't forget to ask, "Who would this first-person narrator be in our world today?"

▷ And, for giggles, don't forget to ask, "Which current Hollywood celebrity would play this speaker?" Because, who's with me, Christopher Walken would be the perfect creeper Duke.

14

What's Going On
with the Title?

14.1 Lifted Directly from the Text

Titles are never unimportant. The author will likely have made one of two choices for the title. One, the author will have elevated some noun or word or phrase lifted directly from inside the text to a position of titular prominence. If the author has promoted this thing/word/phrase to the hyperprominent position of title, you can assume that it is central to your understanding of the overall message. Consider it a major clue, because there it is, front and center in the spotlight.

For example, let's say you've just finished reading Anton Chekhov's short story "The Lady with the Dog." Before you begin reading the story, you would reasonably expect to see this lady's dog in a starring role. Yet after you finish reading, you realize that the dog is by no means a major player.

A wealthy woman brings a yappity Pomeranian along on an otherwise solo vacation. Chekhov doesn't say much about this dog and neither do the characters. We get a hint of adorable paws sticking out of a purse, maybe a cute doggie outfit. That's about it.

In fact the story is not about a dog at all. It's about a casual vacation hookup that suddenly gets all heavy and serious. If it weren't for the title, you might not think twice about a sweet pet that makes a cameo appearance at best. But this dog has advanced all the way to the title. It is safe to conclude that Chekhov promoted this Pomeranian on purpose. So now you're forced to reconsider the role of this no-bite nugget of a lapdog.

Since it doesn't play much of a role in the *literal* plot, you are forced to read the dog as a metaphor. How do you do that? Just ask how dogs usually function in our culture. Dogs are man's best friend, famous for their loyalty, celebrated for following us around as if they wholeheartedly admire our every move, which may be why we love them. "Wait a second. Is Chekhov saying that the lady's *lover* is like a foofy Pomeranian, following her around like a smitten puppy? Is Chekhov saying that all human romantic relationships are fluffy little comforts, like pets who help us handle the stress of being alive?" Bingo!—which, incidentally, was a dog's name in a famous song. Now you're well on your way to figuring out a takeaway for this particular story.

14.2 The Unrelated Title

What if an author opts for a title that isn't even mentioned in the text? The same principle applies: it's still your job to connect title and takeaway. Now the task shifts slightly, this time with the challenge of figuring out how an unrelated word or phrase relates to the text's main message. You can count on even a seemingly irrelevant title to provide a metacomment on the thematic trajectory, so don't ignore a title that seems, on first reading, a bit random. For example, say you read all the way through William Faulkner's classic short story "A Rose for Emily." A southern belle murders her boyfriend, Homer Barron, and then (spoiler alert) sleeps with his decaying body in her bed for forty years. You, the alert reader, have read this story carefully. It's got everything *except* roses—incest, racism, arsenic, stained glass, rats! The only time the word *rose* appears is in reference to the color of the faded curtains and light shade in the dead guy's room.

Without the presence of literal roses, we're obliged once again to think metaphorically. To get a handle on *that*, the

Yet, go figure, Faulkner did not title this story, "A Stinky Corpse for Emily."

best strategy is to ask how actual roses function in our culture. We often associate them with romance. Red roses mark passion and true love. And they're gendered. Pink and white roses often are given to honor a beloved woman, a mother or a grandmother, living or recently deceased. We see roses at major life events: prom, engagements, weddings, and funerals.

So if a rose is supposed to function as a ceremonial tribute to a woman, let's ask the next logical question: Is this story supposed to honor Emily and what she represents? Emily's been having sex with her corpse for four decades. Most of us say, Ew. She can't let go of something that's over, something that's dead. Wisdom tells us to bury a corpse, not embrace it. Does the story give this woman a typical "rose," a tribute? Does it admire Emily's decision to commune with what is dead and over? "Ignore the haters, Emily! You courageous gal, you! You're a brave visionary who goes after what she wants when the whole world is going a different direction!"

Maybe. You could make an argument that this woman's refusal to live by class expectations and social codes is eloquently subversive. After all, she braves a long, possibly intimate, relationship with a man whose role the townsfolk appear to overlook: the "Negro manservant," Tobe. Emily and Tobe live together alone under the same roof for decades until her death. Yet the townsfolk never seem to see Tobe as a man. In fact the narrators use language that consistently *un*mans this man, which tells us a lot about the vision of the Caucasian townsfolk. **If somebody in a text fails to see something that seems obvious to you, that's a terrific thing to write about.**

What these white southern townsfolk do see is a man lacking in power and intention. They assume Tobe is unmanly because he carries a market basket and keeps a kitchen (170). As Tobe ages over the forty years, the narrators describe him as "graying," "stooped," and "doddering" (174). Yet when Emily dies, he suddenly stops playing the servant they have insisted on seeing. After Tobe opens the front door for the town ladies one last time, he "walked right through the house and out the back and was not seen again." Curious, yes? Tobe's conclusive exit implies neither unmanly impotence nor doddering hesitation. It suggests just the opposite, that Tobe is a man of intention and defiance.

And if Tobe is a man of intention and defiance, might he not have killed Homer Barron *for* Emily? In that case he'd be more, so much more, than a faithful servant. If an old-guard, rich southern white woman was boldly hiding an interracial relationship in plain sight of those whom it would have appalled—well, that's what I call subversive! Was Tobe an accessory to murder? Could it have been Tobe, and not Homer Barron, who was the love of Emily's life? The question is: Tobe or Not Tobe? (Get it? Faulkner's little joke actually makes a smart allusion to *Hamlet*.)

An alert reader would also note that mental illness runs in Emily's family. Reading a text is not like reading a menu: you can't just pick and choose. If a detail appears, you have to assume that it's important, especially if it occurs as part of a larger pattern. Into this story Faulkner quietly scatters a whole trail of breadcrumbs regarding mental illness. The principal one, of course, is the shockeroo of Emily's refusal to accept death as terminus, as ending. In fact you could say that for Emily, Homer's death is not an ending at all but a beginning. I think we can all agree that postmortem sex would bring something new to any relationship. She'd be totally in charge, a position of pure power.

However, Emily's signature refusals appear in other ways, too, as part of a larger textual pattern that you, the alert reader, are swift to identify. We've got Emily's great-aunt Wyatt, mentioned twice, who went "completely crazy at last" (170). We've got Emily's refusal to admit that the former mayor, Colonel Sartoris, had been dead for ten years (169). Then there's Emily's insistence that her own father is not dead when her family shows up to help her dispose of the body (171). When Emily denies her own father's death, the narrators remark, "We did not say she was crazy then" (171)—meaning, ouch, that they said she was crazy later. What if the challenging circumstances of Emily's life have triggered latent mental illness? Thus you could just as easily position Emily as a *victim* of those same class expectations and social codes. Maybe the rigid gender and class codes of the Old South made her determined to reinvent herself from victim to survivor!

So maybe the story is not giving her a rose in the conventional sense of an honor or a tribute. Maybe the "rose" is tongue-in-cheek. "Gee, Emily, what a bummer you went nuts and became a creeper necrophiliac. Sorry, condolences!" If the "rose" in the title is ironic, maybe the story is attacking the *townspeople* for their lack of compassion, their ongoing classism, their racist inability to see Tobe as an adult man with independent hopes, dreams, and relationships. It's no accident that the nosy townspeople never even bother to learn Tobe's name. They call him "the Negro" (169) and the "manservant" (168). Tobe is described only in terms of his usefulness to white people. Thus we could make the argument that this anonymous community group is basically *doing the same thing they're criticizing Emily for.* Emily's highbrow family may have "held themselves a little too high for what they really were" (170–71), but, sheesh, look who's talking. Like Emily, these folks are arrogantly clinging to something putrid: their racist values. Personally, I feel that if anybody in this text deserves a "rose," it's Tobe. Give that man a whole bouquet, and throw in a pension plan with a retroactive raise, 'cause whatever he was making, it wasn't enough.

However you decide to interpret baffling words in the title of a text, decide right now that titles are too dang important to ignore. Then write about them.

Let's wrap it up

- ▷ Ask, "How can I read this title as an expression of the author's main message?"
- ▷ If the title has been lifted from a phrase inside the body of the text, be prepared to read the title both literally and symbolically. What larger meaning attaches to it?
- ▷ If the title does not recur elsewhere in the text, it is trying to comment *on* the text. What is it saying?

15
Is There Anything That Repeats?

15.1 Find the Pattern

When you are writing about something you've read, one of the smartest things you can do is write about stuff that repeats. If it happens once, okay. If it happens twice, it's important. If it happens *three* times, it's a pattern. And by *it* I mean *anything* that the text chooses to repeat. Actions, objects, specific words, images, comparisons, references to the weather, allusions to other texts, long awkward sentences, short pithy sentences, profanity, colors, characters who should be there but aren't, characters who are far too present, like helicopter parents. The sky's the limit with repetition, which is why this strategy is so useful.

However, there's a catch. You can't just list a bunch of random things that repeat and then turn in your list as part

Panties that deserve to be seen.

Cottonup

of an academic essay. It's not enough to locate a series of dots. You actually have to *connect* them. Let's say you are reading a personal narrative essay on a childhood incident that an author remembered, and in this text the author refers to how things smell four times. Any decent college reader will notice the plurality of olfactory images. But a *good* reader analyzes what function they serve. What is the author trying to say about fragrance, odor, memory?

15.2 Connecting the Dots

Since you can practice these reading/writing skills on texts of any stripe, let's pick a visual image this time. We haven't done that yet. Here's the sort of ad you might expect to see in a typical contemporary women's magazine.

When you're reading visual images, especially ads from print media, it's important to be savvy about context, content, and intention. For instance this visual image tells you, bottom line, that Cotton Up, an underwear company, wants you to buy Cotton Up underwear. In this sense the ad, like all ads, demonstrates a claim of solution and policy: "You should open your wallet and purchase our product." But get ready to enter the Wiggle Room, because there might be a very interesting gap between what the ad explicitly says and what it tacitly implies.

At this time I invite you to jot down a list of stuff that repeats within this visual text. If you see it at least twice, note it. Your instructor may let you do this task in small groups. It's more fun that way. Plus the comments of our peers often kindle observational sparks that we might not have otherwise noticed.

Just now I'm alone with my cat, who prefers a prolonged belly rub to a list of stuff that repeats. So my list might not be as rich as yours. But here's what I wrote:

▷ Repetition of blue (calming color)
  blue panties
  blue mug

▷ Repetition of white (color of purity, innocence, day-time, cleanliness)
  white top
  white chair
  white walls
  white window casing
  white urban view
  white sky
  stark contrast of white pops against black
    the white word *seen* jumps out because the rest of the text message is black
    the white label *Cotton Up* has crisp visibility be-cause the computer screen is solid black
  white circle of light like a halo around the model's crotch and upper thighs

▷ Repetition of daytime office references
  lots of light
  workplace 9:00-5:00 setting
  modest professional top
  hair in a tidy bun

mug suggests coffee break

tasky file folder on desk signals busywork

computer screen is positioned directly in front of the window, as if more important than the view

model leans on the desk where the work takes place; a metaphor for an employee who leans on a job

absence of window curtains or blinds points to office environment rather than loft apartment

as in most offices, people will be coming and going (they are presumably the ones who will see these deserving panties)

Somebody must bear witness to panties that deserve to be seen. The text implies that this is a typical office, with people coming and going

▷ Reinforcement of coffee break

downtown setting signals a financial district

height of building suggests a skyline with skyscrapers, the site of many business organizations

mug of coffee juxtaposed against file folder; on a coffee break we set down the latter to pick up the former

model is relaxing before getting back to work

▷ Wholesome references

slim boyish figure

plain clean makeup

panties offer comfy coverage rather than cheeky seduction

model has modest downcast eyes
natural manicure
model's outfit argues for understated simplicity
polka dots are cute, fresh, and youthful
no nudity, no cleavage, absence of sexual innuen-
do, model vertical rather than horizontal

▷ Woman-doesn't-need-a-romantic-partner vibe
model is the only person in the frame; one rather
than two
no wedding ring; no picture of partner on desk
nothing seductive
model employed and clearly providing her own
paycheck

Taken together, these textual repetitions accentuate an intended message of female empowerment, right? These images,
coupled with the ad's stated message, are telling readers that
women will feel empowered if they show off their cute panties—not because they are manipulating anybody with their
sexiness but because revealing the cuteness of their panties
on purpose will make them feel clean, strong, wholesome, and
confident.

Quick look again at the ad. Maybe it's because they are
the only fun patterned thing in a roomful of austere solid sur-
faces. Or maybe it's because the halo effect draws our eye to
the dead center of those polka-dots. Or maybe it's because
most of us would be surprised to come across a half-dressed
colleague peacefully enjoying a cup of joe. No matter how you
slice it, though, what the viewer sees first is panties, panties,

panties!

Q: What do we associate panties with?
A: The part of the female anatomy they cover.

If you're just now starting college, you might not know this word: *metonym*. Good word to know. It's a subset of metaphor, meaning something that an author uses as a substitute for the thing with which we ordinarily associate it. This author (Cotton Up) is not interested in showing a woman's naked heinie and vagina, since the object is to get us to purchase the panties. But the author is very much interested in getting us to accept the panties as a metonym *for* the genitals.

When we do so, we agree to the text's tacit message, that making public what is usually private will empower the woman. Armpits, nose hair, gums, and earwax are usually private too. But who, besides our friend Mrs. Child, wants to look at earwax? This ad is not telling us to make *all* private parts public—no, it is implying that we should invite the public gaze to the female netherparts specifically. Panties this cute deserve to be seen. Genitals this cute should be admired, with the assistance of cute panties!

Interestingly, at first glance this ad seems to *affirm* female agency. It stages the action in a professional, wage-earning scenario. It withholds anything that might gesture toward female dependence on a partner. Yet at some point we must ask: How empowering is it, really, for women to equate the display of their genitals and/or panties with empowerment? Isn't this just another way of repackaging the same ol' objectifying gaze? Seems to me that what would really empower men and women is a proud display of what's in our minds, not our pants.

I'm all for self-sexualizing in the right context, particularly when the context turns on consensual intimacy in a private setting. But to use the human body as a form of currency to purchase a feeling of empowerment—well, that smells fishy. It raises some serious ideological questions. In your parents' day wolf whistles and harassment on the job were tolerated, even expected. Today that sort of objectification should be old news. What's new is how the same message has sneakily morphed into something that claims to be the very opposite of objectification. Cotton Up is participating in this new cultural message, and this visual text ups the ante. Back in the day, straight men objectified women. Now women are being asked to objectify *themselves* ... and to pretend that if they author the choice, they become stronger and more satisfied individuals. Since when is genital brio a form of empowerment?

I'll tell you when. When you are looking for romantic action. For sure drawing the public gaze to your metonymic "secret" may be just the ticket if what you want is to attract a sex partner. But how helpful is it if you already have a partner? What if what you want is a college degree, professional respect, parity in salary, and achievement in the workforce? What if what you want is to make a difference in the world? What if what you want is to be a steadfast friend, a supportive partner, and a loving parent? Shall we all show our collective metonymic underpants? Dear Cotton Up, dear wholesome model on your coffee break, we do see your panties. We see your polka dots.

And we can connect them.

Let's wrap it up

▷ Always notice what the author/director/artist chooses to repeat.
▷ Always ask why that repetition is happening.
▷ How do the repetitions serve the whole shebang, the overall agenda of the text's main message?
▷ If the repetitions direct the reading, do you accept the direction?

16 What's Going On with the Context/Setting?

16.1 How Does It Connect?

We read the details of a physical space just as we read the words on a page. And we do it so fast, sometimes, that we don't even know we are reading, assigning, connecting, and concluding.

By *setting*, I mean the whole package of time frame, culture, scenery, physical space, location, all of it. Remember the Freudian question "When is a cigar just a cigar?" When is a setting just a setting? The answer is "Never." God is in the details, as Flaubert said.

If you have ever visited Disneyland, see if you can recall the attraction called the Haunted Mansion. The tour begins in the foyer of what is supposed to typify the upscale manor of yesteryear. It makes sense that Disney chose to set the feature

Walt Disney World's Haunted Mansion

in the 1880s because at that time Americans had a crush on parlor spiritualism: crystal balls, séances, levitation, all that. When the Disney feature begins, we encounter a painting of a pleasant young woman with a parasol. The lights flicker and dim. A thunderclap, spooky effects! Suddenly the painting begins to stretch by an unseen force that pulls the eye down, down, down—Oh! Turns out the young woman is not out for a walk in the park at all! Turns out she is balancing precariously on a tightrope above a pit of alligators! Thank you, Walt Disney, for the instructive lesson you taught us when we were six. **When the vision takes context into account, the message changes.**

In other words, you don't just read the pleasant young lady. You check to see what she is standing on. When the text is an essay rather than a story, you focus on **context** rather than **physical space**. This means you are asking how the author's argument connects to a larger cultural framework: the assumptions, details, and contemporaneous events that have shaped what and how the author is writing. When the text does provide a description of actual physical space, you look at the significance of that. Nonfiction and fiction texts invite similar skills from the reader. One key difference is that in the former, context hovers *around* the writing, as ideas about nineteenth-century séances hover around our experience of the Haunted Mansion; in the latter, context appears *inside* the text, like the ghost who shows up in our car at the end of the ride. Whether inside or outside, context is important.

16.2   Allow the Setting to Guide Your Interpretation

If you haven't yet read Ernest Hemingway's pithy little story "Hills Like White Elephants,"[1] do that now. Since it's very, very short, it'll take you only a couple of minutes to read it.

Most anthologies include a date of publication for every text. I usually start there when I purpose to think about context and setting, because the time frame may change how I read the piece. This Hemingway story was published in 1927. Right away I'm thinking about flappers, jazz babies, Prohibition, and people trying to assert new social freedoms. Even though this story takes place in Spain, not America, it's strong on booze. And it features a pregnant young woman who has staked everything on asserting her freedom from traditional sexual mores. At a train station somewhere between Barcelo-

---

1   Visit link: https://goo.gl/D7Ucjk

na and Madrid, an unhappy couple sits in an outdoor café and bickers about the future: abortion, yes or no?

Since we have a publication date of 1927, our first question should be, "Is this story set in the 1920s, or earlier?" Remember, an author is free to set a story in any decade whatsoever. This story firmly identifies Spain by city names, not some made-up place with aliens or hobbits. The 1920s, on first reading, seems a likely decade for two reasons. One, the couple talks about drinking absinthe, which was a trendy cocktail for affluent hipsters in the 1910s and 1920s. Two, the unidentified narrator uses telltale language to describe the bickering heterosexual couple. The guy is "the American." The girlfriend is "the girl with him" (176). Today, thank goodness, young adult women are not called *girls*. They are called *women*—rightly so, since they are adults, not children. Calling an adult a *girl* seems like a blast from the past because it is. This helps us date the story's action to a time when men were men and women were girls. Interestingly, the narrator goes on to identify the café server as "the woman," as if there is a huge age difference between the server and the girlfriend. The suggestion is that this story was written when *women* were old, unattractive, or working class, while *girls* were the preferred romantic partners.

My second question would be, "Were abortions legal and safe in 1927?" This question of context is a game-changer. If the American is pressuring Jig to have a black-market, illegal abortion, our reading of the American's character instantly changes, and not for the better. The thing the American keeps coming back to is the putative ease and safety of the abortion procedure. He describes an abortion as "an awfully simple operation "and "not really an operation at all." Assuring Jig that she "wouldn't mind it," the American says, "It's not really anything. It's just to let the air in" (177). In 1927 abortions were indeed illegal in England, Spain, and the United States. Unless the American is planning to whisk Jig away to Bolshevik Russia, where abortion is legal in the 1920s, he is advocating a black-market abortion. Knowing this, we can accuse this man of overt deception. A black-market abortion was not a safe procedure, not by any stretch. In the United States alone, 15,000 women died each year from illegal abortions in the 1920s.[2]

So already our reading is being directed by details of setting. Now let's look at the passages I would have skipped when I was a kid. The narrator describes two scenic vistas, which can be viewed from opposite sides of the station platform where the couple is waiting for the train to Madrid:

> The hills across the valley of the Ebro were long and white. On this side there was no shade and no trees and the station was between two lines of rails in the sun. … [The hills] were white in the sun and the country was brown and dry. (176)

This description emphasizes a barren landscape (long white hills, no trees), a harsh sun (no shade), withered grass (brown and dry). This is the sad sort of landscape that you would rath-

---

2 Leslie J. Reagan, *When Abortion Was a Crime: Women, Medicine, and the Law in the United States, 1867–1973* (Berkeley: University of California Press, 1998): 139.

er pass through than settle for. Who would want it? Indeed, when Jig likens the hills to white elephants, we are reminded that a white elephant is something we donate to a thrift store or yard sale, something unwanted.

A second scenic description gives an abrupt contrast to the first:

> The girl stood up and walked to the end of the station. Across, on the other side, were fields of grain and trees along the banks of the Ebro. Far away, beyond the river, were mountains. The shadow of a cloud moved across the field of grain, and she saw the river through the trees. (178)

Just the opposite, right? This time the landscape is lush, fertile (field of grain, mentioned twice). This crop, unlike the former landscape, is *wanted*. It's been planted and tended, and somebody is eagerly waiting the harvest. There's the promise of rain (shadow of a cloud), plenty of water (river, mentioned twice), growing things (trees, mentioned twice). It's no coincidence that Jig is looking out at the lush, growing landscape when she says, "And we could have all this" (178). Hemingway is using the two opposite landscapes to help us visualize the two choices that this couple has.

More importantly, these scenic descriptions are actively **guiding our interpretation**. Hemingway is making the lush, fertile side look an awful lot more appealing than the dry, shriveled side. Since Jig is the one who longs for the fertile landscape, it's fair to infer that she is imagining a fructive future with a husband and a much-wanted baby. But it's not just

A Hemingwayesque train station in Flåm, Norway

Jig who thinks that this future would bring happiness. The *speaker narrating the story* thinks so too. Some narrators describe dry desert landscapes in magnificent terms. Not here.

Then there's the physical space the couple occupies. They wait on a wee platform, a tiny pause between two landscapes and two trains moving in two different directions. Two, two, two! Yes, we get it: twoness represents choice, and this couple is considering only two choices. They will keep the baby. Or they will abort it. Tellingly, it is Jig, not the American, who crosses the platform to look with longing on the side that represents fertility. Jig and her man have only forty minutes between trains, a short stop. In other words, they don't have much time to make this decision. Whether they choose to terminate the pregnancy or settle down and raise their child, they're stuck with whatever they decide. Once they board the train, there's no getting off.

If we skipped the importance of setting, we'd miss the big picture. And the irony is that the big picture provides nuanced meaning rather than sweeping generality. Can you understand a text without attention to context? Sure. But you'll have way more to write about if you take that context seriously. It's there for a reason.

You may find it helpful to imagine this story in today's setting, here, in twenty-first-century America. If you do, you'll probably be struck with a whole host of options Jig doesn't even consider in the story. Today she might sensibly refrain from drinking alcohol while pregnant. Since she wants the baby, she might dump the icky boyfriend and become a single mom. She might decide to get a job and learn Spanish. She might rustle up a support group or go get counseling. She could demand child support from the American, and, if he denied paternity, she could get a DNA test. These are all perfectly viable ideas for the woman of today who, like Jig, would like to keep the baby. But the real use of considering these options becomes instantly clear when you ask the next logical question: "Why can't Jig do any of these things?" Ah. Jig has put all her eggs in one basket, no pun intended. In the 1920s a decision to pursue a premarital sexual relationship may well have burned bridges with home and community. Meanwhile, since Jig relies on the American for everything, we can assume she has no money of her own. Who would hire her, and for what kind of job?

We don't know why Jig originally decided to traipse around Europe with a man who has no legal responsibility to foot her bills. She must have known that it was a calculated risk. When she left her community of origin, was she renouncing conventional morality, or naively expecting it? In other words, did she reject the idea of marriage, or was she hoping for a proposal? What to expect when you're expecting? Not an engagement ring. This is 1927. Women in Jig's situation didn't have many options. Which explains why, at story's end, Jig is smiling, seated on the side of the platform that overlooks the *dry brown landscape*. The fertile scenery is no longer in view. She cannot see it. For her the two choices have already shriveled to one. Thus she is preparing for the unsafe abortion she doesn't want, telling herself and her man that she feels fine. She feels so fine she says it twice.

She feels fine, see.

Let's wrap it up

▷ Details of context and setting don't merely echo the author's position. They *deepen* it.

▷ Look for in-text clues to decade, epoch, or season.

▷ Ask, "How would this scenario be different today?"

Who Lives Here

Go stand in the doorway of your dorm room or at the threshold of your personal space. Just stand there for about thirty seconds and pretend that you are seeing it through the eyes of a stranger. What kinds of first impressions would this space make on someone who didn't know you? Notice everything. Organization or chaos, neatnik or free spirit, folder or wadder? Details of decor, implications of taste or budget? Clothing choices, hygiene routines? Preferred music, study habits? See any textbook titles from where you stand? What about evidence of social or leisure activities?

Now retreat to a neutral space and freewrite for ten minutes solid, without lifting your hand from the paper or keyboard. What would you expect one who occupied such a space to be like? Hook up each expectation to the thing in the space that suggested it.

If you're not squeamish about somebody else's eyes on your stuff, you might also want to ask a casual friend to stand in the doorway of your room and jot down some impressions. (Don't clean up first. Let your friend see the space as you usually occupy it.)

Afterward, compare notes. Of course your friend may have noticed different details than the ones that drew your own eye, or the friend may have made unexpected connections between the details and what they might suggest. It's quite possible that your friend's conjectures about who you are as a person are scary-wrong or laugh-out-loud funny. Right or wrong, they show how we all inevitably assign meaning to details of setting.

17 Where Does the Author End It?

17.1 Profound Last Words

Today when we get the call that a loved one is dying, it is customary to drop everything, is it not? If we are in position to have advance notice of such things, we buy a plane ticket, cancel our appointments, call the boss. People expect us to do this. Bosses aren't thrilled, but they usually do cut us some slack. A death in the family is a legit reason to take time off work.

Wouldn't it be outrageous to get fired for trying to make it to a beloved parent's deathbed? Note that in these situations, provided that we have established personal integrity and reliability over time, pretty much everyone backs up to give us a little bit of space, some additional flexibility. This is because American culture honors the importance of saying good-bye to a beloved relative, friend, or partner. If you consider yourself a writer and you get one of these tragic calls, you write a poem or essay about the experience afterward. If you don't consider yourself a writer, you still write about it, but on Facebook. Endings are milestones. They are important. Words are important. What we say about endings is important.

Did you know that in bygone centuries Americans had another reason to cluster around the bed of a dying loved one? Oh yes: they wanted to say good-bye. But they also wanted to hear what the beloved's last words would be. Most American cultures affirmed the existence of an afterlife, and a beloved's last words might be uttered in crossing that threshold into the next life. Maybe those last words would offer a glimpse into Heaven! Or maybe, in the passage to some unknowable eternity, the beloved's last words might provide a gem of otherworldly counsel, some precious insight that would improve reality for those left behind. And so it was common for folks to write down the last words of their beloved, to meditate on their possible meaning, and to share them with friends. In this way death put a period on life, but it also opened up a whole new discussion.

Think of the author as a beloved on a deathbed, getting ready to wrap it up with something profound. The end approaches, the text is short, here comes the final takeaway! You, the reader, must lean in and pay attention at this critical moment. The author has not given up or gotten bored. She has not run out of things to say. She is working up to the *piqure*, the punch line, if you will. Where she stops, she stops on purpose.

All roads lead to Rome

Long ago I studied with the great American poet Donald Justice, whose nickname in literary circles was "The Master." I was in a class of eager young writers, and we were all on fire to become better poets. We hung on Donald's every word, just like nineteenth-century mourners around a dying loved one. In the 1980s Donald Justice was very much alive, committed to helping us develop our poetics. In workshops he'd repeatedly ask us the same question. It wasn't a rhetorical question either. He really wanted to know our answer. Plus he'd just sit there in terrifying silence until we gave him one. "Is the last line the best line?" he'd ask. "If not, why not?" For Donald Justice all poetic lines lead to the last line, just as all roads lead to Rome. The moment of cessation was more important than all the moments that preceded it because *they existed to take us to that one moment.*

Stories and poems and articles and essays all have one thing in common: they are short. In the span of a few pages, the author has to make weighty choices about what to include and what to exclude. Details have been selectively arranged and presented. The whole text is like a display window in a store. Although the store presumably stocks a lot of items, it's only *these* items that have made it to the display window. Whoever organized the display wants you to see not just these items but these items in relationship to each other. These items are representative of, but more important than, all the other items in the store. If the author has done his job right, you will be able to glimpse the larger world implied by his text. You will be able to glimpse the world of essay, story, or poem beyond the spot where the action stops. There's a big back-story, too. Then there's the implication of a coda, a sequel, a what-happens-next. And it is precisely because the author has located the ending on a time continuum that the author's end zone matters so much. An author's ending reveals time-management skill at its most significant. Here is a spot, here is a moment, that somehow contains all moments.

And so a good reader learns to take last lines into account. In fact a good reader (and, by extension, a good writer) knows that the entirety of an interpretation can hang from the peg of an ending.

17.2 Shifting Interpretations: Sylvia Plath's "Daddy"

For a test case on endings, let's take one of the most popular poems in America's college anthologies. Distilling a text into a few words helps you get at the essence, sort of like juicing an orange, so here is my helpful headline summary of Sylvia Plath's 1962 poem "Daddy."

HATER COMPARES PERSONAL PAIN TO HOLOCAUST

You really do need to read it for yourself, though.

Daddy[1]

by Sylvia Plath

You do not do, you do not do
Any more, black shoe
In which I have lived like a foot
For thirty years, poor and white,
Barely daring to breathe or Achoo.

Daddy, I have had to kill you.
You died before I had time—
Marble-heavy, a bag full of God,
Ghastly statue with one gray toe
Big as a Frisco seal

And a head in the freakish Atlantic
Where it pours bean green over blue
In the waters off beautiful Nauset.
I used to pray to recover you.
Ach, du.

In the German tongue, in the Polish town
Scraped flat by the roller
Of wars, wars, wars.
But the name of the town is common.
My Polack friend

Says there are a dozen or two.

---

1   From *The Collected Poems* by Sylvia Plath. Copyright © 1981 by the Estate of
Sylvia Plath. Used with permission from HarperCollins Publishers.

So I never could tell where you
Put your foot, your root,
I never could talk to you.
The tongue stuck in my jaw.

It stuck in a barb wire snare.
Ich, ich, ich, ich,
I could hardly speak.
I thought every German was you.
And the language obscene

An engine, an engine
Chuffing me off like a Jew.
A Jew to Dachau, Auschwitz, Belsen.
I began to talk like a Jew.
I think I may well be a Jew.

The snows of the Tyrol, the clear beer of Vienna
Are not very pure or true.
With my gipsy ancestress and my weird luck
And my Taroc pack and my Taroc pack
I may be a bit of a Jew.

I have always been scared of *you*,
With your Luftwaffe, your gobbledygoo.
And your neat mustache
And your Aryan eye, bright blue.
Panzer-man, panzer-man, O You—

Not God but a swastika
So black no sky could squeak through.
Every woman adores a Fascist,

The boot in the face, the brute
Brute heart of a brute like you.

You stand at the blackboard, daddy,
In the picture I have of you,
A cleft in your chin instead of your foot
But no less a devil for that, no not
Any less the black man who

Bit my pretty red heart in two.
I was ten when they buried you.
At twenty I tried to die
And get back, back, back to you.
I thought even the bones would do.

But they pulled me out of the sack,
And they stuck me together with glue.
And then I knew what to do.
I made a model of you,
A man in black with a Meinkampf look

And a love of the rack and the screw.
And I said I do, I do.
So daddy, I'm finally through.
The black telephone's off at the root,
The voices just can't worm through.

If I've killed one man, I've killed two—
The vampire who said he was you
And drank my blood for a year,
Seven years, if you want to know.
Daddy, you can lie back now.

There's a stake in your fat black heart
And the villagers never liked you.
They are dancing and stamping on you.
They always *knew* it was you.
Daddy, daddy, you bastard, I'm through.

Many readers respond to this poem with the uneasy sense that this speaker may be pushing the envelope past where it ought to be pushed. The uneasiness isn't about the speaker's ongoing rage or the fact that she still feels tortured decades after a bad experience with her father. People who have survived a childhood of horrific parenting certainly don't need our permission to feel angry about it, nor do they need to process the experience according to any cultural timeline.

Interestingly, most of my students *want* to like the angry speaker. "Good for her for having the courage to tell her story!" In point of fact, literature is full of creepy dads who molest their daughters. That's not exactly a new plot. No, my students are troubled by something else altogether. Their uneasiness is *structural*. It comes from a shocking comparison. This speaker, who is not Jewish, has made the jaw-dropping choice to compare her personal suffering to the collective suffering of six million Jews.

Historians will tell you that there were imbricated economic, moral, and ideological reasons why Hitler selected Jews for persecution, but at bottom most of us would acknowledge that the Holocaust was an extreme example of religious persecution. Hitler's Holocaust was an attack not just on Jewish bodies but on the very ideas that Jewish people lived and died for. Plath's speaker makes a startling comparison when she equates her personal pain to the pain experienced by a multinational ethnic faith group. One of her, six million of them. Throughout the poem the speaker describes a series of emotions (hatred, rage, fear, confusion) and actions (trying and failing to speak, trying and failing to commit suicide, trying and failing to marry away from Daddy). Notice that every emotion, every action, is reactive. That is, everything the speaker does is a response to the dad's abuse, as if the speaker's whole identity is built on who she is in relation to him.

By contrast, the Jews of the Holocaust would have been Jewish with or without Hitler. This is because their identity was not based on an abuser at all. Their identity was established via ethos, heritage, community, and calling; moreover, it formed thousands of years before Hitler ever lived. The Jews cited in this poem were therefore not *reactive* but *proactive,* in the sense that they were seeking to *move toward* something rather than *running away* from something. Judaism seeks to honor God and community in accordance with a long-established faith tradition. However, the speaker of this poem is not attempting to move toward anything. Rather, she is attempting to move away from an abuser. When we consider that the Jews of the Holocaust were moving toward a goal that had nothing to do with the abuser, this comparison is indeed abrupt, unexpected, and jarring. Should we even be comparing the pain of a single reactive speaker to the pain of a proactive group?

Nevertheless, my students are quick to build a case against this unseen malevolent Daddy. It doesn't take long for them to arrive at an incest reading. True, not all of my students go there, but in every class some do. And those readers find persuasive textual support in the speaker's ongoing sense of physical violation by a hated father who bites, kicks, drinks, screws (lines 56, 49, 73, 66). Readers are troubled by a series of strange details, for instance, "The tongue stuck in my jaw"— "Whose tongue?" my students demand. If the speaker wanted to claim the tongue as her own body part, it would be more natural to use a possessive adjective pronoun. In other words, most speakers would say "*My* tongue stuck in my jaw" (line 25, emphasis added). When the pronoun is omitted, we can't help but wonder if that wasn't *Daddy's* tongue sticking in her jaw. Ew. Daddy has a "root" (line 23) that keeps getting put where it ought not to go. And so on. Then there is the hyperbolic list of entities that Daddy gets compared to:

- a black shoe
- a ghastly statue
- a bag full of God
- Hitler
- a train to a death camp
- a Fascist
- a brute
- a stern teacher
- an abusive husband
- a devil/Satan
- a black man
- a vampire

The sheer number of metaphors in this poem argues for the utter failure of language. Not only was the speaker, as a child, unable to articulate her misery or ask for help; now as an adult she is still unable to overstate the evilness of this daddy. She moves restlessly from comparison to comparison because no single comparison can do the trick. He's that evil, see. The speaker meanwhile tosses off some ugly implications, and not just about Daddy. She disrespects people of faith by making God seem egocentric and arrogant; she insults African Americans by equating blackness with moral badness. When she freely disses people of faith and African Americans, she suggests that her own experience is far, far worse than the abuses sustained by other groups who have been oppressed.

Um. Wow. Okay.

And then someone in every class notices that the shocking comparisons might not be so shocking after all. What if the speaker is not really equating her own personal pain to the far wider degree of suffering documented by the Holocaust? What if Plath's hater is speaking on behalf of not one suffering female but all of them? Fifty percent of the world's population since the beginning of recorded history? What if the intention is something other than to narrate the story of private sexual abuse? Maybe this speaker is suggesting that something abusive has been built right into the culture's foundational gender paradigms that, like the Daddy, are pure evil. These gendered paradigms elevate Daddy (the patriarchy). They perpetuate power imbalance for women, who, whether or not they are actually molested by individual daddies, are indeed molested by a corporate structure of oppression.

Well, that changes things. Suddenly what on first reading appeared to be an overreaching statement of personal rage begins to read as a powerful call to community. The whole point is that Daddy's oppression works through the mechanism of isolation, by taking away the voice of the oppressed and making her feel alone. But she is not alone, and she now knows it.

The last lines

And so we come to the End Zone, the final lines of a text that shape our reading of it. In the last stanza we suddenly get a sea change. In every other stanza it was a solitary, isolated speaker versus Daddy, one woman against The Man. Then in this final stanza something different happens. Suddenly we get a whole crowd of people. Villagers! It takes a village!

> And the villagers never liked you.
> They are dancing and stamping on you.
> They always *knew* it was you.
> Daddy, daddy, you bastard, I'm through.

Isn't it cool that just as this poem is about to end, the *I* has become a *They*? People are wired to connect. Even when oppressed, people manage to reach out to each other, dancing and stamping in defiant unity. You could even say that one of the results of oppression is connection, A causes B.

Where does the author leave it? A declaration of rupture, a strongly voiced assertion that it's finally over. Here's a gal who once described herself as a poor white foot who barely dared to breathe or Achoo. Now this same gal is giving voice to a statement of closure that is daring indeed. And I get it that some readers choose to interpret this line as the ultimate irony. Nothing says "stuck in the past" like a grown woman who still calls her father Daddy. The speaker claims to be severing Daddy's power over her, but the ironic reading says, Puh-lease, no way. If this speaker still needs to trash-talk Daddy the Bastard, then she can't possibly be finished with him. She obviously can't stop talking about him and, in doing so, perpetuates his power over her.

Yet what if we interpret the last line with an eye to the power of the united villagers? What if we read the last line to mean, "Because I finally understand how to resist systems of oppression, you no longer have power over me!" If we read the last line as a call to community, then our interpretation of the whole poem changes. We can no longer interpret the speaker as a victim who lacks perspective and self-awareness. Instead, our understanding of the ending becomes an eloquent example of the very thing the poem is trying to demonstrate: how to resist oppression. Oppressed people of the world, unite! Let your stories dance and stomp all over those who tried to stomp on you!

Let's wrap it up

Your interpretation of every text needs to take the last line into account. Do not underestimate its importance. The last line/scene/sentence may seem abrupt or random. It may seem to leave you hanging. But it's part of your job to interpret it. These questions will help:

▷ Why did the author choose to end here and not somewhere else?

▷ What does this ending imply about the future?

▷ What does this ending tell me about the author's values?

▷ How does this ending change what I have read at the front end?

Likewise, when you are writing a text of your own, put some thought into where you want to end your discussion. Most professors will say that in a college essay the most important sentence is the thesis, which comes at the beginning. And I would agree. But the last words are a close runner-up. Your thesis will plant the grade your essay earns, but your last words yield the reader's harvest.

18
Top Three Worst Usage Errors for a College Student

18.1 How to Play the Grammar Game

Please consider the thought that grammar may be the last bastion of unexamined privilege in America. It's the sleeping kind of privilege, which is often harder to detect. Privilege can be sneaky. In practice, what do grammar rules do? They perpetuate the success of those in the know even as they punish the folks who don't have access to the "rules."

You might think that with the advent of texting and fast-paced email, traditional grammar protocols would have already gone the way of calling cards and wedding china. Who has time today to worry about comma splices? Who cares about fragments when we're in a hurry? Ah. I am sorry to report that the very people who will be in charge of evaluating, hiring, and promoting you may be using your grammar as a measure of your professional competence. In some ways you could call these people gatekeepers, because they decide who gets hired and who does not. Remember that it's perfectly legal for an employer to chuck your cover letter because it contains a comma splice.

Thus America's ongoing grammar anxiety will not vanish anytime soon. It is a fire stoked by celebrity bloopers, by newscaster hypercorrections, and by virtually every utterance that proceeds from the mouth of a certain former governor of Alaska. In August 2008 the Oprah magazine, *O*, ran a piece in which Ben Affleck strongly urged all readers to purchase and master the Strunk and White grammar manual *The Elements of Style*.[1] This grammar manual was first published in 1918. For reference, 1918 was the year that Trotsky became leader of the Reds. A lot has changed since 1918, and many grammarians today would agree that *The Elements of Style* is seriously outdated. Does that stop people from secretly revering it and from giving it as a graduation gift to their neighbor's son? Nossir. If Ben Affleck says we need it, it must be true!

Let's say that an insightful, smart student objects on principle to learning the conventions of modern English grammar. This hypothetical student might say something rational such as, "C'mon folks, I think we'll all understand each other even if our writing contains a couple of comma splices!" Here's the deal. When comma-splicers cry out against the grammar rules, who is going to take the comma-splicers seriously? The gatekeepers might roll their eyes and say, "You,

---

1   Visit link: https://goo.gl/EvFBvZ

sir, don't even know how to write! You, ma'am, make comma splices on your memos, there in your low-level management position at a chain drugstore!"

It is only when a writer *has mastered the conventions of basic grammar* that she is permitted to speak in the realm of reputable public discourse. We all do have access to some fundamentally democratic forms of uncensored public speech. For instance, we can tweet and blog about anything at all, as demonstrated by the free-for-all that is the Internet. Whether you would like to discuss your circadian rhythms or share a step-by-step guide for teaching your cat to use a flush toilet, you have some pretty radical freedoms available to you. You don't have to be famous; you don't even have to have credentials, an academic degree, or measurable expertise. Yet note the relationship between these easy-access venues and conventionally bad grammar. Bad grammar won't stop you from getting into a chat room, or from creating a quirky profile on a dating site. Bad grammar won't stop you from posting your thoughts on time travel, or from writing an open letter urging the establishment of an intramural club fencing program at every college. "*En Garde!* Top Hundred Reasons Why Fencing is Bad and Boujee!" So sure, you can get your writing out there. But can you gain access to the highest cultural echelons without good grammar?

Just sayin'.

I didn't make the rules, and I can't single-handedly change them. What I can do is put the ball in your court. *You* decide what to do with this information. If you want to go down feisty and swingin', pronouns akimbo, by all means: it is your right to tweet/splice as you murderously please. If, on the other hand, your aim is a decent GPA and a career after college, I urge you to consider the impact of the Top Three Worst Usage Errors for a College Student.

These three usage errors are not the most frequently occurring ones in college prose, thank goodness. They are at the top for severity, not frequency. Of all the usage errors you can make in college, these are the most cringeworthy. They all send a mixed message whose fundamental contradiction cannot be reconciled. Since these usage errors occur in writing submitted for a college grade, they say, "I value and pursue the goals of higher education." But they simultaneously say something incompatible with the first thing. "Too bad I don't know what a sentence is!"

The idea is that a college-level scholar really ought to be able to communicate a complete idea in the basic form of written English designed for that purpose. This basic form is the sentence. Personally, I think we ought to be able to use *any* form of communication, such as hand gestures, tunes played upon the nose flute, and/or haiku. But college administrators tend to disagree. So without further ado, I give you the Trifecta of Shame.

▷ Comma Splice
▷ Fragment
▷ Run-On

18.2 Comma Splice

Of these three usage errors, the comma splice is the most common at the university level. It happens when you make a mistake in hooking up two complete stand-alone sentences. There are lots of perfectly cricket ways to hook up two stand-alone sentences, but a comma all by itself is not one of them. Here is a basic no-frills comma splice:

> I forgot my umbrella, it started raining.

Both of those two chunks can be sentences all by themselves, so you can't hook them up with just a comma. This is what a comma splice might look like in a college-level paper:

> In *Operation Fly Trap: LA Gangs, Drugs, and the Law*, urban anthropologist Susan Phillips describes the bureaucratic ideologies and methods of law enforcement, including police and FBI agencies, **then** she shows how Los Angeles gang culture has adapted to a culture of chronic surveillance.

On first glance, the academic splice looks like a passable sentence, right? It's long enough and smart enough, and in every other way it passes muster. But check out how the two sentences have been connected. I see this particular structure frequently. My students have alerted me to the logic behind this usage error. "But I didn't use just a comma to connect these two sentences. I used the word *then* too!"

Bad news: you're not supposed to use a random word to

connect two sentences. There are actually rules about what you can and cannot use. Fortunately you do have lots of options. In fact, the only thing that *isn't* okay is a comma all by itself. So, to recap, here's what you cannot do:

> Folks on social media sometimes detail their dreams, this is helpful information for us all!

Now let's look at what you *can* do. Here comes a list of examples that connect two stand-alone sentences in ways that are **perfectly acceptable**. Indeed, you've got a veritable potpourri of options when connecting two stand-alone sentences.

▷ **semicolon**

It's easy to overshare on social media; the permanence of written language invites risk.

▷ **colon**

I know a young man who didn't want to be trapped by language: he has become a mime.

▷ **em dash**

This young mime bravely performs at street fairs— yes, he does the thing with the imaginary box.

▷ **ellipsis**

Our friend the mime wants to be heard ... I, for one, am listening!

Plus you can use any of the classic FANBOY conjunctions to

hook up two complete sentences:

- ▷ **F**or
- ▷ **A**nd
- ▷ **N**or
- ▷ **B**ut
- ▷ **O**r
- ▷ **Y**et

On a style note, though, I don't recommend using *for*, even though it's perfectly correct. It's too formal for contemporary American prose. It invokes the image of a tweedy gentleman orator with a pipe and elbow patches:

> Let all mimes arise and gesticulate, for this is a democracy!

Finally, you can use a handy conjunctive adverb to hook up two complete sentences. These take a special punctuation treatment. Here are the most common hitches:

- ▷ ; therefore,
- ▷ ; however,
- ▷ ; thus,
- ▷ ; consequently,
- ▷ ; moreover,
- ▷ ; nevertheless,

Be careful, though. Some conjunctive adverbs are sipping a glass of sherry with the tweed gentleman:

> Trajan, the first-century Roman emperor, exiled mimes for their indecency; hence, we may infer that Roman mimes were not merely doing the thing with the box. Ergo, we may even conclude that Roman mimes were making some objectionable gestures.

Hence and *ergo* often seem dated, unlike the timeless appeal of a mime!

18.3 Fragment

I'm presenting these three maximum-impact usage errors in order of the uh-oh factor, from least to most. Fragments are slightly more appalling than comma splices. This is because they send the signal that you can't even articulate a complete thought. A fragment is a partial sentence in which you're missing a key grammar thing, either the subject or the verb, or even, yikes, both.

Here let's stick to the most common form of the fragment at the university level. A university fragment usually happens in a specific scenario, when a student writer is attempting to connect two sentences with a semicolon. That's great. You can and should occasionally connect two sentences with a semicolon in your academic writing. It becomes a usage error only when the student forgets something of major grammatical importance. Namely, whatever comes *after* the semicolon needs to be a stand-alone sentence too. In a typical college fragment, the first part before the semicolon is usually okay. But the part after the semicolon is a freeloading parasite, like a barnacle that clings to a shark.

> Benjamin Franklin could have easily been a loyalist; **so-cializing in England with British aristocracy.**

Read the barnacle bit after the semicolon; read it out loud. You will hear that it is not a stand-alone sentence. It needs to be.

There are plenty of good, solid grammatical fixes for the usage error we call *fragment*. Here are two of the easiest fixes.

> ▷ **Convert the second part after the semicolon into a stand-alone.**
>
>> Benjamin Franklin could have easily been a loyalist; he frequently socialized in England with British aristocracy.

> ▷ **Replace the semicolon with a comma.**
>
>> Benjamin Franklin could have easily been a loyalist, socializing in England with British aristocracy.

18.4 Run-On

The run-on is also sometimes called a *fused sentence*. You might think this error would be referring to a sentence that goes a-ramblin' down a long yellow brick road, like Dorothy. No. The toodling yellow-brick-road sentence may be a yawner, but a long sentence isn't necessarily a usage error. There's no rule about how long a sentence should be. Use common sense. And somebody tell Henry James.

But there is a rule about writing two separate sentences and hooking them up with nothing at all. This is like trying to glue two things together with no glue. It's an intriguing choice: not sure I get the logic, but I admire the optimism. One sentence runs into the next, so the two attempt to become one. But without stopping. Without even *pausing*. At least with a comma splice you get the sense that the author took a breath. But here, nada. No punctuation of any stripe.

This is pretty much the all-time worst usage error. With a run-on, you're still sending the signal that you don't know what a sentence is. But now it's a double whammy, because you're also saying, "Perhaps I shall exercise my right to spin a couple of circles before settling down!" I admire this behavior in dogs; who doesn't? But unfortunately we will not be hired if our sentences turn in circles like our Schnauzers.

To be fair to the undergraduates I teach, I rarely see this usage error. When I do see it, though, I am quick to pull the student aside and ask what's going on with the grammar. A handshake and a diploma ain't gonna get you a job.

A run-on in academic work looks like this:

> Murphy believes that tiny houses are a form of "appropriate technology"[2] because they are easily customized and more economical than homes whose conventionally installed systems must accommodate wasteful building codes tiny houses can adapt easily to a variety of building sites.

As a reader I can follow what this writer is saying, but I shouldn't have to work that hard. The run-on forces me to

---

2 Mary Murphy, "Tiny Houses as Appropriate Technology," *Communities* 165 (2014): 54–59.

experience a moment of real confusion. Your goal should be to *prevent* confusion. If grammar rules have any one redeeming thing going for them, it's that they can help us express ourselves with clarity.

The fix for a run-on is reasonable enough. Stop when one sentence ends. Take a breath, use a period, have a healthy snack, such as dried kale chips. Or, I know, wasabi peas! Then begin again. If you are thinking, *But how do I know when one sentence ends?*, then it's time to go to the writing lab and ask for a tutor who can explain it you.

How do I know if a sentence is a complete sentence?

If a sentence is complete, you will be able to find a stand-alone chunk in which a person or thing (subject) does some action (verb). You need both a subject and a complete action, right there in front of you, in the same sentence.

Not complete:

| Reading Schopenhauer before bed.

Who, you might ask, would read Schopenhauer before bed? Scholars, mostly. However, the word *scholars* is missing from the so-called sentence, so the above snippet is a sad little fragment.

Also not complete:

| Doyo reading Schopenhauer before bed.

Now we know who's doing the reading. Our subject is present and accounted for (Doyo). But now the action is incomplete. Sometimes verbs come with bits that help us get the tense right (is, was, am, are, were, be), or bits that help us ask a question (does, do), or even bits that give us the right shade of meaning (should, could, might, etc.). Sometimes the verb comes in a couple of pieces, stretched out like an accordion with lots of little helping words. *Doyo reading* is a structure with one of those words gone missing. Doyo *was* reading before bed. If you have only part of a verb, no cigar. You have written a fragment.

And this, too, is incomplete:

| Before he turned out the light and went to sleep.

Now we've got a real subject (he), doing not one but two complete actions (turned the light out, went to bed). However, this wannabe is still messed up because it is not yet a stand-alone. You know those golf flags that stick out of the ground to mark the hole? English has a group of words that stick out of the sentence to mark extra information. The extra information might be fabulous, it might be compelling, it might even illuminate Schopenhauer. But, grammatically speaking, it will always be *extra information*. It won't be the actual sentence. It's fluff.

The group of flags is called **subordinating conjunctions**. *Sub* means *under*. These conjunctions are subordinate because they are under the authority of a host sentence, which means that the chunk of information they begin cannot be a freestanding sentence. I should probably mention that after college you will never hear or say the term *subordinating conjunction* again, unless you are the sort of person who likes to read Schopenhauer before bed. In fact if at a social event you exclaim with enthusiasm, "Hey, what about those subordinating conjunctions!" don't be surprised if your friend spots an old acquaintance across the room.

You know how we all multitask? I can mud drywall, teach English, or make cinnamon buns, depending on what's needed. Same person, different function. Likewise, in grammar, many types of words can shape-shift according to how they are used in any given sentence. Like all of us, subordinating conjunctions can wear different hats: now a preposition, now a relative pronoun, now a flag for a noun clause. If it sounds complicated, it is. Serious writers often choose to take a grammar class to firm things up, which I'm happy to say you can do in one solid semester. However, you may have zero interest in being a serious writer. Fine. But keep in mind that grammar competence involves more than memorizing a bunch of subordinating conjunctions.

Thank goodness you can be a decent writer without studying grammar. Skim this list of some of the subordinating conjunctions we use most often and tell yourself, very loosely and provisionally, "These words often begin a chunk of extra information. If I use a chunk like that, I still need to complete my sentence with a stand-alone structure."

before	because	after	although	when
where	rather than	unless	whether	whereas
until	though	if	that	while

as   as if   as soon as   since   whenever

Remember that chunks with subordinating conjunctions get mistaken for sentences because they do contain both a subject and a complete action. Nonetheless this chunk is not a full-fledged sentence. It may be helpful to think of these chunks (adverb clauses) as wee alien monsters incubating in the abdominal cavity of a human host. They need to be *inside* a sentence. Aliens *need* us, see.

Sentence Relays

Students number off into relay teams who form lines perpendicular to the whiteboard. The instructor gives the front-runners a marker. On the whiteboard in front of each team the instructor writes a different five-letter word, for example, SCRAM.

When the instructor shouts "Go!" the front-runner dashes to the whiteboard and writes a word beginning with the first letter. Then he runs back and hands the pen like a baton to the second runner. She dashes up to create the second word of a sentence, but it must begin with the second letter of SCRAM. The goal is to be the first team to create a bona fide sentence, complete with subject and verb:

I Sailors clip roses at midnight.

 or

I Somebody's carpet roasts a mosquito.

The sentences will no doubt be silly, but that's the whole point—our language has structural rules that apply no matter what we are saying! Even nonsense sentences have subjects and verbs, and it empowers students to be able to identify them. An added bonus is that the relay sentences often seem to hint at a hidden meaning, like cryptic passwords in a bad spy novel.

In subsequent rounds, I like to up the ante with longer words, depending on the got-game factor. It's distinctly more of a challenge with nine or ten letters. Once a group proudly produced this semicoherent whopper for the word ESTABLISHMENT:

> Eastern Siberian tales about Bob's legendary igloo suggest history might exaggerate nomadic tents.

Be honest! Haven't you always secretly wondered if we can trust history on the important subject of nomadic tents?

19 The Orator's Dilemma

19.1 Your Grammar, Your Choice

Right now it is fashionable for social media and cultural texts such as television, magazines, and movies to urge young people, "Just be who you are! Put yourself out there! Ignore the haters!" This is such a great message that I am reluctant to make an observation that is, dang it, sort of undeniable.

Success requires a bit more than confidence.

The plain truth is that it's not enough to be confident, either in your college classes or your job search after you graduate. If you confidently utter the wrong pronoun, people will (a) judge you and (b) have a concrete reason to move on to the next applicant. I am not making this up. The very company to which you are applying may be seeking a simple, incontestable, legal way to thin the applicant pool. We all know, of course, that it is illegal to discriminate based on race, age, sexual orientation, or ethnicity. But discriminating on the basis of bad grammar is perfectly legal, and many employers do it. You want to give yourself an edge over the other four applicants who have made the short list for a dream internship? Keep reading.

Recently I was invited to serve as one of three judges at an oration competition. The judges' task was to award an honor to the strongest orator, who would deliver a speech in front of a thousand spectators. The participating orators had written effective speeches. The orators demonstrated presence, charisma, and poise, which was why they had advanced in the competition. And the speeches reflected substantive original content.

Yet one of the speakers had made a bold decision to use "wrong" pronouns on purpose. I am using hang quotes here to reflect the orator's dilemma. She had written a speech that described one person's isolation. The sense of alienation seemed even greater because the lonely individual was surrounded by a crowd. Modern English grammar gives us only four pronoun options to talk about a single person: *one, he, she,* and *they.* All of these choices seemed sketchy to the orator. *One:* too formal. *He* or *she:* sexist, because either pronoun would exclude the other gender. *He-or-she*: awkward to repeat over and over during a speech. *They*: not yet fully established as a respectable pronoun choice.

Grammar rules do change as culture evolves, and we have to make savvy decisions about when and how we keep pace. The idea of using *they* as a singular pronoun was already on the rise when the orator was making her decision about whether to go for it. In 2015 *The Washington Post* had officially okayed the use of *they* as a singular pronoun.[1] In May 2017 *The AP Stylebook* gave a thumbs-up to the single *they* in cases when the plural version would be awkward.[2] Yet even though singular *they* was on the uptick, scholars were still sort of tiptoeing around it, as indeed they still are. For example, in the excellent *Garner's Modern English Usage* (2016), style authority Bryan A. Garner frames the national hesitation as a kind of iffy tolerance: "Where noun-pronoun disagreement can be avoided, avoid it. Where it can't be avoided, resort to it cautiously because some people may doubt your literacy."[3] Time for a *Dirty Harry*, Clint Eastwood–style question: *Do I feel lucky?* Will folks doubt my literacy, yes or no?

Thus the orator's dilemma: Which was more important, an outgoing grammar rule or global gender inclusivity? The orator chose the latter. She decided to go with *they*. The orator totally knew that using *they* to talk about one person might

---

1   Visit link: https://goo.gl/5vSbMK

2   Visit link: https://goo.gl/JMKsnP

3   Bryan A. Garner, *Garner's Modern English Usage* (New York: Oxford University Press, 2016), 195.

cause confusion, but she decided the risk was worth it.

I happened to know all about the pronoun angst because the orator and her coach had explained their position in a note to the judges, which we received in advance of the speech. On the night of the event the speech was powerful; the delivery, poised. But the orator didn't win. The judges agreed that the use of *they* to describe one person had created significant confusion. The emphasis was supposed to be on *one* person's profound feelings of inadequacy and loneliness, even as this one person was part of a crowd. Who was the *they*? Was the they supposed to refer to the alienated individual or to the surrounding crowd? We couldn't tell.

We understood the logic. We got the decision. We respected the choice. But here's the kicker. Objecting to grammar issues **doesn't make them go away**. What I'm saying is, you can make an eloquent, insightful argument about the sexist/classist/racist implications of traditional grammar rules, and you will find people like me to nod and give you an intellectual thumbs-up for having had the chops to pull back the curtain, like Toto in *The Wizard of Oz*. But at the end of the day the clarity of your communication will still be judged by bosses, supervisors, professors, editors, proofers. Please understand that I'm not saying you should accommodate the professional preferences of this privileged class. Nor am I saying that the grammar gatekeepers should have the power that they do have. No. I'm saying two very different things:

1. When you start your career, your bosses are the gatekeepers.
2. Your grammar, your choice.

20

Why People Make Such a Big Deal about Pronouns

20.1 The Practical Application

Before you decide that now would be a good time to write a thank-you note to your aunt for that nice "Donner & Blitzen" Christmas sweater, let me mention that this next usage error occurs way more often in college writing than splices, frags, and run-ons. Although I can name many issues of more weighty global significance, this one does have immediate relevance to your academic performance in the short term and to your career plans thereafter. Namely, you will get a bumper return on your investment if you take the time to master the difference between subject and object pronouns.

    I would not be wasting your time with this if it did not have an immediate practical application. Knowing this seemingly obscure grammar distinction is one of the best things you can do to boost your wow factor, both in speaking and in writing. You will seem better prepared if you do not cover your pronoun with a discreet little cough.

Yes, I know: in critical moments like job interviews it is theoretically possible to sidestep iffy pronouns altogether. You can be so quick on the draw that you avoid the whole problem by constructing a brave new sentence that does not include any pronouns at all. That way the interviewer won't *object* to your grammar. But wouldn't you rather she be *impressed* by it? A breezy, confident *whom* is like a firm handshake. It adverts to brisk preparation and professional force. Like the firm handshake, a confidently uttered object pronoun says, "I may wear the occasional reindeer sweater in the privacy of my own home, but I will never embarrass this company!"

Everything I tell you about pronouns will empower you to make intentional choices about your grammar. As a bonus I will also address the age-old, panic-inducing question, "When do you use *whom*?" I will not assume a grammar background. If you don't need a review, skip ahead.

20.2 Subject and Object Pronouns

A subject does the action. An object receives it.

| Last night **Mitch** grilled **burgers** on the deck.

Pronouns are smallish words that substitute for the nouns: *He* grilled *them*.

You can see that even when we substitute a pronoun for a noun, the pronoun is still performing the same function.

A scarecrow and a man do the same thing: they scare crows, even though the first is just representing the other. My husband is still doing the action even though now we are calling him *He* instead of *Mitch*. The burgers are still just sitting there being grilled, even though now we are calling the burgers *them*. We need these little pronoun substitutions. Without them we'd go around sounding like idiots, repeating the same nouns over and over.

I am sorry to report that English offers a bewildering variety of pronoun categories. The good news is that only three of them present usage problems for most college-enrolled native speakers.

Subject pronouns

Subject pronouns, like scarecrows, have to perform the action of the original subject. This is a grammar rule you can count on 100 percent of the time. Also, it makes total sense to call them *subject pronouns*, because they have to substitute for an actual subject or its restatement. If you want to sound pretentious and/or outdated, you can also refer to subject pronouns as *nominative pronouns*. We can take our pick of the following subject pronouns, depending on the gender and quantity we need for our sentence. A moment of silence, please, for the scholar who came up with the ubiquitous pronoun chart!

Who and *whoever* are wild cards, like *x* in algebra. They're merely placeholders in the sentence, the equation variables we use for someone whose name we don't know yet or for someone whose name we don't want to repeat yet because we've just said it. Sometimes we might not know the

	Singular	Plural
First person	I	we
Second person	you	you
Third person	he, she, it, one, who, whoever	they, who, whoever

name of a single person. Sometimes we might not know the names of a whole group of folks. It doesn't matter. Just use the same subject pronoun: who. It signifies somebody or a group of somebodies who are actually doing the action:

> **Who** likes prune soup? Nobody, that's who!
> (singular)

> **Who** makes prune soup? Mennonites, that's who!
> (plural)

Native speakers can usually negotiate the ins and outs of subject pronouns with no problem at all. But there is one curious circumstance when, like the London Bridge, we all fall down. Consider this elementary math equation: 2 + 2 = 4. Whatever comes before the equal sign (2 + 2) is another way of saying whatever comes after (4). We can all agree that (2 + 2) is another way of saying (4). If I wanted to, I could even flip the order: 4 = 2 + 2. The reason I can flip them, the reason that the order is interchangeable, is that I am talking about the *same number* on both sides of the equal sign. That's how equal they are. Equal! The same! This logic also translates into subject pronouns. Let us think of the linking verb *is* as an equal sign.

| Rhoda is a Mennonite.

| A Mennonite is Rhoda.

We're talking about the same prune-soup-making person on either side of the verb. If you want to restate the subject in another way, with more information, or with less, go right ahead.

| Rhoda, the author of this textbook, is Mennonite.

You can do that as often as you please. But you gotta use a *subject* pronoun because you are still referring to the person who is doing the main action.

| She is a Mennonite.

| A Mennonite is she.

So far, so good. At least we are in the land of logic.

Now imagine you and your siblings are home for the holidays, sharing a bathroom. It is 7:20 a.m., and the bathroom has been occupied for a good long time. You're pretty sure you know who's in there, since the best predictor of future behavior is past behavior. You bang helpfully on the door. You and your older sister exchange an eye roll.

"Who is it?" Your little brother sounds peaceful, as if he

might be napping there on the toilet.

"It's me, and FYI, there's a line out here!"

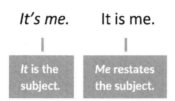

It's me.   It is me.

It *is* the subject.   *Me* restates the subject.

Yup: what I'm saying is, *It's me* is grammatically incorrect. You need a subject pronoun if you want to restate your subject. If you glance at the handy subject pronoun chart above, you'll see that in the first-person slot, *me* is not even an option. The word is, gulp, *I.*

Uh-oh. How is that possible? Who on earth would stand urgently outside the bathroom door in Scooby-Doo pajamas and shout, "'It is I!" Not you. Not your older sister. Not even this English professor. That is, I might wear the Scooby-Doo pajamas. But would I channel Sir Ian McKellen with a noble Shakespearean "'Tis I"? Only if it would help my student get an internship.

These sentences are all dead wrong:

| That was me who called you at midnight last night.

| Not gonna lie, it was us who complained about the barking.

| The one favored to win in the lightweight fight is him.

| They have a bigger boat than us.

Technically speaking, it was I who called, it was we who complained, the favored fighter is he, and the neighbors have a bigger boat than we.

When you're making a comparison between two things, you're assigning these two things the same grammar status in the sentence, as when comparing apples to apples:

| They have a boat. We have a boat.

You would never say *Us have a boat*, would you? So if you are making a comparison, use subject pronouns when you are comparing two subjects. Use object pronouns when you are comparing two objects:

> Bridge prefers the steampunk Sherlock Holmes played by Robert Downey Jr. to the more subtle Sherlock Holmes played by Benedict Cumberbatch.

> Bridge likes Steampunk Sherlock more than he likes Subtle Sherlock.

We are comparing two objects that just sit there and receive the action of being liked by Bridge. The status of these two objects is grammatically the same. Neither Steampunk Sherlock nor Subtle Sherlock does a single thing in this sentence. In grammar terms, they exist solely to be liked, disliked, watched, or compared, by Bridge. Since both Sherlocks are objects, you can substitute an object pronoun to talk about the general superiority of one Sherlock to the other:

| Bridge likes Steampunk Sherlock more than **him**.

And yet, in a perverse twist that Sherlock Holmes himself would applaud, the following sentence is also completely correct:

| Bridge likes Steampunk Sherlock more than **he**.

Meaning that Bridge's roomie, Alan, also flirts with steampunk. Alan admires Robert Downey Jr.'s Sherlock as well but in a distant kind of way. It's not as if Alan has a Sherlock poster above his bed or anything. Bridge not only has the poster; he's been known to do the little wink.

Thus, we may say that

| Bridge likes Steampunk Sherlock more than he [Alan].

Steampunk all the way.

Does this sound ridiculously irrelevant to life as we know it? Does this suggest that grammarians have a whole lotta free time on their hands? Has anyone else noticed that even if I make a grammar mistake and say *They have a bigger boat than us*, all English-speaking persons will understand my meaning? The one who feels your pain is I, my friend.

Object pronouns

Now let's take a look at object pronouns as a group. Since objects are the opposite of subjects, we will use this group of pronouns as substitutes for words that just sit there and receive the action.

	Singular	Plural
First person	me	us
Second person	you	you
Third person	him, her, it, one, whom, whomever	them, whom, whomever

In each of the three sentences below, Granny is doing the action. Dear Granny! She's such a lovebug, always hugging and giving. Because Granny is doing all the action, she's the subject.

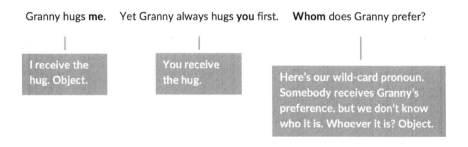

Granny hugs **me**.   Yet Granny always hugs **you** first.   **Whom** does Granny prefer?

I receive the hug. Object.

You receive the hug.

Here's our wild-card pronoun. Somebody receives Granny's preference, but we don't know who it is. Whoever it is? Object.

Not every sentence will have an object. But if it does, you will be able to find it because it's the one just sitting there, absorbing all the action like a sponge.

As with the subject pronouns, you can use object pronouns as often as you please. Just make sure that when you use them, you are using them as substitutes for actual objects.

> **Me** and Timmy found $6 in the parking lot.

Terrific. Spend it wisely. But since you and Timmy are the subjects who are doing the action, you need a subject pronoun. Timmy and *I* found six bucks in the parking lot.

> Timmy told **me** we should use the $6 to buy a card for Granny.

In this sentence, who is receiving the action? Somebody is being told something. Timmy is the teller (subject); the speaker is the told (object). That is, the speaker just sits there and receives the action. Thus *me* is correct. Object pronouns replace objects.

20.3 Hypercorrection

Okay, so. Now that you know the difference between subject and object pronouns, it's time for me to alert you to a usage error that often makes educated folks wince. This is a particular kind of plebiscite. By *plebiscite*, I refer not to the familiar political definition but to a common social practice that signals a lack of education. A *plebeian* is a commoner, someone lacking in refinement or class awareness. Personally, I find the term a bit offensive. But if you think that's offensive, wait'll you see this.

The plebiscite I want to bring to your attention is the most common form of what grammarians call *hypercorrection*. This happens when people kerfuffle their pronouns in a way that suggests they are trying to impress you with their level of education. Somewhere along the line, most Americans have heard that it's taboo to say "It's me" or "Me and Timmy went to the store." Now if these same Americans have never actually studied grammar, if they heard only a stray grammar scold from their teacher in eighth grade, they might have come to the not unreasonable conclusion that the word *me* in and of itself presents some kind of major grammar problem. These same folks might conclude that using the word *me* is an underclass gaffe, not unlike affixing a large bouncy chrome pair of—well, a tribute to the male anatomy—to the bumper of your Ford 250.

If you were to become vaguely suspicious of using the word *me*, it might seem reasonable to switch over to the opposite pronoun, *I*, a whole lot more often. You might go out of your way to use *I* on the grounds that, fingers crossed, it sounds more refined. You might utter hypercorrections like these:

> I'll have you know that this anatomically correct bumper ornament was given to he and I as a gift!

> One day I, too, aspire to have a classy bumper like he.

> Nothing underscores nuance like a family of gun stickers in the rear window and a free-swinging chrome ornament on the bumper. Such a vehicle is an homage to they that use chew.

A regular ol' pronoun error such as *Me and Timmy cut class* reveals that you don't know much about standard usage. But it also says you don't care, which is kind of cool. Jaunty indifference is one of the reasons we like the defiance (and attendant smackmouth) of rap and hip-hop. The musical artists are offering an eloquent middle finger to many social conventions, including grammar. Interestingly, the kings and queens of hip-hop don't typically include hypercorrection among their preferred grammar violations. A hip-hop hypercorrection would be an oxymoron, because the whole point of hip-hop is to foreground your rebellion and indifference. Hypercorrection, on the other hand, says you do care. You care deeply. You care so much that you are trying way too hard to get it right. Which, alas, is uncool.

Allow me to break down the concept of *cool*, which hinges on two related forms of social confidence.

1. It is cool to be so confident that you purposely take the road less traveled, like the Underground Kingz, Tupac, Dr. Dre, and Robert Frost.
2. It is cool to be so confident that you take the main road, knowing exactly where to turn because you looked up the directions ahead of time.

Have you ever seen a TV caricature of an American invited to high tea at a proper British gathering? The standing joke is always on the American. Trying way too hard but not knowing any better, she might accept the teacup with pinkie finger held aloft. Meanwhile the other guests are acutely embarrassed for her. They think the extended pinkie is sad and amusing.

Hypercorrection is worse, socially speaking, than going to a tea party and crooking your pinkie. On the one hand, the speaker's hypercorrection suggests that she is too careless to get her grammar up to speed. On the other, it confesses latent class anxiety: "How I long to impress you with what I hope is a highfalutin pronoun!" Ouch.

You can't see this right now, but I'm typing with my pinkie extended in solidarity with everybody who feels that grammar is kind of mean-spirited.

How to avoid hypercorrection

For those of you who would prefer to sidestep hypercorrection, I cite two methods that work pretty well. One you already know, if you can now tell the difference between something that performs the action and something that receives it.

> ▷ **If it is doing the action, use a subject pronoun.**
> ▷ **If it is receiving the action, use an object pronoun.**

The other method is to use a reliable shortcut, but it's reliable only if you can identify a preposition. Prepositions are those small throwaway words that point to time, space, and relationship: *in, on, between, to, with, under, over, of, from,* to name nine. The English language offers a teeming mess of prepositions, so many that most folks don't bother trying to memorize them. However, here's a list of some common ones if you geek grammar.

aboard	throughout	of
due to	along	unto
past	inside of	between
about	till	off
during	along with	up
per	instead of	beyond
above	to	on
except (for)	amid	upon
prior to	into	by
according to	toward	onto
for	among	via
regarding	like	concerning
across	under	opposite
from	apart from	with
round	near	contrary to
after	underneath	out (of)
in	around	within
since	next (to)	despite
against	unlike	outside
including	as	without
through	notwithstanding	down
ahead of	until	over
inside	as far as	

Prepositions aren't important all by themselves. Their role is minor. They deliver a kernel of extra information that is nice but rarely necessary to the main structure of the sentence. For example:

> Let's meet at the park by the thing with the sign about picking up after your dog.

If in real life you and I were actually planning to meet, you would need to know where to find me, and so these instructions would come in handy. Grammatically speaking, though, most of this sentence is extra information. If you trim the optional bits, what remain are subject and verb—that is, people who do the action, and the action itself:

> Let's meet.

Everything else consists of a string of optional units called *prepositional phrases*. Notice that each little informational nugget begins with its own preposition:

> **at** the park

> **by** the thing

> **with** the sign

> **about** picking up

> **after** your dog

And so we come to the third helpful method for deciding what kind of pronoun to use. **If your questionable pronoun comes after a preposition, you need an object pronoun.**

Here is the most embarrassing form of hypercorrection:

> Just **between** you and I, on Amazon you can purchase several types of upscale bouncy chrome bumper ornaments.

And here is a sentence that is not at all embarrassing, unless you count the items hanging from the bumper

> Just **between** you and me, Santa might bring you a handsome chrome ornament for your vehicle, to go with your sexy cowgirl mud flaps!

If you can spot a preposition, get ready with your object pronoun. In the English language, there are actually three separate occasions when you need an object pronoun. Weirdly, though, the situation with the preposition is the one that results most frequently in hypercorrection. That's the one to watch for.

20.4   Hypercorrection with Reflexive Pronouns

You already know what hypercorrection is and why it makes the gatekeepers squirm. There's one more form of it that you might want to know. This usage error has to do with a third category of pronouns called reflexive pronouns. We don't use this group very often compared to subject and object pronouns, but unfortunately, there is no situation in which hypercorrection does not smell like desperation. Here is your reference chart for the group called **reflexive pronouns.**

	Singular	Plural
First person	myself	ourselves
Second person	yourself	yourselves
Third person	himself, itself, herself, oneself	themselves

We can use reflexive pronouns in two ways without giving folks the heebie-jeebies.

Totally okay:

1. When the speaker is performing an action on self. Somebody does something to himself.

   | He cut himself shaving.

   | She injured herself on the clean-and-jerk.

   | They bought themselves a set of quality ratchet straps.

2. When the speaker wants to create a spot of extra agreement or emphasis. In this case the reflexive pronoun functions like a tinkly bell on a bicycle: nice but extra. Notice that in these examples, the sen-

tences would sound okay if you skipped the reflexive pronoun altogether, even as you can ride just fine without the tinkly bell. Here the reflexive pronoun functions as an extra synonym for the word *too*.

> Is that a shark eating an alligator, or Godzilla with a sick tummy? I sometimes draw Godzilla myself. Let's put your drawing up on the fridge!

> Jacob's new roommate likes thrash. Fortunately Jacob is a metalhead himself.

> Let's skip the pricey zip line and go for a hike instead. We're on a budget ourselves.

Most native English speakers have no problem at all using reflexive pronouns in the two correct ways described above. The problem happens when they opt for a rogue third way. Still on the theory that any pronoun sounds more highbrow and respectable than a homey object pronoun, some folks use reflexive pronouns as a hopeful substitute. This kind of hypercorrection occurs when someone is trying hard to sound smart and culturally literate. Typically writing that tries to sound smart is the kind of writing that wears a power suit— you know, formal tone, authoritative pronouncement, corporate memo, essay with footnotes. What happens is, the speaker uses a reflexive pronoun as **the last element in a list that always follows a preposition.**

Sadly, this is not the time for a reflexive pronoun. Remember, you need an *object* pronoun after a preposition. You can't go around substituting a reflexive pronoun. That is, you can, but don't be surprised if people suddenly study their fingernails, embarrassed at your pretentious grammar. And now, for your grammar pleasure, I give you the formula to avoid this specific kind of hypercorrection. If you are alert enough to recognize this one pattern right now, you will be able to sidestep the usage error for the rest of your writing life.

The memo was sent **to** Kao, Werner, and **myself**.
(Should be: Kao, Werner, and *me*.)

Preposition starts a list. **Hypercorrection comes at the end of the list.**

The ultimate responsibility lies **with** the research team and **himself**.
(Should be: the team and *him*.)

Preposition launches multiperson list again, and once more **the last element in the list is the hypercorrected pronoun.**

I remember the first few months after a recent presidential election. At the new president's first press conference this otherwise august, polished politician hypercorrected his pronouns, using a subject pronoun instead of the correct object pronoun. In the weeks that followed the president went on to hypercorrect reflexive pronouns, too, so ouch. In those first months he was regularly called out for it. For example, in the *New York Times*, Patricia T. O'Conner and Stewart Kellerman, authors of *Origins of the Specious: Myths and Misconceptions of the English Language*, observed that since the national election four months earlier, the president had been "roundly criticized" for hypercorrection.[1] O'Conner and Kellerman went on to document specific instances. Did I think that the president's hypercorrection compromised his ability to lead a powerful nation? No. But, interestingly, somebody did, and not just O'Conner and Kellerman.

Shortly after the brouhaha about the president's hyper-corrected reflexive pronouns, I began to notice what seemed like an overnight fix. Suddenly the presidential pronouns were living happily ever after. To me this strongly suggested that an advisor had made a persuasive case for a private grammar lesson or two.

Imagine the gravitas, the moral responsibility, of be-ing elected to the highest office in the land. Imagine all the weighty issues you'd face as an incoming president: free trade, international terrorism, global warming, gay marriage, abor-tion, health care, Supreme Court appointments, economic, ra-cial, and ethnic tensions of every possible permutation. This is a job that doesn't leave you with a lot of spare time. Isn't it curious that the president of the United States found hyper-correction a big enough deal to merit his personal time and attention?

20.5   How Not to Be Thrown into a Who/Whom Tizzy

Sorry in advance for some bad news.

---

1   Visit link: https://goo.gl/aah4D3

In academic and professional writing you aren't supposed to use the relative pronoun *that* to describe a person. It's for things and ideas, not people.

If you are like my own students, right about now you are saying "Whaaa—?" Almost everybody commits this usage error hundreds of times a day. Would you even notice that the following sentences contain usage errors?

> The Italian philosopher **that** I am reading right now is Benedetto Croce.

> Ludacris is a singer and actor **that** everybody's heard of.

> The cousin **that** I told you about is coming for a visit.

What do Benedetto Croce, Ludacris, and my Mennonite cousin Waldemer have in common? Not much, it is true. But they are all people. Because they are all human beings rather than things, I have to use *who* or *whom* when I talk about them. Indeed I would like to talk about this trio at length and how they might respond to one another, especially if all three were to walk into a bar. Just kidding! Mennonites don't drink.

People started using *that* everywhere, for every situation, but not because they were making some democratic push to simplify pronouns. They were doing it because they wanted to avoid the *who/whom* tizzy. Step around it, man! Step around it like dog poop on the sidewalk! Not knowing the difference between *who* and *whom*, they did step around it. Meanwhile our day-to-day writing got more and more casual with the advent of texting and social media. Few readers of casual writing noticed, and even fewer cared. And now it sounds familiar enough to seem correct.

It isn't. This is why, in your shoes, I would learn the difference between *who* and *whom*.

But what about using *that* with animals?

I cannot say why my students always ask me this question. Also, they ask with an urgency, as if their life depended on using correct pronouns for a nice doggie in a handsome kerchief. If this question seems off topic to you, skip to the next section. Shout-out to all my students with pets.

Use *that* for animals that you would like to eat or swat, but not for your beloved pet. A hunter might say, "I shot a bear that weighed 400 pounds!" If this hunter is married to the professor, he might bring her the bear in four Hefty bags, and she would be forced to try her hand at bear lasagna. Which, I'm sorry, tastes like sponge. Our son took the entire 400 pounds off our hands, saying:

> Bear **that** tastes like sponge is no problem with plenty of ketchup.

A pet owner, however, personifies her animal with the pronoun appropriate for people. Her pet is not some freeloading, untidy raccoon **that** may or may not have rabies. Her pet is a Great Dane **who** likes to slow-dance with her. It is easy to see yourself in intimate relationship with a Great Dane **who** weighs a splendid 169 pounds and looks a little like Humphrey

Bogart, especially when lipping a fake cigar.

The Jennifer test

And now a classroom-tested trick called **The Jennifer Test**. I named it after a former student whom I was helping when I hit on the shortcut.

> I know a guy (who/whom paints fences).

> The guy (who/whom you hired) called about the fence.

In The Jennifer Test, you isolate the chunk made scary by the pronoun stress. You'll know you've correctly isolated the chunk if what remains is a complete stand-alone sentence (*I know a guy. The guy called about the fence.*) Once you've identified the scary chunk, substitute *Jennifer* for the pronoun.

> I know a guy (Jennifer paints fences).

Jennifer paints fences. Does that sound okay?

If *Jennifer* sounds okay, use *who*. I know a guy *who* paints fences. (Or you can just reason it out, since you also now understand that if the person is doing the action, you need a subject pronoun.)
How does this one sound?

> The guy (Jennifer you hired) called about the fence.

Jennifer you hired. Sounds lousy, right? If the chunk sounds bad when you plug in *Jennifer*, use *whom*. A guy *whom* you hired called about the fence.

| **Who**: "Jennifer sounds good."

| **Whom**: "Jennifer sounds bad."

During many an office hour I have invoked the name *Jennifer* with reverence and thanksgiving. I'm the kind of writer who wants to understand my grammar choices, but I get it that some writers just want to fix the problem and move on. The Jennifer Test saves time.

The Day That Grammar Died

Field trip! In groups of two or three venture out into the world, to a street or coffeehouse if your campus is small enough. If your university is too big for that, find an on-site coffee shop or gathering place. Your goal: in a conversation with a random stranger, make a major pronoun error on purpose. Your classmates must hear you do it.

▷ No fake accents

▷ No apologies or explanations after you make the pronoun gaffe

▷ Keep it brief. Ask a question such as "Her and me are lost. Can you tell us where x is?" Or make a ho-hum remark such as "Two lattes for my friend and myself, please." Etc.

▷ The silent partner observes the stranger's reaction, or lack of it.

When you assemble for the next class session, be prepared to answer two questions:

1. Did you receive any responses that suggested surprise or judgment?

2. How hard was it to make a pronoun mistake on purpose and then walk away? Your response will tell you how invested you are in grammar as a system of social governance.

21

How to Add a Pop of Crisp Clarity

21.1 Intentional Clarity

Usually when we say that someone is a clear writer, what we mean is that the writer's *ideas* are lucidly presented. The writer doesn't waste a lot of time with fancypants jargon, as if trying to call attention to his or her scholarly currency or huge vocabulary. The writer communicates well and easily, so that the reader is struck by the originality of the intellectual contribution. The writer doesn't muddy the waters, in other words. Scholars do an awful lot of background reading and research in advance of crafting their own arguments, and sometimes all that thoroughgoing preparedness can seem to take center stage. In that way an author can accidentally seem to be tooting his own horn instead of entering a larger scholarly conversation. I don't know anybody who would do that on purpose, do you?

If you are ever asked to read a dense, opaque piece of scholarly writing, know that folks are not merely showing off. There really is a huge amount of background reading and research that goes into the production of academic writing. Scholars are expected to demonstrate their knowledge of the field to which they contributing, and part of their job is to document the previously published material that their own ideas are responding to. Moreover, some scholars reason that since their published work will be read mostly by other professional scholars, they don't need to bother with the clarity of the prose.

I'm a fan of intentional clarity. Like so many of the skills we have talked about in this textbook, clarity is not an accidental by-product of writing a lot. If it were, every publishing scholar would be a clear writer. Rather, clarity happens when we seek to make it happen. And the first and most obvious thing we need to say on this topic is that the clarity of a writer's ideas cannot emerge unless the writing itself is clear. Thus this chapter deals with three structural things you can do at the basic level—the stuff going on in the sentences, on the page—to add a pop of clarity so that your good ideas are free to shine. I want to show you a couple more usage errors that I frequently see in college writing. All of these have the same effect. They interrupt the flow and make me say, "Wait a sec. What—?" Then I have to double back for a second to figure out what the student writer is trying to say. I'm happy to report that I can almost always follow along, but wouldn't you rather propel the reader with your insightful analysis than detour the reader with fuzzy prose?

21.2 Proofing Your Work

Antecedence

The other pronoun errors we have discussed can hit your oral presentation, too, but this is one that most people won't notice unless they see it on your page. It's called an **antecedence** error. Basically it just means that you have created a moment of accidental pronoun confusion by failing to specify the person or thing you're referring to. Take this sentence:

> Sylvia Plath sets her poem in a psychiatric facility, creating a young female protagonist who struggles with depression. As we know, she is mentally ill.

Who is mentally ill, Sylvia Plath or the character? Grammatically speaking, the reader isn't just supposed to *assume* what the writer meant to say. The reader is supposed to go with what the sentence actually does say. Ah, grammar: such a black-and-white little world! The pronoun always refers back to the nearest noun that agrees in gender and number. In the sentence above, then, it's the *character* who is mentally ill because, when you traipse backward from the fuzzy pronoun *she*, the first actual person you find is *young female protagonist*. If you meant to suggest that it's *Plath* who is mentally ill, well, that's not what you said. The word *Plath* isn't the nearest preceding noun.

Your task as a writer isn't merely to think and create and respond. You actually have to take responsibility for craft at the sentence level, too. Even if your goal is modest—you aspire to get decent grades rather than book contracts—it is still your responsibility to anticipate pronoun confusion and clear it up when it happens. Clearing up the confusion often involves restructuring the sentence, moving things around so that the identity of the thing/person your pronoun refers to is crystal clear.

Even seasoned professional writers make antecedence errors. This is because when we are writing, we certainly aren't thinking about anything as lame as pronouns. Sheesh, we'd never get a thing written if we let ourselves be paralyzed by the inevitability of stray usage errors. *Of course* we're not thinking about grammar when we write. We're thinking about the thing we're writing about. Plenty of time to check for usage errors later.

Checking for usage errors

The preceding paragraph should alert you to the fact that there must be at least two phases for everything you write: the drafting stage and the proofing stage. I can suggest two ways to check your work for usage errors, if you don't count Grammarly. And I definitely do not. You wouldn't call yourself a mechanic and not know how to work on cars, would you? Owning a wrench doesn't make you a competent mechanic any more than Grammarly makes you a competent writer.

The first way to check for usage errors (providing you can recognize them when you see them) is to proof your own work. But this activity depends on wise time management:

1. Finish writing your draft at least one day before it's

due.

2. Read something else that has nothing to do with what you've just written, such as a news story about the discovery of many tiny Ice Age camels in Oregon.
3. Call a friend and tell her that you can apparently catch cold from camels. Who knew?
4. Come back to your document and read your work out loud.

I find that reading aloud is a reliable way to spot pronoun errors, especially those involving moments of ambiguous antecedence.

The other way would be to wheedle your buddy into proofing your work for you. This works really well if you are surrounded by friends who have PhDs in English. However, it may be contraindicated if you are surrounded by friends who are indifferent to pronoun errors or, worse, who confidently hypercorrect their pronouns. Whatever method you end up using to proofread your work before you turn it in, make sure you build in the time for this ultra-important step.

If you don't know whether you need extra work to get up to speed with issues at the sentence level, you might want to do yourself a favor and take responsibility for your own writing. How hard is it to just ask? It takes, what, thirty seconds? March right up to your instructor after class. "Professor, can you give me a heads-up if you see any grammar issues in my work that need attention?" Your instructor is much more likely than your peers to have accurate feedback on this front.

Warning: Peer review groups

One last thing about proofing. Red light, danger! Loud beeping noises, like a truck backing up in the alley! If you are in a composition class that uses Peer Review groups, do not attempt to use these groups to get your paper proofed. That is not what Peer Review groups are for.

Proofing a writing assignment is like personal hygiene. If the person wants to clean it up, he will make it happen without your assistance. If you are the kind of person who would love to point out a peer's misplaced modifier, I strongly urge you to hush the grammar mouth and focus instead on the task at hand.

Proofing is a personal responsibility, not a group task. It is a very different thing from giving an author feedback. Also, proofing comes as the very last step in the writing process. It comes *after* you get feedback on content and strategy. It comes *after* you have written a second draft that incorporates the feedback of your peers.

A Peer Review group is supposed to provide the opportunity to give and receive feedback on the big things, the main things, such as thesis and topic sentence, efficacy of introduction and conclusion, commentary on quotations and close analysis. The Peer Review group is supposed to help you rethink the first draft so that your second draft will be even better. The Peer Review group is not designed to be an editing service. Peer Review groups are not the time to identify issues at the sentence level. If a colleague in one of those groups tries to comment on your grammar, politely redirect the conversation. "But what do you think of my close analysis in the second paragraph? How could it be stronger?"

21.3 Misplaced Modifiers

Proofing a document out loud is also the only way to prevent pesky misplaced modifiers such as

| Applauding wildly, the tenor bowed to the audience.

When you're writing such a sentence, in your head it is perfectly clear that the audience is encoring the tenor. But something gets lost in translation between brain and keyboard. This sentence presents us with the ludicrous image of an opera singer who is wildly and enthusiastically applauding *himself.* I, for one, would really enjoy a self-affirming opera star! Misplaced modifiers are sillier than most usage errors. The reader tends to chuckle because a description has gone wonky. A chunk of extra information that is supposed to describe one thing has somehow gotten in the wrong spot, and thus it is describing the wrong thing.

Imagine if a standard adjective (a single word that describes something) got in the wrong spot:

| My passport eventually turned up in my jacket pocket lost.

The word *lost* is an adjective. But it's supposed to be describing *passport*, not *pocket*. The pocket isn't lost at all. It's in the jacket, right where you would expect it to be. But it sounds as if the pocket is lost, because *pocket* is the nearest preceding noun before the word *lost*.

It's the same with modifiers, which are merely longish adjectives in the form of a chunk of extra information. You can put modifiers anywhere in the sentence ... as long as they are next to the things they are supposed to be describing. Anywhere else will be a usage error, and if you snug that modifier up against some *other* noun, prepare to amuse your reader.

> **Calling me from work**, I told my husband I would hold dinner for him.

According to the sentence above, I am calling myself from work. That would be truly strange, would it not? Too bad the grammar of the sentence forces me to read it this way. Unfortunately, after the highlighted modifier, the very next word is *I*. If you think about it, of course, you do figure it out. I am not calling myself. It's my husband who is calling *me*, letting me know that he'll be late for dinner.

Misplaced modifiers speak of carelessness at best, laziness at worst. If you don't want your professors to think you are sloppy or lazy, remember: that essay ain't done until it's proofed.

21.4 Malapropisms

Mrs. Malaprop is the name of a busybody character in Richard Brinsley Sheridan's 1775 comedy of manners, *The Rivals*.[1] Her

---

1   Visit link: https://goo.gl/rHXNFh

Mrs. Malaprop in the Huntington Theatre Company's production of *The Rivals*

role is to provide comic relief. Her M.O. is to mix up two words with different meanings but similar sounds. "She is as headstrong as an allegory on the banks of the Nile!" she exclaims. What she means to say is, "She is as headstrong as an *alligator* on the banks of the Nile." The audience hoots at the thought of an allegory crouching low and dangerous like a reptile in its Egyptian habitat.

For a teensy pleasurable moment we are forced to imagine a ferocious scaly allegory, and maybe some menacing fables, hiding in stubborn congregation there on the Nile. That's supposed to be delightfully nutty. The audience in 1775 did laugh, and not just at the headstrong allegory. They chuckled at Mrs. Malaprop's every lame utterance through the whole play, each time her character came on stage. They laughed, we infer, because it's painful and funny to see someone overreaching. Mrs. Malaprop was ignorant, she was embarrassing—and, good lord, she didn't even know it! *That's* why folks laughed.

Thanks to Sheridan's character, the word *malapropism* was coined. When somebody soberly announces he has *prostrate* cancer, that's a malapropism. It is a malapropism to warn somebody about a wolf in *cheap* clothing, or to suggest that Michelangelo created a belletristic masterpiece by painting the *Sixteenth* Chapel. Recently while my husband and I were in bed singing southern spirituals, I paused to challenge his lyrics as he belted out "Swing Low, Sweet Chariot." Who was a-comin' after me, *a band of* angels, or *abandoned* angels? I argued that angels, an independent group, require no supervision. So why would be they abandoned? I mean, right? But my husband was not in the mood to discuss angelology. He was in the mood to sing, and so he nipped my argument in the *butt*.

You, a college student, may not yet have reached the stage of life where it is fun to sing in bed. But you have indeed reached the stage of life where you might want to sidestep malapropisms in your academic essays. Shakespeare actually used malapropisms a couple of hundred years before Sheridan's character made them memorable. When Shakespeare did it, he wasn't making fun of uneducated people. He was making fun of people who tried too hard to impress. Malapropisms may come from any honest mix-up of soundalike words. But the effect is sadly the same. They make your writing sound jejune.

Here's a double whammy I often see in freshman writing:

> It seems reasonable to imply that school uniforms would prevent bullying, but the problem does not lay in the

It seems reasonable to *infer*, not *imply*. And the problem *lies*, not *lays*.

Too bad there's no easy trick to teach us the difference between words that are often confused in college writing, *affect* and *effect*, *lay* and *lie*, *elude* and *allude*, and the like. Either you know the difference or you don't. If I were weak in this area, and if I had only limited time to give this issue, I'd narrow down the field to the single most problematic pair and work with that one until I got some victory.

Lay/Lie

And here it is, the single most problematic malapropistic pair. *Lay/lie* is the bugaboo of college students everywhere. By freshman year most students have given up, and I don't blame them. But grammar gatekeepers *will* blame them. The problem isn't the meanings. No, the meanings are clear. In fact the definitions are really easy:

> ▷ **lie: tell a lie; say something that isn't true**
>   I had a flatmate once who lied about having been Madonna's personal chef.

> ▷ **lay: put it down; set a specific thing down**
>   Lay the cylinder on top of the refractometer.

▷ **lie: recline, stretch out**
Dad is out back, lying in the hammock.

Most of us can nod at these three separate meanings. What's hard is tense. Watch how weirdness begins to happen when we scoot these words into the past tense.

	Today I ...	Yesterday I ...	I have often ...
To lie (tell a lie)	lie	lied	lied
To lay (set it down)	lay	laid	laid
To lie (recline)	lie	lay	lain

See the confusing overlap? On the day when verb tenses were decided, the genius who gave us *lay* and *lie* must have had an epic migraine. Poor fellow, he should have **lain** on the couch until he felt better.

My goodness, there goes America, nitpicking about the difference between *lay* and *lie*, when it could be focusing on more important things, such as funding Large Wild Cat preserves! At Cat Haven in Dunlap, California, it is certainly not the large cats' fault that sometimes they maul the volunteers. Cheetahs and mountain lions need love too! Let us pledge our emotional support to organizations such as Cat Haven, which are at least as consequential as the difference between *lay* and *lie*!

Preoccupied with their global vision for large-cat preserves, Americans have understandably defaulted to *lay*. They have neither the time nor the desire to learn the difference between *lay* and *lie*, and, given the sheer number of large cats who need our protection, who can blame them? Also, when it comes to rarely used participles such as *lain*, it is far easier to cover your mouth a little, as if clearing your throat, and move on.

Use *lay* when you are setting a thing or a person down somewhere.

| Lay the apron on the counter.

| The paramedic laid the child on the stretcher.

| In 2016 the critic laid out two competing interpretations.

Use *lie* when something or someone is stretched out, supine and horizontal.

| The apron is lying on the counter.

| The child was lying on the stretcher when she opened her eyes.

| The answer, said the critic, lay in a factor that had been overlooked.

The first step to figuring out *lay* and *lie* is the lightbulb moment when you suddenly go, "Wait a second ... are you saying that it is impossible to go to the beach and *lay out*?" Righto. Laying out is not an option, even with good sunscreen.

21.5 Two Tense Errors to Watch for in College Writing

A tense error works against you whether it comes from your mouth or pen. The good news is that a tense error almost never results in lasting confusion. Tense errors are more likely to result in a light pity, a condescension that falls gentle as snow. When I was your age, the number-one tense error to watch for was some version of *I seen it already*, a version of the present perfect tense that invoked an image of loose gatherings under the bleachers. The error seemed to ask, like the stoners of yesteryear, "Know where I can score an ohzee?"

Today the tense errors I come across in the writing of undergraduates fall chiefly into two camps. In my humble opinion, these two tense errors would be the ones to address for maximum impact. Even if you think of yourself as pretty strong grammatically, you might want to keep reading. Lots of students (and professors!) make these tense errors. I make them myself, unless I am paying attention.

Tense error #1: Ignoring the past perfect tense ("Lalalala, not happening!")

Let's draw a nice timeline called Tyler's Party.

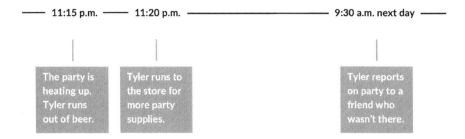

The next morning, when Tyler is talking to his buddy, he may want to describe how the party heated up so fast that he had to make a beer run before midnight. The party is now over, a pleasant memory. It started in the past, and it ended in the past. Thus if Tyler wants to talk about the party now, he must look back into recent history. We've got two actions, and both of them are in the past:

> ▷ an earlier action
>   (running out of beer)

> ▷ a later action
>   (going to the store)

Tyler's party was a good party, that's all. No hangovers, no decisions he regrets. The actions of yesterday evening do not impact the present, except that Tyler wants to talk about the party with his friend. Notice that the two actions that happened last night had a distinct relationship to one another. The earlier action started and ended before the second one even commenced. Therefore, Tyler correctly tells his friend, "I had to go to the store because we **had run out** of beer."

So many people ignore the past perfect tense altogether that I am going to make a prediction. I am guessing that the following sentence will sound okay to you:

> I had to go to the store because we ran out of beer.

To the grammar-savvy, though, that sentence confesses the underexposure of the speaker. Some grammarians suggest that the past perfect tense will soon become extinct, like the pterodactyl. Personally, I wish it Godspeed on its evolutionary course. But while this tense remains, which will probably be throughout your lifetime, I suggest that its correct use in your writing is crisply practical. So few undergraduates use the tense correctly (or at all) that your writing will soar breezily above the rest, like our friendly pterodactyl.

In a past perfect sentence you will always find the exact same relationship between actions that happened in the past. It doesn't matter whether the sentence is about something casual, like a beer run, or something ideological, like Foucault's social theory of panopticism. Once you get the relationship between past events, you get it. The second action didn't happen until the first one ended—it's that simple. Luckily there are no exceptions to the rule. So, to recap: when an earlier past action finishes before a second past action starts, we must use a past participle (had + past verb) for the earlier action.

> In December 2016 the journal *Current Biology* called attention to the discovery of a semitranslucent piece of amber about the size of a dried apricot. It contained the 99-million-year-old tail of a junior coelurosaur, a thero-

pod from the mid-Cretaceous period. Until its discovery, science **had never seen** a dinosaur tail with feathers.

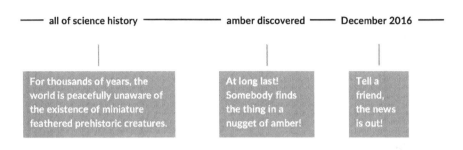

—— all of science history ——————— amber discovered —— December 2016 ——

| For thousands of years, the world is peacefully unaware of the existence of miniature feathered prehistoric creatures. | At long last! Somebody finds the thing in a nugget of amber! | Tell a friend, the news is out! |

A good writer clarifies chronology, tagging the earlier action with past perfect. Before scientists discovered the amber, they **had never seen** such a wondrous junior dinosaur!

The thing to remember is that you cannot trust your instinct here, because you hear this tense error so often that the usage error will sound just fine to the ear. I'll give you a good tense worksheet, but first let's look at the other tense error that sabotages otherwise good college writing.

Tense error #2: Surprise mistake when you're pretending

We reserve the right to speak and write about imaginary things. We like to speculate and pretend. Whom would we invite if we could ask any ten historical figures to a dinner party, and they would all show up with a bottle of wine and some flowers? What ten modern conveniences would we put in our Conestoga wagon for our pioneer trip on the Oregon Trail? When we write about pretend things, we use a special hypothetical tense designed for that purpose. To wit, at the imaginary dinner party I **would seat** Lao Tzu across from Martin Luther. The mistake comes when we use this special hypothetical tense. However, we typically make a usage error only with a certain verb, and only in a certain situation.

In my program at UCLA the grad students organized a game involving celebrity sightings. Points were awarded for fame, place, time, and celebrity activity at moment of sighting. For a while the record was televangelist Tammy Faye Bakker at a Marshall's, in the valley, on a Wednesday morning, with Bakker pushing a cart of discount merchandise and saying to the lucky grad student, who happened to be me, I mean I, "Dear, I wish I had some of your height!"

The famed Tammy Faye Bakker sighting

Some weeks later my Tammy Faye Bakker sighting got

bumped when a fellow grad student named Jake witnessed 90s rapper Ice-T in a Denny's at 2:00 a.m. on a Monday night. Jake was awarded maximum points because Ice-T happened to be ordering a Grand Slam pancake breakfast.

Who can beat Ice-T with pork links and a stack of buttery pancakes?

Ice-T remains securely in the lead until alert romanticist scholar Leilani, ordering an ice cream cone at the Baskin Robbins on Sunset, spies Warren Beatty in same. Leilani pays for her ice cream and runs outside to the car, where she madly texts everyone she knows that she has just seen Warren Beatty. Then she realizes she is so starstruck that she has left her ice cream cone in the store. She goes back in and says, "Excuse me, I think I left my ice cream cone—?"

Warren Beatty turns to her, smiling. "It's in your purse."

Which is to say, if you are not pretending—if that man

might really *be* Warren Beatty—then you say, If that man **is** Warren Beatty. If you are pretending, which Leilani clearly was not, you would say, If he **were** Warren Beatty.

I don't know about you, but I'm in the mood for some Mocha Almond Fudge. If I **were** at an ice cream store right now, I'd be tempted. Sadly, I am not in an ice cream store. I am sitting at my computer wearing my husband's pajamas. If my husband **were** to purchase better pajamas, perhaps I might wear them in public, on an ice cream run.

Grammarap

Create a new Word document and format it into two columns. Choose a rap song and type up the lyrics in the left column, citing recording artist and release date. Try to pick a song whose lyrics and message move away from the stylistic conventions of academic writing.

Now translate the lyrics, line by line, into the right column, using standard academic English, paying close attention to tone and grammar. Frame all content in language that is acceptable in an academic setting. You may have to free the lyrics of profanity, since most hip-hop/rap songs are not clean. You may have to invest significant thought into your grammar translation. The absence of conventional punctuation, coupled with the presence of prolix and generalized obscenity, will force you to ask, "What are these lyrics actually saying?" In such a way you'll see that bad grammar and sloppy language can obscure meaning. But you'll have fun doing it.

Finally, on an additional page that has not been formatted into columns, answer these questions in one paragraph:

▷ Assuming that the rapper's English differs substantively from standard academic English, we may analyze the rapper's grammar as proactive, deliberate, and argumentative (in the sense that the rapper's grammar actively controverts many of the standards that govern academic English). What argument is the rapper making? How do the rapper's grammatical choices propel this argument?

22

Style Rescue

22.1 The Development of Style

Have you ever heard a professor say that a student is a stylish writer? What a huge compliment, and rare. It *is* surprising when an undergraduate develops personal style. It's not that it can't be prioritized at this stage of your professional preparation, but many undergraduates are simply not aware of the big payoff that an investment in style yields.

And then, too, the development of style (which is a major part of the study of craft) takes a long time. There's a funny story about a writer at a cocktail party. A medical doctor asks the writer how his current book is coming along. "Great, thanks," says the writer. The doctor says, "You know, I've always wanted to write a book. One of these summers I'm just going to have to sit down and do it." The writer doesn't miss a beat. "You know, I've always wanted to become a medical doctor. One of these summers I'm just going to have to sit down and do it." The writer's point, of course, was that even as you cannot become a medical doctor in one summer, neither can you become a publishable writer in one summer. Unless you are a prodigious savant, you will probably agree that excellence requires time, and study, and mastery of craft. The development of personal style is a significant part of the craft, just as important as learning specific skills such as explication or comparison/contrast. And while style is an ongoing study, it can start now, here, in this class, at the beginning of your college education. The sooner you start working on style, the greater your chances of becoming a memorable, competent writer even during your college years. It's a practical investment no matter what your major is. You have probably figured out by now that style is one of the things that distinguishes an excellent grade from a good grade.

A charcoal sketch, a videography assignment, a calculus problem—all call for various kinds of language, if we use Bakhtin's definition of *language* as any sort of human communication. Writing, by definition, uses words. When you put words together, you've got speech. When you've got speech, you've got style. So while it is true that not all writers have *distinct* styles, all writers do have style. It might be boring, it might be predictable, it might be doing the bare minimum to pass a composition course. But it's a style.

That's not the thing the surprised instructor is complimenting. When you hear someone complimenting a writer's style, the compliment is this, in a nutshell: *Wow, this writing is the opposite of IMPERSONAL!* If the professor in question were to hear this essay read aloud by, say, the random guy at the pontoon party, and if the pontoon guy did not name names, the professor would still be able to tell whose writing it was. The giveaway wouldn't necessarily be the logic, or even the content. The giveaway would be the way the sentences flow, eddy, and tickle. The overall tone. The mood, the pizzazz, the fingerprint. The hand under memory's chin. The hard-to-name thing that makes the writing recognizably yours.

I can imagine a pre-law major or a biochem major immediately objecting: "But I don't want my writing to have personality! I want it to seem neutral, competent, and professional!" Neutral, competent, professional, gotcha. But consider this. The law firm, the research lab, is now reviewing 314 cover letters with attached writing samples. They have two positions to fill. All 314 writing samples are neutral, competent, and professional. All of them are grammatical. (Because the screeners have already chucked the ones that aren't! Note to self.)

Among 314 stellar overachievers, whose writing are they going to remember?

Yes. The writing with style. This is because style is the cherry on top of academic competence.

Many freshman composition classes don't even mention the development of style, as if it's a skill to be saved for much later, after everybody practices research papers and footnotes. Nonsense. Good style is *achievable for any writer*, not just for the occasional smartypants who aces an internship, not just for the quirky bard who publishes in the campus fine-arts journal. You qualify to develop style no matter who you are. And you start to develop it the moment you start working on it, whether in your freshman year or your senior year. You can be any sort of writer, from any tribe or nation, with any level of exposure or underexposure. The democracy of this process is actually sort of mind-blowing. Like the possibility of upward mobility, the option for developing style inheres in the very fabric of the American culture! You can be a non-native speaker, a comma-splicer, a pontoon partyer! You can be Jeremy Meeks, the unusually attractive felon who from time to time releases stylish photographs of himself to the media!

Mug shot of Jeremy Meeks

More glad tidings. The only thing you really need to develop your style is the same thing you need to get a college degree: a hearty combination of intention + practice. You can nail the grammar course. You can produce killer lab reports. You can get a gold star for a polished term paper. But you'd still need to train in order to develop style.

22.2   Selfies with a Larger Purpose

When I was in college, undergraduate writers were not encouraged to develop style. They were encouraged to deliver tidy term papers in bland but mechanically correct prose. So today's emphasis on style is a relatively New Deal, like what FDR would have funded, if only he had thought about it. Go ask your grandma if you don't believe me. She'll give you an earful about how it was considered wrong even to use the first-person pronoun "I" in an academic essay. Today we no longer pretend that the essay's writer does not exist. In fact, we collectively agree to admit that the writer of every paper brings to the task a unique set of individual biases, assumptions, and experiences that shape the writing.

Consider, if you will, the function of a selfie. A selfie says to the world, "Hey, this is who I am at this moment in time, this is what I'm doing right now, look at me!" Note the impromptu whimsy that defines the genre. It's not rehearsed, it's not staged. Your friends didn't show up in order to take a selfie. Snapping a selfie is an outcropping of some other activity, a casual and fun result of the reason you gathered with your friends in the first place. If you think about it, this change in how we see ourselves, and how we want to be seen, is the perfect national selfie of our times in the twenty-first

century. That's why the selfie genre seems so fresh and irresistible. It comes after a century of carefully constructed, pre-posed daguerreotypes, studio portraits, and media stills.

Are you fortunate enough to have faded historical photographs in your family? If so, think of those old-school formal wedding portraits of your great-grandparents, the ones where your great-granddad is standing, frowning, beside your great-grandma, she who sits there with about as much expression as an icebox. Shutter speed was part of the deal, of course. They had to hold still for the camera. But have you ever asked why they chose to hold still with a blankness, as opposed to a smile? We can only assume that your ancestors were normal people. In real life they didn't go around with an expression of emotional paralysis, as if a snake had bitten them and they had no opinion about it. No, your great-grandparents laughed just like you. They loved their partners, they sang the song about "Dinah Blow Your Horn", they scolded their kids for playing Poop Stick in the house.

The lack of expression in these historical photographs reveals the cultural values of the people who posed for them, just as the spontaneous goofiness of your own selfies reveals something about your own culture. The traditional Wedding Pose frames the husband as the standing authority (literally standing, ready for action, symbolically in charge) with the wife as the subordinate helpmate (seated, symbolically beneath her man). The lack of momentary, transient facial expression says, "This is our public face as a couple, and if we choose to sing "Dinah Blow Your Horn" very loudly in the privacy of our own bedroom, it is none of your business." Thus the photograph is a statement of a private identity intentionally concealed, even as it is a declaration of a public identity that accommodates mainstream gender roles and heterosexual norms, such as a white dress to signal the bride's virginity and a power tie to signal the groom's earning capacity.

My mom used to tell me that Great-Aunt Nellie had an epic behind. Not knowing anything about portraiture iconography, Mom and her sisters figured, giggling, that their Aunt Nellie was seated due to anatomical shame. As a little girl, I used to think that the size of her burden, and the weight of its sorrow, explained the stern expression. "On this my wedding day, my thoughts turn persistently to my robust buttocks."

Great-Aunt Nellie (left) in the selfie of yesteryear

Today's selfie makes its own statement of larger identity. The selfie says, "This is what I am doing/feeling right now, and by refusing to pose or plan the photograph, I am making a statement of my own authenticity. I am not reflecting who my culture wants me to be—I am reflecting my own thoughts and experiences."

This is dangerous stuff, all the more so because the experience of taking a selfie is usually fun, not serious. When something consequential presents as something trivial, look out! It pays to notice the larger meanings in the minutiae of everyday life. You can't get much sillier and smaller than taking selfies and posting them. To us in the twenty-first century the process seems healthy, just as keeping a journal must have seemed to our ancestors. Indeed, selfies are a form of visual record-keeping, and so much more: a shared language, a tool to build community, a refusal to conform, an assertion that we are okay with who we are. And while all of these things are great, a danger quickens when something becomes so natural that we do it without thinking. Ironic, eh? Of course we take selfies without thinking. In fact, that's the whole point—we're not *supposed* to think about them. We are purposely *unintentional*. It's exactly because this ideology is so pervasive that incoming college freshmen often have a hard time understanding the function of style in university writing, where style cannot advance *except by intention*.

College essay assignments never call for a selfie. Even the personal essay assignment is not a selfie because it asks you to make connections with what other people think and say. On the one hand, in college you may develop style in every kind of writing you do, whether traditional academic analysis or personal reflection. That sounds selfie-like, right? But on the other hand, the purpose of college writing assignments departs abruptly from the purpose of the visual selfie: to declare who you are to others. The purpose of college writing assignments is to *grow* who you are, not declare who you are.

So here's the first rule of thumb in developing style. If you post a fun tidbit, a thoughtful anecdote, a complicated personal narrative in your writing, your selfie must have a larger purpose. You can't use your selfie to say, "Hi everybody, this is what I think!" Instead, use it to connect your personal experience to a larger point that somebody else *has already made* about the world.

Developing style in your writing is a much bigger deal than including the odd snippet from your experience or the occasional juxtaposition of your own convictions against those of others. Training your style is actually a matter of the structural choices that sculpt your writing. Without strong style, you will still have a vehicle for your ideas. But without a distinct style, nobody will remember them.

23

Up Your Game by Avoiding These Five Things

23.1 Spotting the Problem

In *David and Goliath: Underdogs, Misfits, and the Art of Battling Giants* (2013), Malcolm Gladwell tells the story of a dad, Vivek Ranadivé, who, having no basketball experience, decided to coach his twelve-year-old daughter's National Junior Basketball team. With the exception of two committed players, Ranadivé's team members were less interested in playing basketball than in reading, science projects, ski vacations, and future careers. Gladwell describes Ranadivé's players like this: "They weren't all that tall. They couldn't shoot. They weren't particularly adept at dribbling. They were not the sort who

Malcolm Gladwell speaking at the 2008 PopTech! Conference

played pickup games at the playground every evening."[1] Read: these kids were not very good at basketball.

Given his players' divided interests and uneven skills, Ranadivé spent some time in serious observation. He noticed that the league's strongest teams, the ones with the tall players who could shoot and dribble well, were able to push their advantage when the weaker teams defended only a fraction of the physical space on the court. Ranadivé, from Mumbai, had fresh eyes to see that most of the American teams were defending only twenty-four feet of a ninety-four-foot court. When a weaker team defended only a fraction of the court, it was easier for the stronger team to practice all the skills that had made them better in the first place. Ranadivé decided that his players would no longer give away the advantage. No, his girls would play a full-court press every time, every single game. This meant

---

1   Malcolm Gladwell, *David and Goliath: Underdogs, Misfits, and the Art of Battling Giants* (New York: Little, Brown, 2013), 19–21.

that his players would go for it across the full length of the court, all ninety-four feet, trying to stop the stronger players from advancing the ball.

To everybody's surprise, Ranadivé's once-medium team ended up going to the national championships.

Malcolm Gladwell tells this story to illustrate how and why the little guy can win, an event, he notes, that happens statistically pretty often. Political scientist Ivan Arreguín-Toft crunched the numbers. In the past two hundred years of warfare, the less powerful country won 28.5 percent of the time, despite being outnumbered and disadvantaged. And the victory rate shot up to 68.6 percent when the underdog had the perspicacity to identify his own weakness and change up the strategy. That's what Ranadivé did. In order to strengthen his team, first Ranadivé had to notice the unhelpful things his team was doing. Isn't it amazing that the trajectory of an entire team could have experienced such an astonishing reversal in one season? **Spotting the problem and doing something different brought immediate results.**

Your writing instructor, like Ranadivé, can help you spot the problem. Your writing can improve right away. Here are five things you may be doing right now that are not helping you out. If you spot the problem and try something else, you too can see immediate results.

23.2   Trim Your Pairs

Here's a clever trick to know if you've written a shaggy sentence that needs a trim. How many pairs of words come marching two by two, like animals to Noah's ark? If your sentence has two pairs—a two-prong verb, a compound subject, two words that describe the same noun, two anything—it's time for a trim. Too many pairs in the same sentence dilute the oomph.

Which pair do you love? Keep that one. Then go back and whittle the other pairs down to singles, so the one pair that you like doesn't have to share the spotlight. When you start out writing a first draft, you're writing off the top of your mind, adding a little of this and a little of that. This pair, that pair, another pair over here! Before you know it, you have accidentally written a sentence that sounds puffy and fatigued:

> The toxic dangerous algae bloom that originated and spread in Lake Okeechobee, swiftly infecting other beaches and shores, has been caused by fertilizer sewage and manure pollution, and has resulted in a state of emergency and an environmental disaster in Martin, Lee, St. Lucie, and Palm Beach counties.

A good writer pays attention to word patterns that repeat too often and too soon. In the Okeechobee sentence, six clusters are spreading, not unlike the algae bloom.

| toxic and dangerous

| originated and spread

| beaches and shores

| sewage and pollution

| emergency and disaster

| Martin, Lee, St. Lucie, and Palm Beach

Let's say that of these six sibling clusters, the one that matters most to you is *sewage and pollution* because you think it's important to name both things that have produced the algae. Find the keeper. Now whittle down the remaining pairs to singles:

> Fertilizer sewage and manure pollution have caused the toxic algae bloom that has now spread from Lake Okeechobee to beaches in three counties.

Notice that your sentence gets it mojo back when you trim the pairs. A nice surprise feature is that trimming the pairs shortens the sentence, so you say more with less.

23.3 Bye-Bye, Passive

If you are interested in sharp, clear writing, know that you have to learn the difference between active and passive voice to get it. There are no shortcuts, alas. Since we all unconsciously default to the less admirable passive voice, we have to go out of our way to learn what active voice is and how to practice it. If I had to name just one sentence-level thing that represented mediocrity, it would be passive voice.

Please know that passive voice isn't a grammar issue. It's a style issue. Don't let anybody tell you that the passive voice is grammatically incorrect. It isn't. Passive writing often comes across as a grammar issue because it's another hallmark of high school writing. It is for this reason that so many college-level instructors identify passive-voice verbs as usage errors. Your instructors *want* you to bump it up a notch. In America passive-voice writing comes off as lackluster and weak.

Pretend for a moment that you are sixteen years old. You have just come home with a driver's license. Exultant and bold, you ask to borrow your dad's new Prius. He lets you. (Hey, it's an imaginary scenario.) Later that evening, briefly glancing at a text out of the corner of your eye, you suddenly slam on the brakes for a family of raccoons. The Prius rolls twice, whopping the guardrail and shattering the windshield. You, phone, raccoons: unharmed. The front end, the windshield, the guardrail: trashed.

Thankfully, all hypothetical raccoons left the scene unscathed.

It is now time to go home and 'fess up. Here is your dad,

wearing embarrassing short-shorts and a T-shirt that says

I USED TO BE ADDICTED TO THE HOKEY-POKEY THEN I TURNED MY-SELF AROUND

because that is what dads do. Perhaps he is also enjoying a liverwurst sandwich and playing air guitar. Perhaps he is merely clipping his toenails, there on the couch. The damage to the Prius will surely cost more than the $1,000 deductible.

Okay, deep breath. Which would you rather say?

> **Option #1, Passive Voice**
> "Dad, your car was wrecked."

> **Option #2, Active Voice**
> "Dad, I wrecked your car."

You'd rather go with the first one, right? This is because *Dad, your car was wrecked* buys you a tiny delay. For this one wee moment, this first option allows your dad to think that the wreck may not have been your fault. Option #1 invites a brief conjecture. Perhaps someone else wrecked the car! Perhaps the blame rests squarely on the itinerant raccoons! Perhaps your driving was excellent, your judgment sound, and your motor skills superb!

However, Option #2 puts it all right out there, front and center, with no possibility of anything other than taking full responsibility for your own poor decision making. I was the one who wrecked the car, Dad. I was the one who read a text while driving. Yup. I did that.

This is the difference between active and passive voice. In an active sentence, the subject does the action and the sentence spells it out. It's super-clear who does what [I wrecked it]. In the passive sentence, the opposite is true. The subject doesn't do the action. It just sits there and *receives* the action [Car was wrecked by somebody or something]. Thus the passive sentence creates an information delay. It stalls for time. It creates a convenient little tunnel of ambiguity.

When to go with active voice

American culture admires a straight-shootin' admission of agency. Have you ever heard the phrase popularized by President Harry Truman? He liked it so much that he kept it as a little sign on his desk in the Oval Office: THE BUCK STOPS HERE.

President Harry Truman with his famous "The Buck Stops Here" sign

I freely translate this as, "I will not blame other folks for my problems, like a weasel! No, I will accept full responsibility for what I have done!" The idea is that Americans and their sentences *ought* to prefer candor. If we wreck our dad's Prius, dang it, we should have the chops to say so!

This vision of American agency is why college instructors prefer the active voice, even when they are not English professors. And the cultural preference goes far beyond academia. Although few writers in the blogosphere practice the active voice with any degree of consistency, pretty much everybody prefers it. It makes your writing pop. It crisps things up. By contrast, passive sentences seem sluggish and furtive, as if they have something to hide, and as if they are too lazy to get up off of the couch and fix their verbs. They make the reader ask, Who's doing the action? So why isn't he taking the responsibility for the action that he himself decided to do? Think about cagey political sidestepping, about how often a politician's language hides behind the dodge of passive voice:

> The allegations of sexual misconduct have been documented and reviewed, and a committee has been organized to investigate the situation further.

Documented where? Reviewed by whom? Exactly who is on this mysterious committee, and who is in charge of organizing it? Sounds as if somebody is pursuing his constitutional right to say something without saying anything. Don't be that guy.

When to go with passive voice

Of course you can't announce human agency all the time, and there will be some occasions when the passive voice does make more sense than the active verb. For example, lab reports are much less interested in who did it than in what was done. A sharp college lab report would never say:

> An observation was made by the team that ontogenetic color change at sexual maturation can be considered as an identifying factor for an appropriate mate for some organisms.

No. Reed College cites an example of a well-written lab report with *this* as the first sentence of the abstract:

> Ontogenetic color change at sexual maturation can be useful in identifying an appropriate mate for some organisms.

This lab report doesn't care that the team is doing the observation. It doesn't care because it's *assuming* what is perfectly obvious: that humans are the ones conducting the observation. So the lab report isn't going to bother with all that. What it wants to know is what the ontogenetic color change is doing. Take a look at the report's second sentence, also well written.

▷ **Active subject does action**:
  Largus californicus individuals undergo two ontogenetic color changes.

Notice that even in science writing, the student writer is shooting for active voice whenever possible. I'm no scientist, but it's perfectly obvious that these *Largus californicus* individuals are busy. They are undergoing something! Looks as if Carey Booth Box, the author, has deliberately sidestepped the limp passive version, which would have looked like this:

▷ **Passive subject receives action**:
Two ontogenetic color changes <u>were observed</u> in *Largus californicus* individuals.

Largus californicus individuals are bugs that might make a humanities professor flap her hands and shriek in a little circle, helpful-like. Too bad her husband isn't home to squish them with his thumb while making his signature terminator noise:

Largus californicus (Bordered Plant Bug)

"Djjidge!" Yet human beings are not the only ones who can lay down an active verb. Things and ideas can be active too. In my world a *Largus californicus* individual might *infest, menace, scurry,* or *scoot under the stove.* I'm guessing that in a science class the *Largus californicus* individual is better behaved. Maybe he *changes, undergoes, manifests,* or *displays.* You just have to find the right active verb for the kind of writing your subject happens to be doing at the moment.

In sum, it may take some tweaking, but you can almost

always improve a sentence by changing the action from passive to active.

The Massive Passive

Few writing activities are as helpful as writing badly on purpose. Here is a game that invites you to invent a hideous hypothetical essay assignment. In partner pairs, imagine a preposterous, untenable, boring, outrageously ridiculous essay prompt. Here are a couple of gems my own students have proposed:

1. In a twenty-five- to thirty-page paper, analyze the evolution of pubic hair, paying special attention to Darwin's principle of evolutionary adaptation. Based on its history, what does the future hold for pubic hair? You may use any source, as long as you locate it on Wikipedia.

2. What is the social relevance of the demotion of Pluto from planet to celestial object? What are the moral and intellectual implications of this demotion as they relate to global warming and especially to the recent controversy surrounding Wal-Mart's alleged refusal to provide spousal insurance to same-sex employees between 2011 and 2013? Please confine your remarks to thirty pages.

Turn in your fake assignments, all of which your instructor will throw into a hat. Each team selects one of the silly essay prompts.

Now comes the fun part. Your assignment is to coauthor a single page from this hypothetical assignment. You may feel free to

---

quote from real or made-up sources. The catch is that every single sentence must be heavily passive, bloated like a tick.

For your general inspiration and reading pleasure, here are two excerpts that respond to the prompts above.

"Evolutionary Pubic Hair—You Wish!"

A startling development can be seen in prehistoric eras when body hair was thought to be prodigious, and when clothing was not yet needed. In *Our Friendly Pubes*, it is asserted by Bernard Slum that in certain cave drawings, freak amounts of pubic hair can be observed, a veritable explosion of hair that is clearly admired by all the figures in the drawings, including pets. It is further posited by Slum that the largest amounts of pubic hair can be correlated with sexual dominance. Indeed one of the female figures is presumed to be bowing down in respectful worship to the alpha male's hirsute pubic region. This can also be applied to our society, in which the Sasquatch, known for his shaggy personal hygiene, is still regarded with respect and enthusiasm.

"The History of Pluto: Demotion from Planet to Celestial Object"

Pluto's demotion was caused by many various aspects, all of which were mentioned by the panel of celebrity judges. Some quibbling was heard, however, with reference to three of the aspects—the fact that a decrease in the overall mass of the planet had been measured;

.the fact that a shift in Pluto's orbital pattern had been detected, and the fact that one fewer cosmic gas had been documented on its surface. It was whispered that at least one of the celebrity judges had remarked that Pluto's orbit was strained, its performance easily overlooked, and its legacy already all but forgotten. Another celebrity judge, who was rumored to be high at the time, was reported to have said, "Poor Pluto! It can't be blamed for Wal-Mart's bad behavior! And Pluto's remaining gases could really be considered kind of cute!"

Next session, bring two typed copies of your Massive Passive assignment to class. Give one to your instructor, who will train her eye like a lighthouse on one question, and one question only. "Is every sentence passive?" 10/10 if every sentence is passive!

Take the second copy and swap with another pair in class. Don't worry that the assignment is bad, the logic is bad, the thesis is bad. You can't try to make it smart because it ain't smart. What you can do is change every single passive verb to active. The instructor may want to invert the grading scale for the rewrites, taking off one point for every stray passive verb that remains.

My students enjoy the useful trifecta of this assignment, which taps creativity, presents a hearty style challenge, and uses collaborative learning.

Key for Massive Passive Prompts. All verbs are now active. [Note how the switcheroo shortens the paragraphs, which, though still ridiculous, are much tighter.]

Pubic Hair

A prehistoric cave drawing depicts an image of a nude, hirsute *Homo erectus*. In *Our Friendly Pubes*, Bernard Slum notes an exaggerated amount of pubic hair on the focal figure, an alpha male. All other figures in the drawing, including pets, cluster around him; therefore, Slum correlates abundant pubic hair with social and sexual dominance. Indeed one of the female figures bows down, venerating the alpha male's hirsute pubic region. Traces of this veneration appear even today, in contemporary portrayals of the shaggy Sasquatch. Sightings of the mythical predator inevitably pair descriptors of hairiness with size and strength.

Pluto

The panel of celebrity judges cited several reasons for Pluto's demotion. However, they disagreed on three points: the decrease in Pluto's mass, the shift in its orbital pattern, and the number of surface gases. One judge remarked that Pluto's orbit was strained, its performance unremarkable, and its legacy irrelevant. Another observed, "Poor Pluto! We cannot blame it for Wal-Mart's decision to settle the lawsuit regarding its putative failure to provide spousal health benefits to same-sex employees between 2011 and 2013. And Pluto's remaining gases are kind of cute!"

23.4 Squeeze the Sponge

If it's obvious, don't say it. The light of your personal voice cannot shine if you hide it under a bush of phatic phrases. I strongly recommend self-editing, even in your fun writing. It is only through practice that you train your prose to concision. The more practice, the easier the concision. Over time it becomes downright pleasurable to squeeze the sponge. Let's say that in an email you tell a friend:

> I was thinking in my head that true altruistic heroes, like that guy Sully who landed the plane in the Hudson, are pretty rare.

Any words or phrases that don't need to be there? Sure. You can omit *in my head*, for starters. Where else would you be thinking, in your foot? Second, you don't even need the first part at all. The punch line of the sentence isn't your thought process or where it occurs. The punch line is the rarity of heroes.

In a first draft we all write whatever comes out of our heads. But a good writer always reads over every sentence for function. If you know what a sentence is trying to do, make sure it does that thing. In a sentence that's supposed to be about Sully's heroic landing, how about you focus on Sully's heroic landing rather than on your own thought process?

> True altruistic heroes, like that guy Sully who landed the plane in the Hudson, are pretty rare.

Better!

23.5 Don't Get All Fancypants Until You Know Your Business

Nobody ever mentions this, and someone needs to. Here goes. Your academic success in college won't depend on sounding smart. It will depend on *being* smart. Your professors can tell the difference. Thus you don't want to create sentences whose pants are too fancy. You've heard the expression *too big for his britches?* Check out this gem:

> One of the many stereotypes that scrutinize the body for reification of abstract ideologies appear in the "community" discourse, which disappears from the discourse of the individual alltogether.

Part of the problem here is that the grammar is a bit wonky. Let's say, though, that your reader can chill with subject-verb agreement errors. Also the reader is willing to take the misspelled adverb in stride. Yet even if we discount the usage errors, the sentence is *still* hard to follow. This is because the writer is attempting to be smart rather than clear. What is this sentence even trying to say? Here's my best guess.

> We project cultural ideas onto the human body.

Most academic subjects require us to stretch our vocabularies as we develop expertise in new areas. That's a good thing. But there's a fine line between deploying a competent vocabulary and using jargon to show off. A pyrotechnic vocabulary is fine if that's where you want to go. I can think of many successful published critics and scholars who are famously "difficult," meaning their writing is way harder than it needs to be. But I urge you to make sure you have steps one and two under your belt before you start dazzling your reader with highfalutin words (reification, discourse).[2] First you need to clear the underbrush (step one). Then you need to clean up the grammar (step two). If you prematurely try to display an erudite vocabulary *while making grammatical errors*, your reader will smile. That's not the effect you're going for.

After you have achieved basic competence, though, you are free to develop your vocabulary style as you please. You can even do what the poet Wallace Stevens did. He used his lunch break to scour the dictionary for new words. This always makes me feel sad. However, he did become one of the greatest poets of the twentieth century. So there's that. I wish I didn't always remember his effortful lunch hour when I am reading one of his poems, though. Didn't he have any friends he could grab a sandwich with?

23.6 Downplay the Expletive

Here we're not talking about angry oaths or interjections. We're talking about a certain type of sentence with a low-energy **expletive construction**, meaning a sentence that wastes space with a dummy subject up at the front. The sentence

---

2   There's a word that means "a person who enjoys using real whoppers." I am not making this up: *sesquipedalian.*

eventually gets around to naming its real subject, but it takes its own sweet time about it. It doesn't have much forward momentum because its sole purpose is to declare the existence of something. In other words, it's not saying what the thing does or causes, only that it exists.

| There is a trick to peeling garlic.

| There was a free-love movement in the nineteenth century.

With both of these examples, you can probably intuit what the next sentence will offer. We expect to see, respectively, the actual trick to peeling garlic and an elaboration of free love in the nineteenth century. These expletive constructions happen constantly and naturally in our writing because we need a little stepping-stone between what we've just been talking about and the point we would like to make next. Sentences that declare existence are not grammatically wrong, just flat, like a balloon before you blow it up. That's why I try to keep a lid on the number of sentences that start with these phrases:

| There is

| There was

| There are

| There were

On the one hand, expletive structures make your writing seem easy and casual, like natural speech. On the other hand, they don't achieve very much compared to sentences in which the real subject begins the sentence.

If all the sentences in your essay were riding a tandem bicycle, these would be the slackers not doing any actual pedaling. When I'm proofing an essay before I send it to a publisher, I always check for existential overload. Kierkegaard would be proud.

24 Up Your Game by Doing Five Things on Purpose

24.1 Alternate Your Sentence Length

At this time I would like to suggest five quick fixes that will dramatically improve your style. In the last chapter we looked at a couple of things you could stop doing. Here we're moving in the other direction. These are five things that you can proactively do for immediate results. But you have to do them on purpose, because they don't happen gradually, all by themselves.

Long sentences are part of the academic game. We're all thinking in complicated ways about our material, and it makes sense that our sentences would have complicated syntax to reflect that. But change it up. If you've got a long sentence, make the next one short-n-sweet.

Many students overuse the same ho-hum declarative

rhythm because they have never realized that it is their responsibility to make variety happen. Variety does not happen all by itself. I know a woman who claims that her husband fixed a tuna sandwich for lunch every day ... for *twenty-six years*. You do not want to turn your college essays into twenty-six years of tuna sandwiches. The time has come to try a muffuletta. Varying the sentence lengths doesn't cause the development of personal voice, but it **frees up the prose so that the development can happen**.

24.2 Switch up Sentence Types

English writing has what we call four modes. If you use these modes well and richly, they will help you pace your work. This means that you will be able to speed your readers up, as if by magic, just where you want to create momentum, and slow them down just where you want to pause for a Big Moment. The four types of sentences add four different flavors. All sentences fit into one of these four categories.

Declarative

Declarative sentences make a basic statement with a period. If this mode sounds bland, it can be, unless you intentionally maximize its opportunities. Interestingly, of the four sentence types, the declarative actually offers the most internal variety. You can radically alter the internal rhythm of any declarative sentence depending on where you put the extra information. Check out two declarative sentences that say the same thing with different rhythms:

> In the seventeenth century sometimes a lady might nestle a crabapple into her armpit for up to two months, then wrap and send the crabapple to her fiancé, who would sniff it as a promise of amorous pleasures to come.

> A crabapple nestled for eight weeks into a lady's armpit made a sensuous gift to a seventeenth-century fiancé; as a promise of sensual pleasures to come, the crabapple hinted at the erotic intimacies of the marriage bed.

Either one of these declarative sentences would educate readers vis-à-vis the elusive armpit apple, but one sentence might be preferable depending on the rhythm of the preceding sentence. If the previous sentence begins with an extra-information phrase that sounds like *In the seventeenth century*, then you could go with the second declarative sentence, for the sake of rhythm and pacing.

Interrogative

Interrogative sentences ask a question:

> Didn't the armpit apple stain the lady's dress?

> At what stage in the courtship would you send an armpit apple?

> What if the apple got all brown and nasty while in the lady's armpit?

Imperative

Imperative sentences give a direct command to the reader or listener:

> Note the unapologetically erotic role of body odor in Elizabethan culture.

Exclamatory

Exclamatory sentences deliver a pop of emotion or a rousing call to action:

> You should surprise your partner with an armpit apple today!

The Monotonous Conversation

Your instructor will begin by dividing the class into groups of three or four. Each group chooses a scribe to keep tally. If you have six groups, jot down six intriguing situational topics that might come up in casual conversation, for instance:

▷ Your brother is a struggling actor who just got offered the part of a Q-tip in a commercial. Should he take the role?

▷ You recently met a guy at a party who, over the course of the evening, revealed that he was King Tut.

▷ On the third date it is time to reveal to your new romantic interest that you keep ghost-busting equipment in the trunk of your car.

▷ Your mom's friend recently came back from international travels with a tapeworm. You witnessed this tapeworm in a jar. And the mom's friend seemed kind of proud of her souvenir.

▷ You accidentally claimed the wrong suitcase at the luggage carousel—check it out, the identical suitcase you claimed was full of unopened boxes of saltine crackers.

▷ At your college there's a guy who is trying to make it through all four years without spending a single dime, aside from tuition. People give him hand-me-downs and rides and so on. Mooch or visionary?

Each group picks a topic out of a hat. The instructor will time you, one minute per round. The object is to keep the conversational shuttlecock in the air, with each speaker uttering only declarative sentences, for starters. The scribe keeps tally: How many on-topic declarative sentences are produced as a part of a reasonable social exchange?

It's harder than it looks. Let's say the group has selected the saltine crackers scenario. The conversation must proceed with none of the usual syntactical variety that would typically mark such an exchange—no questions, no exclamations, no imperatives. Like this:

▷ "At JKF I accidentally claimed a suitcase that looked identical to mine."

▷ "That's a major bummer."

▷ "It was filled with fourteen unopened boxes of saltines."

▷ "It would have been much weirder if the boxes had been opened."

▷ "Homeland Security probably opens many food items in the line of their patriotic duty."

▷ "I don't care for saltines."

▷ "Many people, perhaps Homeland Security workers, find them an economical snack."

▷ "Frankly, I prefer Cheez-Its."

As you can see, the syntactical challenge invites a freewheeling discursivity as students struggle to tether the declarative mode. It is the scribe's job to tally responses at the end of the round and to eliminate any responses that stray too far afield from the previous comment.

The instructor collects the six scenarios, shuffles them, and distributes to each group a new scenario. The second round, the interrogative mode, is harder because we do not base our social interactions exclusively on questions. An added bonus is that this round offers an homage to the dialogue in Tom Stoppard's *Rosencrantz and Guildenstern Are Dead*:

▷ "Did you hear about my mom's friend's tapeworm?"

- ▷ "She didn't pick it up locally, did she?"

- ▷ "Haven't you ever heard of getting an intestinal parasite while traveling abroad?"

- ▷ "How did she know that she had a tapeworm?"

- ▷ "Do you really want to hear this story while we're eating dinner?"

- ▷ "Why did you start it telling it, then?"

- ▷ "Are you accusing me of bad manners?"

- ▷ "Dude, am *I* the one who wants to discuss tapeworms over a plate of cavatappi?"

You wouldn't think that the interrogative mode would so speedily devolve into hostility, but, in a related tribute to Chinua Achebe: Things Fall Apart.

The imperative and exclamatory rounds are more challenging still. Trying to converse using these modes provides a helpful illustration of what to avoid in academic discourse and why. I always give my students the option of sidestepping exclamatory mode, because a conversation that consists entirely of exclamations is absurd. And yet the absurdity is exactly why students want to try it. We all know that academic discourse rests on reason, not emotion. Thus it makes sense that the notion of shouting in a college classroom might come as a welcome relief. Everybody secretly wants to shout in college, and who can blame them? Alas, nobody gets very far with exclamatory mode. The scribes have to be quick on the draw with the censor, like Tipper Gore.

▷ "I can't believe that my brother is auditioning for the role of a Q-tip!"

▷ "What an egregious insult to his humanity!"

▷ "Hollywood blows, man!"

▷ "Your brother ought to change his major to marine biology!"

▷ "Not marine biology again!"

▷ "Eff you!"

▷ "No, eff YOU and the seahorse you rode in on!"

An alert scribe would refuse to tally the last two remarks. These get the boot for two reasons. One, they aren't even exclamatory. Technically, they're imperative, commanding the conversant to perform a specific task. Two, times may be a-changin', but obscenity is still taboo in academic writing and college classrooms alike.

24.3 Maximize the Rhetorical Question

One of the hallmarks of high school writing is the strained rhetorical question as first sentence. Somebody out there is telling high school juniors that it's a good idea to get the reader's attention by opening with a rhetorical question, like this:

| Have you ever considered the Peace Corps?

| What would society be like without social media?

| Should cannabis be federally legalized?

Or perhaps

| If the world were to end in two months, would you have
| enough canned goods for the Apocalypse?

Understand, there's nothing wrong with rhetorical questions. On the contrary, they can play a very useful role in our thinking and our writing. They really do help get the ol' ball rolling. So the problem isn't using them. The problem is putting them in the wrong spot. The problem is thrusting them into the limelight, with poufy hair and lipstick, like Honey Boo Boo.

A rhetorical question is probably not the best way to open a discussion because it sounds contrived and artificial. Would you approach a stranger and say, "Sir, have you considered the connection between poverty and crime?" Please don't do that. And don't do it in your writing either. Instead let your rhetorical questions arise naturally out of a discussion that's already underway. Check out this rhetorical question, tucked into the middle of a discussion about Toni Morrison's provocative short story "Recitatif." The story describes a friendship between two girls of different races, Twyla and Roberta. The text never specifies who is Caucasian and who is African American. Pretty soon readers figure out that it's a head-scratcher *on purpose*.

> It's true that in this story we do not know who is black and who is white. But what do we know? We know that the text offers many hints concerning the racial identity of Twyla and Roberta. Some seem to point to Twyla's whiteness; some, to her blackness. What they all do, however, is force the reader to acknowledge that the seemingly irresistible project of assigning a racial identity invokes a series of stereotypes that depict African Americans in a negative light. Thus when the story withholds information about racial identity, Morrison is not saying that race doesn't matter. She's saying that it matters *so much* that we can't create identity without it.

Would you have noticed the rhetorical question if I hadn't called your attention to it? ["But what do we know?"] It was subtle, yes? This is what a rhetorical question ought to do. It ought to usher in further thought without calling awkward attention to itself. Because this rhetorical question is short and to the point, it actually speeds the reader up. The writer is therefore controlling the pace of the discussion. And that's a good thing indeed.

24.4   Vary Your Punctuation

You've got to do this on purpose, too. And to do that, you need to know the vibe associated with each piece of punctuation, not just the grammar rules. I personally feel that your texts and tweets should be a gorgeous free-for-all, with no rules except courtesy. Life is short, splice your commas! Go ahead, bust out a little frownie face, or that cryptic emoji that looks like a sherpa! However, here is an important heads-up. If in your fun writing you do not make it a habit to practice correct punctuation, then in your academic writing you'll be more likely to get it wrong.

Academic and professional writing relentlessly demands serious punctuation. Although I myself might enjoy some more pep in our academic writing—say, some emoticons along with the footnotes, a rabbit trail here and there—I suspect that most professors would not share my enthusiasm. The general expectation is, Do not sprinkle commas in randomly, like pepper.

Semicolon

Use a semicolon to hook up two stand-alone sentences. But not just any two. Both need to have the same degree of importance. A semicolon is like an equal sign. It says, "Now allow me to communicate two significant and related thoughts." Whatever comes in front of the semicolon is important; whatever follows it is equally important.

The vibe is formal and academic-sounding. The semicolon is wearing a tweed jacket. It might mention that it went to school on the "East Coast." If you display many semicolons, you will sound like a newbie trying too hard to sound smart. Useful tip: one per page, no more. A little tweed goes a long way.

Colon

Use a colon in two ways:

▷ to introduce a list

▷ to introduce a second sentence that is more important than what you've just said

> Virginia Smith cites a French architect who in 1626 explained why civilized people no longer needed to take or build baths: the linen undergarment had made bathing utterly unnecessary.[1]

The part about never taking a bath is more momentous than the part about the French architect. So the colon functions like a drumroll for the star of the sentence, which is the linen undergarment that mercifully allowed folks to stop bathing. Taking a bath, besides being inconvenient, would bring on the chilblains and the pox.

Dash

Use a dash in three ways:

▷ to add on some interesting little bit

> When a man named D'Argens refused to quit his trusty linen undershirt for four years, they had to peel it off him—removing his skin with it.

▷ to attach a full sentence, a whole separate thought

> King Louis XIV rarely took a bath—but his atten-

---

1   Virginia Smith, *Clean: A History of Personal Hygiene and Purity* (New York: Oxford University Press, 2007), 193.

dants rubbed him down with scented linen cloths.

▷ to open up your sentence and plop down an extra bit
  into the middle of it

  Fustian—a new mix of linen and wool—eventually
  became a staple of the peasant class, who never
  had access to the fine linen undershirts worn by the
  aristocracy.

As you can see, the mood of the dash is much more casual. In fact the vibe is so casual that you want to be careful. A dash can make you seem scattered and disorganized, as if you can't manage to say what you want to say in the first sentence, and so have to add it on as an afterthought. If you make it a habit to use dashes in the middle of the sentence, know that the cumulative effect will be one of interruption. Don't interrupt yourself too often. That will make you seem like a dog who gives chase to every squirrel.

In sum, do use dashes, even in very formal writing. You want the variety. Just don't use too many, and don't use them the same way all the time. One per page. Keep that dog on a leash.

Parentheses

Use parentheses in two ways:

▷ to insert in-text citations that document your content

  The dust of Homer's decomposing corpse in Emily's bed is foreshadowed by the "faint dust" that ris-
  es "sluggishly about [the aldermen's] thighs" when

they sit down on her couch (Faulkner 174).

▷ to add something that seems slightly tangential but relevant enough to include

Emily's illness results in a distinct shift in public perception. After the illness the townsfolk compare her to one of "those angels in colored church windows—sort of tragic and serene" (139). Emily's new nobility rests in part on a perception of goodness and beauty (angels in stained-glass windows). But Faulkner's language suggests a double reading, as it associates Emily, a white southern belle, with African Americans ("colored church windows").

The vibe for parentheses is chatty, as if you have a lot to say and can't wait until the next sentence to say it. For this reason make sure your parenthetical remark doesn't create extra work for your reader. If you launch a parenthetical aside smack in the middle of your sentence, it will be hard for the reader to pick up the original thread again. Here is an example of what not to do:

None of the townsfolk ever question Emily's long relationship with her "manservant," Tobe. However, modern readers wonder whether Tobe was actually the one who killed Homer (Faulkner's clever allusion to *Hamlet*: "Tobe or not Tobe?"), in order to please his mistress.

It's smart to say that thing about Tobe or not Tobe, but put it at the end of the sentence, where it belongs. Parentheses are the orange cone in the middle of the road. Necessary from time to time ... but they do interrupt the flow.

24.5 Change the Subject

This tip is really useful when you are writing an academic paper that keeps coming back to a specific movement, idea, or person. It's the kind of thing you, the author, might not notice. Your reader will, though. A little minor tinkering with the subject adds a freshness and makes a preemptive strike against the accidental repetition of same-sounding word choices. You might want to take a look at your cover letter, assuming you have one saved on your computer. A typical cover letter might start out something like this:

> Dear Human Resources Representative:
>
> I am currently a health care professional, and I am seeking a full-time position in an assisted-living facility.
>
> I have two years of relevant experience at Rest Haven, where I am a steady and reliable employee. I care deeply about clients, and I treat everyone with equal respect.

As you read this snippet, you are probably struck with a deeply familiar feeling. "Sounds just like all cover letters. That's what cover letters sound like."

No, that's what *average* cover letters sound like.

The purpose of a cover letter is to foreground information about the person seeking employment, so by definition the speaker does need to be talking about self. But watch out. The semantic subject (I) relentlessly invites the same grammatical subject (I), and unless you are paying attention, your cover letter (or essay on Émile Durkheim) will sound repetitious. Your mission in any piece of writing that demands a sustained focus on the same subject is: inject variety to prevent overkill. *I am ... I am ... I have ... I am ... I care ... I treat.* You're at six for six.

Dear Human Resources Representative:

I am seeking a full-time position as a health care professional at an assisted-living facility.

My two years at Rest Haven signal both my steadiness and reliability. Resident care requires respect and cheerful assistance with mobility, meals, and personal hygiene. My supervisor and the residents themselves will affirm that I provide these things, and more.

Now we have *I am ... years signal ... care requires ... supervisors and residents will affirm.*

All you have to do is get in there with a highly visible red or green marker and circle the repeating subjects. Then reduce them by 75 percent. This easy strategy makes a big difference in the maturity of your writing voice.

25 Humor as Paradigm Shift

25.1   An Ending with a Twist

Many composition textbooks work up to the same big finish, ending with a section on how to write a longer research paper. Such information is splendid and useful, but I have two reasons for taking a different approach. The first is that you have already been practicing many of the skills you need to launch a college research paper—how to quote, how to follow up a quoted passage with close analysis, how to craft a central argument, and so on. The second is that while I respect the project of gathering, documenting, and integrating information, I believe there is a skill equally important.

This skill has more to do with insight than information, and sometimes it doesn't get much airtime in composition classes. That's why I've decided to end this textbook with a discussion that some students and instructors might not expect. In this sense, the last two chapters function as an ending with a twist. It is a twist that intends to satisfy rather than surprise. I do not mean to suggest that the protocols of library research are unimportant. On the contrary, they are vital to your education. But I invite you now to shift your focus from what you are learning to *why* you are learning it.

25.2 Humor as Prophylaxis

Humor is like the other skills we have discussed and practiced in this textbook. You rarely use just one writing strategy as the sole basis of organization for a piece of academic writing. Most essay assignments call on you to blend various writing strategies and techniques. Like explication or personal writing, humor is helpful here and there. And like explication and personal writing, humor is something you can learn.

Stop right now and take a second to think of a couple people you personally know who don't seem to have a sense of humor. They don't laugh, they seem uptight. Would you want a romantic partner like that? Would you want a friend like that? Would you want to be like that yourself? If the answer is a triple no, then why would you want to write like that? If you have a sense of humor as a part of your real personality outside school, then the goal should be to narrow the gap between who you are in your personal life and who you are on paper.

Understand, I am not advocating crass humor in your college essays. College-level discourse is polite, mannerly, and self-aware. This will not be changing anytime soon, and neither will the professional discourse that comes after graduation. If you think it's hilarious to belch the alphabet, fine: knock yourself out in the privacy of your dorm room. When I talk about learning the craft of humor, I am in no way suggesting that we defy appropriate academic protocol.

Like the deliberate civilities recommended by etiquette, intentional humor functions as a helpful lubricity in your writing. It is the spoonful of sugar that makes the medicine go down. But the most challenging thing about humor is knowing when to use it. The biggest mistake is to limit it to occasion or genre. That's understandable, since in college we are anxious to be taken seriously as competent thinkers. Yet humor is not an all-or-nothing proposition. You'll come across writing assignments in which you would *expect* to use humor, and in which humor is perfectly cricket. Who would disagree, for example, that humor might enrich a creative nonfiction essay, a personal anecdote, a poem, play, or short story? You'll also come across plenty of assignments that do not ask for humor but that would be the more memorable for its judicious use.

Humorous moments in academic and professional writing are rarely haha knee-slappers. One-liners, jokes, and gags are not very useful in academic writing. The kind of humor we're talking about lends depth and subtlety. It attaches to outlook and perspective. It enhances and matures the academic voice.

Humor is a prophylactic against earnestness. Writers want to seem reliable and sincere, and success in college is a serious business. Yet the quickest way to alienate your reader is to take yourself *too* seriously. How can you tell when the speaker is overly earnest? Ah, it's what's absent rather than present: an overly earnest speaker is marked by an utter lack of humor, which often makes the speaker seem closed, strident, and self-righteous.

Remember Carrie Nation, the radical temperance advocate who took it upon herself to smash up saloons with a hatchet? Between 1900 and 1910 Carrie Nation was arrested thirty times for what she called "hatchetations." Carrie Nation was a formidable woman. Standing six feet tall, she'd stride off the street into a saloon, hatchet at the ready. To the bartender she'd say in a cheery yet businesslike voice, "Good day, Destroyer of Men's Souls!" Then she'd get busy with the ax. Also she would sing and pray while she did the deed.

Carrie Nation ca. 1910

I'm not saying Carrie Nation could have destroyed more saloons if she had had a sense of humor. But I am saying that a passion for a cause could have garnered a more sympathetic response had she been a teensy bit more self-aware.

▷   Irony: funny.
▷   Sanctimoniousness: not funny.

No matter how just your cause, how good your intention, how sharp your ax, writing a hatchetation is not likely to advance your case. A good argument needs to be earnest. But not too earnest.

25.3   Five Practical Strategies to Develop Humor in College Writing

Focus: Self or others?

If your humor principally targets another writer or group, your writing will swiftly devolve into biting satire. Humor doesn't need a specific "target"—that is, somebody to rue or mock. That is, you don't need to serve up a snarkfest in order to inject judicious humor into your writing. Humor can be proactive; it doesn't need to be merely reactive. However, if you insist on choosing a specific target, I suggest that you take the opportunity to target your own foibles, regrets, and mistakes.

If you are poking fun at what you once did or thought, it means you have grown enough to be self-aware about the former condition and about the ways in which you have changed since then. When *other* folks become the exclusive target of humor, the writing suddenly picks up a rolling savage snap, as if the writer is more mean-spirited than insightful, more caustic than kind. Nothing says, "Will you help me carry my personal baggage?" like a sardonic piece of writing. Targeting the self provides evidence of growth. Targeting others suggests lack of it.

Where to stop

It's impossible to know when to stop on the first draft. Keep writing. Then go back and find the best part. Rearrange the humorous passage, if necessary, to locate the best bit or funniest locution at the end of the paragraph.

The other day I met Donna out walking her dog. Donna is one of those folks who disclose odd things at surprising times. "They call me the Plant Whisperer!" she might abruptly confide, or "I have a welt on my shin!" I do my neighborly best with disclosures like these, but sometimes I'm not sure how to respond. On this occasion Donna reported that she and a group of friends had recently dressed up for a night on the town. "So there we were, six middle-aged women all dolled up outside Sophronia's. Suddenly a police officer turns on his siren and starts flashing his lights at us—"

"But why?" I asked. "It's not illegal to hang out in front of a restaurant."

"Oh, it was a huge joke!" Donna's grin broke into a chuckle. "The officer was teasing us. He says, get this, he says, 'Are you *ladies of the evening*?'"

I smiled politely.

"*Ladies of the evening*, he says! Because we were dressed up in fancy dresses! Six women, all in their fifties, in short skirts and high heels! *Ladies of the evening*!"

"Sounds like a great evening out."

"Well, when we got to our table, we couldn't stop laughing! We laughed all night! We laughed so hard, we had to tell the people at the next table why we couldn't stop laughing!"

Guess you had to be there.

Never explain that something is funny. Doing so takes

you past the best moment. For example, don't narrate a personal anecdote and then follow it up with a short commentary on why you thought that experience was rich. That's an example of what we call **overwriting**, writing beyond where you should have stopped.

Nor should you ever use your writing to explain why another writer or text is funny. If you want your reader to see the same humor you saw, quote or cite the humorous text, then finish with the usual close analysis required by good academic prose. If you didn't need anyone to explain the humor to you, neither will your reader.

Syntax and pacing

A humorous passage planted inside a piece of academic writing requires stewardship. Pace it, punctuate it, with care. Humor needs to sneak up on the reader. So move fast. No long sentences, no big words. If your sentences come onstage dressed in semicolons and colons, you're just asking for a wardrobe malfunction.

Surprising configurations

Compare stuff to other stuff. Metaphor is one of the things that sets us apart from the animals. It speaks to our highest longings, our deepest human nature. We yearn to name the unnamable, do we not? This is why we so often say what something is *like*. Yet the very act of coming up with a simile acknowledges that the two things are deeply different, in spite of their shared commonality. A woman called *Honey* by her partner is a living, breathing girlfriend. She is not honey, an inanimate viscid material elaborated out of the nectar of flowers by various bees. Her partner has called her Honey because she's sweet.

An alert listener notices that the partner's comparison, like the bee, is actually working pretty hard. The term *Honey* trails some unspoken associations that act to define the partner's affection. Honey is precious. Honey is delicious. Presumably the partner would like to consume honey, to taste honey ... you see where this is going. The great power of metaphor is the power of suggestion. The great power of metaphor is all the stuff you *don't* say, in addition to the stuff that you actually do say.

Thus an alert use of metaphor is a terrific way to expand the scope of your writing and to manage its emotional tone. Our view of the romantic relationship changes with just one word, a single metaphor. We may infer that this relationship is consensual, but other than that, we don't know a single thing about it. We don't know if Honey is old, young, gay, straight, or prone to hatchetation. But notice how even a one-word metaphor can independently direct our vision. Our idea of the partners' relationship changes if we learn that her partner calls her Peanut. Or Punkin. Or Babe.

Fresh, unexpected similes are the single most overlooked trick of good college writing. Interestingly, you can use metaphor to get exactly the opposite effect: staleness. The way to do this would be to tap a metaphor that you've heard often before.

- high as a kite

- soft as silk

- smooth as glass

- hard as a rock

- strong as an ox

- cold as ice

- cool as a cucumber

If you take the lazy way out and plug in a familiar comparison, you might as well switch to a flowery cursive font and title your academic essay

To My Beloved Grandparents on Their Golden Anniversary

Not that you shouldn't send your grandparents a card on their anniversary. Please do. But don't bring that tried-and-true, nicey-nice language to the academic arena. In our personal lives clichéd language may serve an important function, especially when invested with personal emotion. But in college, fresh language is almost as important as original thinking.

If in a rough draft you have two humorous extended metaphors going, choose the most evocative. Ditch the other.

Direct speech

Indirect speech (reporting, explicating, analyzing, narrating) is rarely as humorous as direct speech. Compare the endings of these two otherwise identical (true) paragraphs to see what I mean.

> We'd been dating just a couple of weeks when I discovered that Mitch, a truck driver, had never read or seen a single Shakespeare play. He agreed to give *Romeo and Juliet* a try. Our local players interpreted Friar Lawrence as a pothead, Romeo as a drama queen, and Tybalt and Mercutio as victims of Roid Rage. Anabolic steroids for one and all! The swordplay was fierce; the boots, thunderous. At evening's end Mitch rose, politely holding my coat. I asked him what he had thought of his first Shakespeare play. "That Shakespeare shore do talk a lotta foolishness."

> We'd been dating just a couple of weeks when I discovered that Mitch, a truck driver, had never read or seen a single Shakespeare play. He agreed to give *Romeo and Juliet* a try. Our local players interpreted Friar Lawrence as a pothead, Romeo as a drama queen, and Tybalt and Mercutio as victims of Roid Rage. Anabolic steroids for one and all! The swordplay was fierce; the boots, thunderous. At evening's end Mitch rose, politely holding my coat. I asked him what he had thought of his first Shakespeare play. He answered that he thought Shakespeare sure talked a lot of foolishness.

Summary is not funny. Don't be afraid to have somebody break into *brief* direct speech smack in the middle of an essay (never at the beginning of a paragraph). Just remember that if somebody speaks in the middle of a piece of academic writing, the direct speech must be handled with clean concision. The person says not one more word than he needs to. A single line of dialogue that comes at the end of a humorous bit, like the Shakespeare line in the first paragraph, can be a great way to bridge to the rest of an essay.

25.4   The Amusement Paradigm

The application of epiphany to humor is the equivalent of an amusing punch line. It is funny **in proportion to its element of surprise**. Its wit, saltiness, or silliness is effective only because it *interrupts* our train of thought with something unexpected. Humor sets up a punch line by making an initial gesture to the expected. It calls on familiar vocabulary. It draws on cultural references we recognize.

The setup is necessary to get us to the punch line, which, depending on its success, makes us chuckle or groan, change the channel, or forward the epiphanic moment to a friend. Whatever the effect, however, the structure is the same. Whether in an oral or written text, it arrives as an abrupt intrusion of the unfamiliar. In this sense a wry moment in a piece of academic writing is like an epiphany, because it strikes us from a place outside ourselves. Like an epiphany, it seems to appear out of nowhere, a teensy jolt from outside our thought process. We didn't see it coming, and it's funny *because* we didn't. In fact it doesn't seem like our own thought. We hadn't considered it quite that way—and, by jingo, that's a good one!

Like a time-release vitamin, you, the writer, release your whammy gradually. It is only when the reader reaches the end that the bigger picture comes into view. The humor has actually been a careful semantic technique, not a way to amp up the entertainment value. If the reader is alert, he will see that you've been using humor as an approach in order to make an argument about life itself. Phrased as a cause-and-effect equation, if life is the problem, outlook is the answer. It is a *weltanschauung*, a strategy, a deliberate sort of seeing that changes the way we experience trauma, conflict, and the human tendency to put our own irresistible selves at the center of the universe.

Humor helps us stay in balance. Balance is one of the things scholars consciously seek. Academic writing is known for its fairness, even-handedness, and significance. Rightly so, eh? Academic writing is supposed to result in change, if not in quotidian life, at least in the intellectual realm. Change is a serious business. Academic writing is supposed to make an original contribution to a larger, ongoing cultural conversation. This standard applies whether you are at the stage where you are publishing your academic writing in a peer-reviewed journal or drafting it for the eyes of fellow students and an instructor.

You may recall a much-discussed image of Kim Kardashian's backside, which at this writing is still part of a larger cultural conversation. Kardashian (un)covered *Paper* magazine with the stated intention of using her butt to break the Internet. Breaking the Internet with one's butt is certainly an uplifting and altruistic goal, raising the bar for humanity! I have created a helpful visual aid on this topic. It illustrates what Kardashian's contribution to our collective national inquiry regarding butts has added in terms of nuance, implication, and consequence.

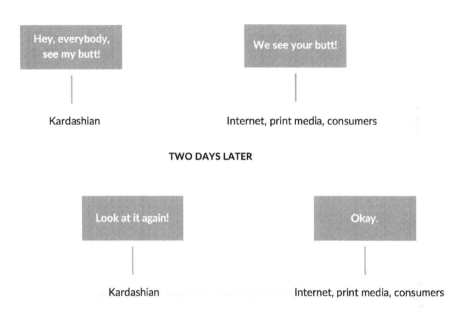

Perhaps this is the moment to suggest that, culturally speaking, we may have been contenting ourselves with a flimsy but entertaining shadow, as in Plato's Allegory of the Cave. Western culture's substitute for humor is thin. It's called amusement, and it's a pale imitation of what humor can actually achieve. The counterfeit does one thing only. It reprises a single equation of cause and effect: if we are amused, then we laugh. Notice that the amusement paradigm restricts the purview of humor to a predictable realm of one-liners, late-night TV, party bloopers, sassy tweets, and so on. Someone makes a funny; we laugh. If this, then that. Look at my butt. Okay, we will.

This amusement paradigm both assumes and reinforces our passivity. We *need* to be amused: it is our collective right! America has become a nation of online gamers. We are movie-goers and TV-watchers, screen-scrollers and phone-diddlers. I'm not against any of these activities, but I would indeed like to suggest that they are the sort of amusements that often contribute to our own objectification. They can turn us into objects by eroding our awareness that we have authority as subjects.

One of the scarier consequences of the amusement paradigm is what I call creeping entitlement. When we agree to let amusements position us in the role of object, we increasingly want and even demand to be objectified by the things that amuse us. Our screens and scripts and games and tweets contribute to the formation of our identity. And this is pretty scary because objects, by definition, do not act. They are acted *upon*. Objects stay where they are put, caught in a passive cycle of stasis and need. (Entertain me, amuse me!)

In such a climate we might not even notice that there is an alternative. But there is. We don't have to settle for the passive self-objectification of the amusement paradigm. We can step up into the role of subject. As subjects, we craft our own humor as part of our distinctive voice. A distinctive voice speaks to the detachment necessary in order to pursue insight. And pursuit of insight should be a mainstay in our academic writing. We should be moving toward insight as well as knowledge. Critical inquiry isn't just the gathering up of a mess of facts. If it were, we could all skip college and check our phones instead.

If you find no humor in the texts around you or in the texts that you yourself are authoring, then I suggest that you may be too close, too invested, too earnest in your personal voice. Moreover, if you cannot detect humor in a challenging situation, it might be time to widen the lens. Your scope may be too small. A narrow scope will cause you to miss that abstract but necessary thing we call irony, and irony has matter-of-factly become both a condition and an expression of our times. Indeed it is hard to think of a canonical contemporary American nonfiction book, film, artwork, or television series that is free of irony. Try to do so and you will see what I mean.

I can imagine a passionate advocate for social justice saying, "But what about sex trafficking? Cancer? Fracking? Chemical warfare? Those things aren't funny!" I agree. Not only are those things not funny, they are downright sobering. But I am not saying that tragic events or conditions are funny in and of themselves. I am saying that as we write about our challenges—our tragedies, traumas, conflicts, diseases, social ills—we can see better and write better when we reach for a pair of eyeglasses called Intentional Paradigm Shift.

While amusement slaps the knee and tickles the ribs, humor is a writing technique that helps us move from A to B. Getting somewhere in your writing is very, very important. You need a takeaway; otherwise why write? The trajectory of humor scoots us beyond predictable cause-and-effect negative emotions like fear and anger, which mire us in stasis. That's why we always feel so drained after a tearjerker or a slasher movie. After two hours of having experienced only one emotion, we are frankly exhausted. Stasis: definitely demanding. But is it interesting?

When deployed with technical competence, humor *is* interesting. This is because it takes us somewhere. It pushes beyond that song stuck on repeat. If you are competent at the craft, humor propels the reader to arrive at insight. And it's no coincidence that insight predicates the ability to take action. Who would bother to inconvenience themselves with action if they didn't believe in the idea behind it? You, the author, are not *seeing* humor in a difficult situation. You're *finding* it. To find humor is to widen the lens, to discover a less predictable picture than the one that invites the same old same old emotional response. Emotions are important. It is important to want to experience them, in life and on the page. But if we allow our writing to become ruled by our emotions, we'll never surprise ourselves, let alone our readers.

25.5 David Sedaris, "Jesus Shaves"

Here's a scenario. Imagine that you are studying a language abroad with only two months' exposure. Smiling hard to show international goodwill, clutching your phone with its translation app, you can barely navigate the subway system.

What emotions would you feel in this situation?

Fear, anxiety, panicky humility. A feeling of out-of-control helplessness. A keen regret that you did not choose to study this language earlier when you had the chance. Your efforts at communication make strangers guffaw. Baby steps! One time in France a stranger asked me how long I had been studying French. I answered slowly, and with great effort, "Four months." Except that what I really said was "Fourteen years." No wonder the stranger burst out laughing! Everyone knows that we must pass through a tunnel of failure in order to arrive at the fluency on the other side. If you were to write about the humiliating experience of studying a foreign language by immersion, and if the writing focused only on the re-creation of predictable negative emotions, *the writing would not be memorable.* This is because it would not be surprising. What's surprising about feeling bad that you can't speak effective French in France?

Check out how David Sedaris, one of America's best-known humor writers, handles the same situation. In the short essay "Jesus Shaves," Sedaris doesn't deny having felt all the typical negative emotions we just named. Oh, he feels them. But communicating his feelings is not the point of this essay. Sedaris is using humor to steer the reader in a more surprising direction.

Jesus Shaves[1]
by David Sedaris

"And what does one do on the fourteenth of July? Does one celebrate Bastille Day?"

It was my second month of French class, and the teacher

---

1   David Sedaris, "Jesus Shaves," *Me Talk Pretty One Day* (New York: Little, Brown, 2000), 174–80.

was leading us in an exercise designed to promote the use of one, our latest personal pronoun.

"Might one sing on Bastille Day?" she asked. "Might one dance in the streets? Somebody give me an answer."

Printed in our textbooks was a list of major holidays accompanied by a scattered arrangement of photographs depicting French people in the act of celebration. The object of the lesson was to match the holiday with the corresponding picture. It was simple enough but seemed an exercise better suited to the use of the pronoun they. I didn't know about the rest of the class, but when Bastille Day eventually rolled around, I planned to stay home and clean my oven.

Normally, when working from the book, it was my habit to tune out my fellow students and scout ahead, concentrating on the question I'd calculated might fall to me, but this afternoon we were veering from the usual format. Questions were answered on a volunteer basis, and I was able to sit back and relax, confident that the same few students would do most of the talking. Today's discussion was dominated by an Italian nanny, two chatty Poles, and a pouty, plump Moroccan woman who had grown up speaking French and had enrolled in the class hoping to improve her spelling. She'd covered these lessons back in the third grade and took every opportunity to demonstrate her superiority. A question would be asked, and she'd race to give the answer, behaving as if this were a game show and, if quick enough, she might go home with a tropical vacation or a side-by-side refrigerator/freezer. A transfer student, by the end of her first day she'd raised her hand so many times that her shoulder had given out. Now she just leaned back and shouted out the answers, her bronzed arms folded across her chest like some great grammar genie.

We'd finished discussing Bastille Day, and the teacher had moved on to Easter, which was represented in our textbooks by a black-and-white photograph of a chocolate bell lying upon a bed of palm fronds.

"And what does one do on Easter? Would anyone like to tell us?"

It was, for me, another one of those holidays I'd just as soon avoid. As a rule, my family had always ignored the Easter celebrated by our non-Orthodox friends and neighbors. While the others feasted on their chocolate figurines, my brother, sisters, and I had endured epic fasts, folding our bony fingers in prayer and begging for an end to the monotony that was the Holy Trinity Church. As Greeks, we had our own Easter, which was usually observed anywhere from two to four weeks after what was known in our circle as "the American version." The reason had to do with the moon or the Orthodox calendar—something mysterious like that—though our mother always suspected it was scheduled at a later date so that the Greeks could buy their marshmallow chicks and plastic grass at drastically reduced sale prices. "The cheap sons of bitches," she'd say. "If they had their way, we'd be celebrating Christmas in the middle of goddamn February."

Because our mother was raised a Protestant, our Easters were a hybrid of the Greek and the American traditions. We received baskets of candy until we grew older and the Easter Bunny branched out. Those who smoked would awaken to find a carton of cigarettes and an assortment of disposable lighters, while the others would receive an equivalent, each according to his or her vice. In the evening we had the traditional Greek meal followed by a game in which we would toast one another with blood-colored eggs. The symbolism escapes me, but the holder of the table's one uncracked egg was supposedly rewarded with a year of good luck. I won only once. It was the year my mother died, my apartment got broken into, and I was taken to the emergency room suffering from what the attending physician diagnosed as "housewife's knee."

The Italian nanny was attempting to answer the teacher's latest question when the Moroccan student interrupted, shouting, "Excuse me, but what's an Easter?"

It would seem that despite having grown up in a Muslim country, she would have heard it mentioned once or twice, but no. "I mean it," she said. "I have no idea what you people are talking about."

The teacher called upon the rest of us to explain.

The Poles led the charge to the best of their ability. "It is," said one, "a party for the little boy of God who call his self Jesus and … oh, shit." She faltered and her fellow countryman came to her aid.

"He call his self Jesus and then he die one day on two … morsels of … lumber."

The rest of the class jumped in, offering bits of information that would have given the pope an aneurysm.

"He die one day and then he go above of my head to live with your father."

"He weared of himself the long hair and after he die, the first day he come back here for to say hello to the peoples."

"He nice, the Jesus."

"He make the good things, and on the Easter we be sad because somebody makes him dead today."

Part of the problem had to do with vocabulary. Simple nouns such as cross and resurrection were beyond our grasp, let alone such complicated reflexive phrases as "to give of yourself your only begotten son." Faced with the challenge of explaining the cornerstone of Christianity, we did what any self-respecting group of people might do. We talked about food instead.

"Easter is a party for to eat of the lamb," the Italian nanny explained. "One too may eat of the chocolate."

"And who brings the chocolate?" the teacher asked.

I knew the word, so I raised my hand. "The rabbit of Easter. He bring of the chocolate."

"A rabbit?" The teacher, assuming I'd used the wrong word, positioned her fingers on top of her head, wriggling them as though they were ears. "You mean one of these? A rabbit rabbit?"

"Well, sure," I said. "He come in the night when one sleep on a bed. With a hand he have a basket and foods."

The teacher sighed and shook her head. As far as she

was concerned, I had just explained everything that was wrong with my country. "No, no," she said. "Here in France the chocolate is brought by a big bell that flies out from Rome."

I called for a time-out. "But how do the bell know where you live?"

"Well," she said, "how does a rabbit?"

It was a decent point, but at least a rabbit has eyes. That's a start. Rabbits move from place to place, while most bells can only go back and forth—and they can't even do that on their power. On top of that, the Easter Bunny has character. He's someone you'd like to meet and shake hands with. A bell has all the personality of a cast-iron skillet. It's like saying that come Christmas, a magic dustpan flies in from the North Pole, led by eight flying cinder blocks. Who wants to stay up all night so they can see a bell? And why fly one in from Rome when they've got more bells than they know what to do with right here in Paris? That's the most implausible aspect of the whole story, as there's no way the bells of France would allow a foreign worker to fly in and take their jobs. That Roman bell would be lucky to get work cleaning up after a French bell's dog—and even then he'd need papers. It just didn't add up.

Nothing we said was of any help to the Moroccan student. A dead man with long hair supposedly living with her father, a leg of lamb served with palm fronds and chocolate; equally confused and disgusted, she shrugged her massive shoulders and turned her attention back to the comic book she kept hidden beneath her binder.

I wondered then if, without the language barrier, my

classmates and I could have done a better job making sense of Christianity, an idea that sounds pretty far-fetched to begin with.

In communicating any religious belief, the operative word is faith, a concept illustrated by our very presence in that classroom. Why bother struggling with the grammar lessons of a six-year-old if each of us didn't believe that, against all reason, we might eventually improve? If I could hope to one day carry on a fluent conversation, it was a relatively short leap to believing that a rabbit might visit my home in the middle of the night, leaving behind a handful of chocolate kisses and a carton of menthol cigarettes. So why stop there? If I could believe in myself, why not give other improbabilities the benefit of the doubt? I told myself that despite her past behavior, my teacher was a kind and loving person who had only my best interests at heart. I accepted the idea that an omniscient God had cast me in his own image and that he watched over me and guided me from one place to the next. The Virgin Birth, the Resurrection, and the countless miracles—my heart expanded to encompass all the wonders and possibilities of the universe.

A bell, though—that's fucked up.

Your sense of humor is located in your mind. It is not an emotion. It is a mental activity, like all the other forms of craftwork we have studied—thesis development, paragraph organization, or close analysis. The craft of humor can be trained and matured like any other form of thinking. We can choose not only what we think but *how* we think it. No doubt you already agree with this, since you have decided to pursue a college education.

In the David Sedaris essay we see how a savvy writer uses humor not ultimately to get laughs but to make us think. Now I want to give you a real-life example of how you can use humor as a mental pushback, a way to help shape your writing voice. This approach, like the one Sedaris uses, illustrates the real work of becoming a writer. It assumes that the writer is never a weather vane, turning here, whirling there, producing material in obedient response to the wind of circumstances. This approach takes the exact opposite strategy. It actively rejects the idea that you will allow your writing voice to be shaped by the usual triggers (predictable emotions, the default focus on self) and by external circumstances (problems, stressors, bad news).

In 2008 I received a doozy of a bad medical report. Nobody expects a death sentence when they jog six miles a day and make their own yogurt. I rapidly cycled through Elisabeth Kübler-Ross's classic Stages of Death & Dying:

1. Denial ("But ... yogurt!")
2. Anger ("Dang it ... yogurt!")
3. Depression ("All that yogurt for nuthin!")
4. Bargaining ("What if I start juicing spinach?")
5. Acceptance ("Might as well have a taco.")

I had six months to say good-bye, make a will, confront my mortality, and write one last book. A terminal diagnosis is the subject of all subjects. If you read a smattering of the cancer books out there, you will see what I mean. There's a pattern. The author accepts that the diagnosis is the subject, which turns the author into the object. And, right on cue, the objectified writer spends the whole narrative reacting to the diagnosis.

I wanted the writing to achieve something more surprising. What's interesting about writing that trots like a puppy on the usual leash? Only two possibilities with that kind of paradigm, right?

▷   Diagnosis + long good-bye = death
▷   Diagnosis + long good-bye = life

Neither approach surprises. A long good-bye in which bad news pulls the author around like an obedient pooch is sad, maybe, but not intellectually interesting. If the author survives, we applaud. But we don't think anything new.

I decided to try something else. When I changed my paradigm on purpose, when I widened the lens to start finding fun and funny surprises in my subject material, I suddenly had a lot more to write about. My character, the speaker, was no longer an object. She was a subject, and so was I, writing the thing now with more insight, more enjoyment, more humor, a gathering sense of where I wanted to go. The illness book I had begun morphed into a romance, then took another turn as it became a meditation on how we construct our identity, on what prevents or accelerates our growth. When my editor received the finished manuscript, she called me chuckling. I had utterly failed to resolve the cancer plot. I had forgotten all about it. Oops. But what a fantastic moment! My omission told me that I had indeed managed to reject the usual paradigm of cancer-as-subject, writer-as-object.

It is only when you do the work of shifting your paradigm on purpose that the old patterns fall away and you are free to develop the voice that you wouldn't otherwise find.

"Jesus Shaves" Discussion Questions

1. What details in the essay demonstrate that Sedaris feels the usual negative emotions that we associate with being out of our comfort zone in a foreign country?

2. This essay is written from the perspective of an American adjusting to France. When did you first notice that this essay is about something far larger than one guy's problems as he makes a cultural adjustment?

3. Use the description of the cigarette-bringing Easter Bunny to comment on the kind of relationship Sedaris had with his family of origin. What details of his home life as a child prefigure his cynicism as an adult? Has he abandoned belief, or did he never believe?

4. Grab a partner and come up with a short list of all the things Sedaris seems to be mocking or making fun of in "Jesus Shaves."

5. Now the hard part. Still with your partner, make a short list of all the things Sedaris reveres.

25.6   What If It's Serious?

Okay, I'm ready. Bring on your objection.

> **We say this respectfully, but you are a scholar with job security. You are speaking as one who cultures her own mung beans and carries an overpriced purse. Have you considered that your intentional pursuit of humor might be an outcropping of privilege? No offense, but one person's cancer journey is very small in the grand scheme of things. What about BIG problems that exist outside of one mind and one body? Surely you can't subject epic global tragedies to a deliberate paradigm shift! An atrocity is what it is—it HAS to be the subject.**

No, it certainly does not have to be the subject. Memorable pieces of writing that deal with global atrocities—Elie Wiesel's *Night*, Susan Southard's *Nagasaki*, Dawn Anahid MacKeen's *The Hundred-Year Walk*, to name a few—are not about the atrocities themselves. They are about how people shifted their paradigms to survive them. In the latter, for instance, Dawn Anahid MacKeen tells the story of the Armenian Genocide as experienced firsthand by her grandfather, Stepan Miskjian, whose journals she found and translated. In the journals Miskjian describes raped and dismembered toddlers, starving people eating a horse, people eating each other, people drinking urine to survive. The violence is unspeakable, graphic, and detailed.

But the single most astonishing thing about Miskjian's

story is a surprise in the structuring of the narrative. Throughout Miskjian's tortured agon, he goes out of his way to write about stuff he finds sweet and amusing. He jokes about lack, poverty, even death itself. How did he do that? *Why* did he do that? Dawn Anahid MacKeen's granddad lived right alongside the 1.5 million other Armenians who didn't make it out of the death camps at Deir Zor. Unsurprisingly, the narrative reveals that the dominant paradigm of this displaced people was one of desperation and hopelessness. In spite of that, the reader understands that Miskjian did not write his story as a tale of desperation or hopelessness. Yes, the writing provides an eyewitness account of genocide, ethnic cleansing, the political turmoil of the Ottoman Empire. That's what makes it memorable history. What makes it memorable *writing* is that one man deliberately shifted his paradigm in order to survive.

Human cruelty sanctioned by law is horrifying. But it is not surprising. History offers a profane pageant of such things for us to study. Indeed, the human record documents many atrocities that both predate and postdate the Armenian Genocide. Even inside the actual structure of the narrative of *The Hundred-Year Walk*, the cruelty doesn't change. The Turks are cruel at the beginning of Miskjian's ordeal, and they are still cruel at the end of it. Structurally speaking, the cruelty is a condition of stasis. As always, to look for the takeaway, we must examine what changes rather than what stays the same. And the only thing that changes in the narrative is paradigm—first Miskjian's, then his granddaughter's a hundred years later as she travels to Turkey herself to retrace her grandfather's journey.

By now you have figured out that in order to develop humor you must be able to make an intentional paradigm shift and that this shift is a structural choice that can apply to any academic assignment. Paradigm shifts don't always turn on humor. However, humor does provide a relatively easy way to help writers refocus. In other words, it helps beginning writers resist predictable patterns that drag the writing down into forgetability. Learning how to widen or refocus the lens at will strengthens your writing.

Thus I recommend the intentional exploration of the craft of humor as a part of every writer's goal to develop a personal voice. Of course this exploration is much harder than being spoon-fed giggles by institutionalized entertainment. This may be why so few writers take the time and trouble to learn the craft.

When we proactively develop humor in our writing voice, we engage in an act of cultural resistance. To be amused in America, all you need is ten bucks and a chair. But developing humor as craft requires that we get up out of the chair that literalizes the very concept of stasis. To craft humor we need to be able to think globally; to make connections between unobvious things; to trace implications; and to see our small expendable selves in right relation to the large ideas we may embrace. Using humor to develop a writing voice requires assertion, practice, and tact. These are not the qualities of a toddler who opens wide for a spoonful of yummy. Developing a distinct writing voice is an adult, sentient activity. And as soon as we step up to the role of subject, the blinders fall from our eyes. If we stop expecting the world to amuse us, if we understand that humor is a tool with which to build insight—ah, that's when we begin developing the habit of mind that characterizes good college writing. That's when we begin to develop voice.

Paradigm Shifting

Paradigm-shifters sometimes take as their goal the worthy practice of thinking outside the box. Depending on the box, that can indeed be challenging. Let's try a more modest goal for a practice essay. Instead of trying to think altogether outside the box, how about switching boxes?

Choose a hot-button topic in today's news media about which you have a strong opinion. Pick something that you feel either passionate about or frustrated by. Now hit the library. Find reputable sources that document what the other side thinks. Write an essay supporting their cause, not yours. Citing sources you have located in library databases, identify how your ideological opponents counter your own position on this issue. This is a hard essay to write because it makes you get up off your dearly held personal convictions long enough to examine and document the other side. The hardest part, of course, will be the conclusion. What's at stake for the folks on the other side of this argument? You know why this issue matters to you. But why does the opposite position matter so much to them?

Paradigm Shifting That Invites Humor

Sometimes it's easier to work on paradigm shifting when you begin with familiar material. Pick one of the prompts below. Create two drafts. In the first, write your familiar material as it comes, without thinking about craft or paradigms at all.

In small groups, read this first draft to your peers. Invite them to make suggestions about what you could do to shift the paradigm. Take notes while your peers are making suggestions, even if you think their suggestions are missing the mark. Then go home and create a second draft in which you intentionally shift your paradigm.

Prompts

▷ Write about someone who is no longer in your life.

▷ Write about a secret you didn't keep.

▷ Write about someone with weirdly bad manners.

▷ Write about the biggest meanness you perpetrated in middle high.

▷ Write about a car trip.

▷ Write about something you spent a long time denying.

▷ Write about having picked out the totally wrong gift for someone.

▷ Write about a time when someone misread your intentions.

▷ Write about how something teensy turned out to be huge.

▷ Write about what you tried to hide.

▷ Write about the kid everybody made fun of.

▷ Write about your worst job.

▷ Write about how you knew something was over.

▷ Write about finally doing something you'd always wanted to do.

▷ Write about being unbelievably embarrassed by your parents.

▷ Write about a form of groupthink that has actually worked pretty well for you.

26 Conclusion

26.1 Take a Chance

I began this book with a story of a college teacher whose approach wasn't very helpful. Remember the connoisseur of matcha who made the class really feel the hugeness of every little thing we didn't know? The matcha professor was indisputably competent and knowledgeable, and I ended up learning what I was there to learn. But I didn't enjoy the experience, and, if you want to know the truth, I emerged from that class with less confidence than I had had going in. Thus it seems fitting to end this book with a very different story, about a professor and a classroom experience that provided a takeaway I wasn't expecting.

As we all know, most majors require a fairly wide variety of coursework to give us depth and breadth in our area of interest. Sometimes you have minimal interest in a particular required course, even though you yourself picked the area, major, or discipline. At such times there's nothing to do but suck it up and soldier on. That was the situation for the class I'm talking about. I had a sweet tooth for English in general, but I had read enough American literature to know that I certainly wouldn't be specializing in colonial literature. This was a requirement I could not sidestep. I apologize for this now, but back then in my mind colonial literature wasn't even technically literature, since it seemed mainly to consist of upper-crust preachers and cranky deacons writing tracts on the various types of sin. And when folks *did* write poems and plays, the focus branched out to include yet another area in which I had no interest: British political incursions on colonial rights and liberties. Page-turners these texts were not. Imagine, if you will, an earnest pamphlet titled *Observations on the New Constitution, and on the Federal and State Conventions.*[1] The professor had a reputation for boundless enthusiasm for this material and for providing an exhausting amount of feedback on student work. She was supposed to be hard. There were lots of texts on the syllabus, and some were bizarrely expensive. I was working two part-time jobs.

Despite my vague self-pity, and my pronounced indifference to colonial politics and religious heresies, I rolled my eyes/sleeves and went for it. Though my GPA was more important to me than the course material, it wasn't long before I started to get interested in spite of myself. And I still remem-

---

1   Mercy Otis Warren, *Observations on the New Constitution, and on the Federal and State Conventions* (Detroit: Gale, Sabin Americana, 2012).

ber how, and why, that happened.

In a class discussion I remarked on the irony that the Puritans, themselves having experienced religious persecution, were always dishing up serious invective against another religious group, the Quakers. Apparently the two groups were at loggerheads. And they were even squabbling face-to-face, not just in print. Quakers, for example, would disrupt Puritan church services by banging on pots and pans and shouting. That's some zealous chutzpah, no? That day in class I was responding to dog vomit. A Puritan writer had insulted the local Quakers by calling them *dog vomit*.

The professor didn't seem disappointed that my only response was a mild interest in the meanness of the metaphor. "Good point. It's extreme language," she nodded. "The two groups must have experienced their differences extremely. For them it must have been more than hairsplitting differences."

Up until that moment I had been privately thinking that both groups must have been pretty immature—I mean, dog vomit? Banging pots and pans on purpose while folks are trying to worship? Who does that? Sheesh. But because my teacher had hooked up my dog-vomit comment to a larger issue, I felt as if I had said something smart. And I suddenly determined to learn more about the extreme differences that had polarized these two groups.

In my first essay for that class, I wrote about the big ideological differences between the Quakers and the Puritans. I mentioned that as the tensions escalated, some of the Quakers were interrupting Puritan church services, marching straight up to the front of the meetinghouse and removing their clothes as a sign that the Puritans were uncovered by God's grace. These Quakers brought a whole new meaning to the term *striptease*! I mentioned that in my research I had come across only Quaker women who went naked as a sign, not men. I didn't speculate about why that might be. But in the margins my professor wrote, "Excellent observation. Is gender relevant here? What if you make this the focus of your research?"

I busted my chops in that class. Sometimes, exhausted after working late, I had to force myself to read the boring colonial tracts out loud. The prof knew I was working two jobs. She cut me no slack. In fact, she never mentioned my schedule at all. She just kept calling my attention, gently and repeatedly, to what was possible.

I knew that colonial literature would never become my main focus. But by semester's end I had written a whole big thing on gender and going naked as a sign, and, here's the kicker, somehow I found myself submitting a proposal to a history conference. I had never even *thought* of putting my work out there in front of my peers. Without that class, without that prof, I wouldn't have even known you could do that. And yet not four months later I was traveling to a different state to present original research on a topic I hadn't even known I was interested in.

This is my wish for you—not that you'll remove your underpants in public or bang your kitchen utensils while folks are trying to concentrate but that you'll take a chance on what you can do. Your college experience will repeatedly push you out of your comfort zone. You will read new things, hard things, boring things. You will come up against hairsplitting distinctions. Distractions will smack their pots and pans when you are trying to focus. But know this. These things will not pull you away from the learning process. They *are* the learning process.

My friend, in the formative years that lie ahead, I wish you the courage to ask questions, the wisdom to listen, and the confidence to identify your gifts. May you become everything you were created to be, and may you find ways to give back what you have been given.

You will have realized by now that this isn't a textbook but a letter. Let me sign it, then, with a heart that believes in your bright future.

Warmly,

Rhoda

CREDITS

INDEX

Kübler-Ross, Elisabeth, 438

L

"The Lady with the Dog"
(Chekhov), 200–216, 249–
250
Lamse, Jourdan, 185
language, value, 45
last words, 279–282
lay/lie, word usage, 353–355
"The Lesson" (Bambara),
50–51
limited omniscient narrator,
230–231
linear time (*chronos*), 172–
174
loaded terms, 45
Locke, John, 55–36
logic
    deductive, 58–59
    inductive, 53–58
Lopate, Phillip, 170
A Lost Lady (Cather), 235–
236

M

MacKeen, Dawn Anahid,
441–442
malapropism, 350–353
Mattingly, Samantha, 156–
162
memoirs
    autobiographies vs.,
    171–172
    first memories, 178–182
    as story of our change,
    190–194
    understanding *kairos*, 174
memory, student exercise,
178–179
metaphors, 148, 250, 421–
422
methodology, 96, 113
metonym, 263
*Misha: A Mémoire of the Ho-
locaust Years* (Defonseca),
177
Miskjian, Stepan, 441–442
modifiers, 349–350
Morrison, Toni, 405
motif, glass slipper as, 37–39
Murphy's Law (cold shoul-
der), student exercise, 17–18
"My Last Duchess" (Brown-

peer review groups, 348–349
period of time (*kairos*), 174
personal essays, 169–176
  student exercise, 194
personal experiences
  autobiographies, 171–176
  complaints against, 176–178
  essay of, 169–176
  memoirs, 171–185, 190–193
  spot the lie, 192–193
  student essay, 185–190
  understanding of time, 172–174
phrases, 96–100, 143–145, 215
physical space, 268–269
Plath, Sylvia, 282–292, 345
point of view
  mixture of types, 232–237
  shifting, 235–238
  types of, 229–232
point-by-point method, 204–207
prepositions, 329–332
pretending, 359–362
problems, spotting, 375–377
pronouns
  antecedence errors, 345–347
  changing attitudes on usage, 312–314
  object pronouns, 325–326
  practical application, 317–318
  reflexive pronouns, 332–336
  subject pronouns, 319–325
proofing your work, 345–349, 390
punctuation. *See* grammar
purpose, 65–68

Q

questions
  quotes, FAQ's, 138–150
  rhetorical, 404–406
  student essays, 190, 262–263
  See also focused questions
quotes
  in conclusions, 125, 140–141
  demonstrating evidence, 126–128
  follow-up to, 139–140, 145–147, 214

Made in the USA
Middletown, DE
24 June 2019